Sport Psychology

The PsychologyExpress series

→ **UNDERSTAND QUICKLY**
→ **REVISE EFFECTIVELY**
→ **TAKE EXAMS WITH CONFIDENCE**

'All of the revision material I need in one place – a must for psychology undergrads.'
Andrea Franklin, Psychology student at Anglia Ruskin University

'Very useful, straight to the point and provides guidance to the student, while helping them to develop independent learning.'
Lindsay Pitcher, Psychology student at Anglia Ruskin University

'Engaging, interesting, comprehensive ... it helps to guide understanding and boosts confidence.'
Megan Munro, Forensic Psychology student at Leeds Trinity University College

'Very useful ... bridges the gap between Statistics textbooks and Statistics workbooks.'
Chris Lynch, Psychology student at the University of Chester

'The answer guidelines are brilliant, I wish I had had it last year.'
Tony Whalley, Psychology student at the University of Chester

'I definitely would (buy a revision guide) as I like the structure, the assessment advice and practice questions and would feel more confident knowing exactly what to revise and having something to refer to.'
Steff Copestake, Psychology student at the University of Chester

'The clarity is absolutely first rate ... These chapters will be an excellent revision guide for students as well as providing a good opportunity for novel forms of assessment in and out of class.'
Dr Deaglan Page, Queen's University, Belfast

'Do you think they will help students when revising/working towards assessment? Unreservedly, yes.'
Dr Mike Cox, Newcastle University

'The revision guide should be very helpful to students preparing for their exams.'
Dr Kun Guo, University of Lincoln

'A brilliant revision guide, very helpful for students of all levels.'
Svetoslav Georgiev, Psychology student at Anglia Ruskin University

'Develops knowledge and understanding in an easy to read manner with details on how to structure the best answers for essays and practical problems – vital for university students.'
Emily Griffiths, Psychology student at Leeds Metropolitan University

'Brilliant! Easy to read and understand – I would recommend this revision guide to every sport psychology student.'
Thomas Platt, Psychology student at Leeds Metropolitan University

Sport
Psychology

Mark Allen
London South Bank University

Paul McCarthy
Glasgow Caledonian University

Series editor:
Dominic Upton
University of Worcester

PEARSON

Harlow, England • London • New York • Boston • San Francisco • Toronto • Sydney
Auckland • Singapore • Hong Kong • Tokyo • Seoul • Taipei • New Delhi
Cape Town • São Paulo • Mexico City • Madrid • Amsterdam • Munich • Paris • Milan

Psychology Express

Pearson Education Limited
Edinburgh Gate
Harlow CM20 2JE
United Kingdom
Tel: +44 (0)1279 623623

Web: www.pearson.com/uk

First published 2014 (print and electronic)

ISBN: 978-1-4479-2396-1 (print)
 978-1-2920-0362-7 (PDF)
 978-1-292-01573-6 (ePub)
 978-1-2920-0363-4 (eText)

British Library Cataloguing-in-Publication Data
A catalogue record for the print edition is available from the British Library

Library of Congress Cataloging-in-Publication Data
A catalog record for the print edition is available from the Library of Congress

ARP impression 98

Cover image © Getty Images

Print edition typeset in 9.5 Avenir LT Std by 73
Print edition printed and bound in Great Britain by Ashford Colour Press Ltd

NOTE THAT ANY PAGE CROSS REFERENCES REFER TO THE PRINT EDITION

Contents

Acknowledgements   vii

Introduction   ix

Guided tour   xii

1 Personality   1

2 Motivation   15

3 Emotion   31

4 Self-confidence   47

5 Concentration   61

6 Coping   75

7 Group processes   89

8 Judgement and decision making   105

9 Mental toughness   121

10 Sport psychology in practice   137

And finally, before the exam …   155

Glossary   159

References   163

Index   179

Companion Website

For open-access **student resources** specifically written
to complement this textbook and support your learning,
please visit **www.pearsoned.co.uk/psychologyexpress**

Acknowledgements

Authors' acknowledgements

We are most grateful to Pearson for the opportunity to publish this book. Their staff, Neha Sharma and Joy Cash, supported us faultlessly throughout the preparation and publication process. We are particularly thankful to the series editor, Professor Dominic Upton, not only for the chance to write this book but also for his help, encouragement and suggestions whilst writing. Thank you also to the reviewers for their constructive advice to improve this book.

Mark Allen: thanks to all my family and friends for their support.
Paul McCarthy: thanks to Lesley, Liam and Euan for making life wonderful.

Series editor's acknowledgments

I am grateful to Neha Sharma and Jane Lawes at Pearson Education for their assistance with this series. I would also like to thank Penney, Francesca, Rosie and Gabriel for their dedication to psychology.

Dominic Upton

Publisher's acknowledgments

Our thanks go to all the reviewers who contributed to the development of this text, including students who participated in research and focus groups, which helped to shape the series format:

Dr Denise Hill, University of Gloucestershire
Professor Tim Woodman, Bangor University

Student reviewers:

Lauren Smith, Psychology student at Leeds Metropolitan University
Thomas Platt, Psychology student at Leeds Metropolitan University
Jessica Lee, Psychology student at Leeds Metropolitan University

We are grateful to the following for permission to reproduce copyright material:

Figures

Figure 2.1 from The 3×2 achievement goal model, *Journal of Educational Psychology*, 103, 632–48 (Elliot, A.J., Murayama, K. and Pekrun, R. 2011), American Psychological Association; Figure 2.2 from *Handbook of Theories of Social Psychology*, 1, Sage (Deci, E.L. and Ryan, R.M. in Van Lange, P.A.M., Kruglanski, A.W. and Higgins, E.T. (Eds) 2012), pp. 416–437, reproduced by permission of SAGE Publications, London, Los Angeles, New Delhi and Singapore, copyright © SAGE Publications, 2012; Figure 2.3 from *Handbook of Theories of Social Psychology*,1, Sage (Weiner, B. in Van Lange, P.A.M., Kruglanski, A.W. and Higgins, E.T. (Eds) 2012), pp.135–155, reproduced by permission of SAGE Publications, London, Los Angeles, New Delhi and Singapore, copyright © SAGE Publications, 2012; Figure 4.2 from A conceptual model of coaching efficacy: preliminary investigation and instrument development, *Journal of Educational Psychology*, 91, 675–776 (Feltz, D.L., Chase, M.A., Moritz, S.E. and Sullivan, P.J. 1999), American Psychological Association; Figure 7.1 from *Group Dynamics in Sport*, 4th ed., Fitness Information Technology (Carron, A.V. and Eys, M.A. 2012), copyright Fitness Information Technology. Reprinted with permission; Figure 9.1 from Advancing mental toughness research and theory using personal construct psychology, *International Review of Sport and Exercise Psychology*, 2, 54–72 (Gucciardi, D.F., Gordon, S. and Dimmock, J.A. 2009), reprinted by permission of the publisher (Taylor & Francis Ltd, http://www.tandf.co.uk/journals).

Tables

Table 1.1 from Normal personality inventories in clinical assessment: general requirements and the potential for using the Neo Personality Inventory, *Psychological Assessment*, 4 (1), 5–13 (Costa, P.T. and McCrae, R.R. 1992), American Psychological Association; Table 8.1 from Individual differences in reasoning: implications for the rationality debate, *Behavioral and Brain Sciences*, 23, 645–726 (Stanovich, K.E. and West, R.F. 2000), Cambridge University Press USA; Table 10.2 from Imagery use in sport: a literature review and applied model, *The Sport Psychologist*, 13 (3), 245–68 (Martin, K.A., Moritz, S.E. and Hall, C.R. 1999), American Psychological Association.

In some instances we have been unable to trace the owners of copyright material, and we would appreciate any information that would enable us to do so.

Introduction

Not only is psychology one of the fastest-growing subjects to study at university worldwide, it is also one of the most exciting and relevant subjects. Over the past decade the scope, breadth and importance of psychology have developed considerably. Important research work from as far afield as the UK, Europe, USA and Australia has demonstrated the exacting research base of the topic and how this can be applied to all manner of everyday issues and concerns. Being a student of psychology is an exciting experience – the study of mind and behaviour is a fascinating journey of discovery. Studying psychology at degree level brings with it new experiences, new skills and knowledge. As the Quality Assurance Agency (QAA) has stressed:

> psychology is distinctive in the rich and diverse range of attributes it develops – skills which are associated with the humanities (e.g. critical thinking and essay writing) and the sciences (hypotheses-testing and numeracy).   (QAA, 2010, p. 5)

Recent evidence suggests that employers appreciate the skills and knowledge of psychology graduates, but in order to reach this pinnacle you need to develop your skills, further your knowledge and most of all successfully complete your degree to your maximum ability. The skills, knowledge and opportunities that you gain during your psychology degree will give you an edge in the employment field. The QAA stresses the high level of employment skills developed during a psychology degree:

> due to the wide range of generic skills, and the rigour with which they are taught, training in psychology is widely accepted as providing an excellent preparation for many careers. In addition to subject skills and knowledge, graduates also develop skills in communication, numeracy, teamwork, critical thinking, computing, independent learning and many others, all of which are highly valued by employers.   (QAA, 2010, p. 2)

In 2010, we produced a series of books under the Psychology Express title and we are proud to note that both students and tutors have found the books extremely valuable. We appreciated that these books, representing the foundation of the Psychology undergraduate course, covered only one part of a typical course (albeit one of the most important) and that there was a need to build on the success of these and produce a series that covered the application of psychology in applied settings, often covered in the latter parts of the Psychology undergraduate programme. This book is part of this new series, although written and designed with the positive attributes common to all in the Psychology Express series. It is not a replacement for every single text, journal article, presentation and abstract you will read and review during the course of your degree programme. It is in no way a replacement for your lectures, seminars or additional reading. A top-rated assessment answer is likely to include considerable additional information and wider reading – and you are directed to some of these readings in this text. This revision guide is a conductor: directing you through the maze of your degree by providing an overview of your course, helping you formulate your ideas, and directing your reading.

Each book within Psychology Express presents a summary coverage of the key concepts, theories and research in the field, within an explicit framework of revision. The focus throughout all of the books in the series will be on how you should approach and consider your topics in relation to assessment and exams. Various features have been included to help you build up your skills and knowledge, ready for your assessments. More detail of the features can be found in the guided tour for this book on page xii.

By reading and engaging with this book, you will develop your skills and knowledge base and in this way you should excel in your studies and your associated assessments.

Psychology Express: Sport Psychology is divided into ten chapters and your course has probably been divided up into similar sections. However we, the series authors and editor, must stress a key point: do not let the purchase, reading and engagement with the material in this text restrict your reading or your thinking. In psychology, you need to be aware of the wider literature and how it interrelates and how authors and thinkers have criticised and developed the arguments of others. So even if an essay asks you about one particular topic, you need to draw on similar issues raised in other areas of psychology. There are, of course, some similar themes that run throughout the material covered in this text, but you can learn from the other areas of psychology covered in the other texts in this series as well as from material presented elsewhere.

We hope you enjoy this text and the others in the Psychology Express series, which cover the complete knowledge base of psychology:

- *Health Psychology* (Angel Chater and Erica Cook);
- *Sport Psychology* (Mark Allen and Paul McCarthy);
- *Educational Psychology* (Penney Upton and Charlotte Taylor);
- *Occupational Psychology* (Catherine Steele, Kazia Solowiej, Holly Sands, and Ann Bicknell);
- *Forensic Psychology* (Laura Caulfield and Dean Wilkinson);
- *Abnormal and Clinical Psychology* (Tim Jones and Phil Tyson).

This book, and the other companion volumes in this series, should cover all your study needs (there will also be further guidance on the website). It will, obviously, need to be supplemented with further reading and this text directs you towards suitable sources. Hopefully, quite a bit of what you read here you will already have come across and the text will act as a jolt to set your mind at rest – you do know the material in depth. Overall, we hope that you find this book useful and informative as a guide both for your study now and in your future as a successful psychology graduate.

Revision note

- *Use evidence based on your reading, not on anecdotes or your 'common sense'.*
- *Show the examiner you know your material in depth – use your additional reading wisely.*
- *Remember to draw on a number of different sources: there is rarely one 'correct' answer to any psychological problem.*
- *Base your conclusions on research-based evidence.*

Explore the accompanying website at www.pearsoned.co.uk/psychologyexpress

→ Prepare more effectively for exams and assignments using the answer guidelines for questions from this book.

→ Test your knowledge using multiple choice questions and flashcards.

→ Improve your essay skill by exploring the You be the maker exercises.

Guided tour

→ Understand key concepts quickly

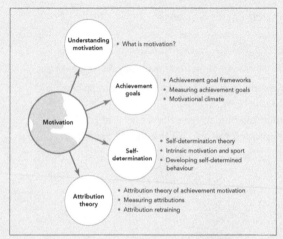

Start to plan your revision using the **Topic maps.**

Grasp **Key terms** quickly using the handy definitions. Use the flashcards online to test yourself.

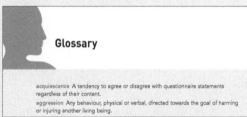

Glossary

acquiescence A tendency to agree or disagree with questionnaire statements regardless of their content.

aggression Any behaviour, physical or verbal, directed towards the goal of harming or injuring another living being.

→ Revise effectively

Hatzigeorgiadis, Zourbanos, Galanis, & Theodorakis (2011): Self-talk and sports performance: A meta-analysis

Hatzigeorgiadis and colleagues performed a meta-analysis of self-talk interventions and sport performance. The meta-analysis included data obtained from 32 previously published empirical studies. The meta-analyses established positive self-talk as an effective strategy for improving sport performance. Several factors were also identified that moderated the effectiveness of self-talk interventions. Self-talk was found to be more effective when learning new skills compared with refining well-learned tasks. Self-talk was also more effective for improving performance in tasks involving fine, compared with gross, motor demands. Moreover, for fine tasks, instructional self-talk was more effective for performance enhancement than was motivational self-talk. Overall, the meta-analysis demonstrated the effectiveness of self-talk as a strategy to facilitate learning and enhance performance in sport.

Quickly remind yourself of the **Key studies** using the special boxes in the text.

Prepare for upcoming exams
and tests using the **Test your
knowledge** and **Sample
question** features.

Compare your responses with
the **Answer guidelines** in the
text and on the website.

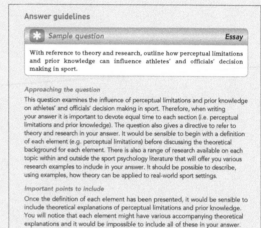

Answer guidelines

Sample question   Essay

With reference to theory and research, outline how perceptual limitations
and prior knowledge can influence athletes' and officials' decision
making in sport.

Approaching the question

This question examines the influence of perceptual limitations and prior knowledge
on athletes' and officials' decision making in sport. Therefore, when writing
your answer it is important to devote equal time to each section (i.e. perceptual
limitations and prior knowledge). The question also gives a directive to refer to
theory and research in your answer. It would be sensible to begin with a definition
of each element (e.g. perceptual limitations) before discussing the theoretical
background for each element. There is also a range of research available on each
topic within and outside the sport psychology literature that will offer you various
research examples to include in your answer. It should be possible to describe,
using examples, how theory can be applied to real-world sport settings.

Important points to include

Once the definition of each element has been presented, it would be sensible to
include theoretical explanations of perceptual limitations and prior knowledge.
You will notice that each element might have various accompanying theoretical
explanations and it would be impossible to include all of these in your answer.

→ Make your answers stand out

Use the **Critical focus** boxes
to impress your examiner
with your deep and critical
understanding.

CRITICAL FOCUS

The primacy effect

In a classic study of judgement and decision making, Asch (1946) demonstrated how
the order in which information is presented can influence how a person is perceived.
Asch presented participants with a number of adjectives to describe a target person
(intelligent, industrious, impulsive, critical, stubborn and envious). Participants received
this information in one of two ways – favourable adjectives first (as above) or unfavourable adjectives first (the order reversed). When participants were asked to report their
impressions of that person, they reported more positive impressions when they received
the favourable adjectives first. This became known as the *primacy effect*.

In sport settings it is also possible that athletes' judgements and impressions are
influenced by the order of information. In a study of football players and coaches,
Greenlees, Dicks, Holder and Thelwell (2007) were interested in whether the order
in which information about an opponent is received would influence the judgements
formed of that opponent. In the study, all participants were required to watch a video
of a target player warming up, but half watched a declining performance pattern
(successful to unsuccessful) and half watched an ascending performance pattern

Make your answer stand out

*Make sure that your answer has structure. You can begin by providing
definitions of the constructs you are to discuss and the general areas you are
going to cover. Then provide detailed descriptions of conceptual models and
be sure to include the research that has supported or refuted elements of the
model (and relationships as yet untested). You can then conclude by outlining
practical suggestions (based on the research you have outlined) and how future
research into some of the untested relationships might lead to further practical
applications of the theory.*

Go into the exam with
confidence using the handy
tips to **make your answer
stand out.**

Personality

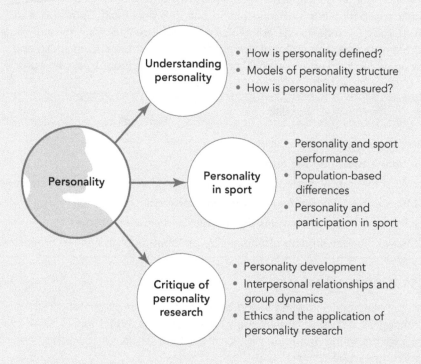

- **Understanding personality**
  - How is personality defined?
  - Models of personality structure
  - How is personality measured?

- **Personality**

- **Personality in sport**
  - Personality and sport performance
  - Population-based differences
  - Personality and participation in sport

- **Critique of personality research**
  - Personality development
  - Interpersonal relationships and group dynamics
  - Ethics and the application of personality research

A printable version of this topic map is available from
www.pearsoned.co.uk/psychologyexpress

Introduction

Personality is a concept that is familiar to us all. We often contemplate our own personality and how it compares with the personality of people we know. Personality theorists are interested in the same types of questions that ordinary people intuitively ask – can people change their personality? Is there an underlying structure or basis to personality? Is personality genetically inherited or environmentally determined? And how might personality affect people's behaviour throughout their lifespan? Personality research in sport has been under investigation for over 70 years and we are only just beginning to understand how personality might be related to athletic success. In this chapter we consider the structure of human personality and the various personality theories shaped by prominent psychologists in the twentieth century. We shall discuss how personality might contribute to sport participation, how personality might differ between discrete athletic populations, and whether sport participation has a role in shaping people's personality. We shall also consider the personality characteristics that might be important for individual and team success, the ethics of using personality assessments in sport, and how an understanding of personality effects can contribute to applied practice.

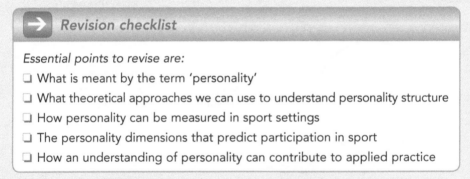

Revision checklist

Essential points to revise are:
- ❏ What is meant by the term 'personality'
- ❏ What theoretical approaches we can use to understand personality structure
- ❏ How personality can be measured in sport settings
- ❏ The personality dimensions that predict participation in sport
- ❏ How an understanding of personality can contribute to applied practice

Assessment advice

- Personality represents one strand of research in sport psychology and although it is studied less intensely now than in the 1960s and 1970s, it still represents an important function to understand, explain and predict behaviour among sport performers.

- Make sure you develop an understanding of the various dimensions of personality and the importance of each personality dimension in various athletic contexts.

- This topic is heavily theoretical, so it is useful to concretise your answers with examples and where possible bring a practical viewpoint to abstract concepts.

- Measuring personality accurately is vital to scientific progress. When you compare and contrast study findings, make sure you consider the different approaches that have been used to assess athletes' personality.

- Many studies include assessments of mood states alongside personality. When reading the literature, make sure that you do not confuse the research findings on mood with the research findings on personality.

Sample question

Could you answer this question? Below is a typical essay question that could arise on this topic.

 Sample question — *Essay*

To what extent has our understanding of personality aided athletics success? Critically discuss with reference to empirical evidence and theoretical explanations.

Guidelines on answering this question are included at the end of this chapter, whilst guidance on tackling other exam questions can be found on the companion website at **www.pearsoned.co.uk/psychologyexpress**

Understanding personality

How is personality defined?

'Personality' is a term we hear frequently in everyday language. We often discuss the personality characteristics of our friends and relatives, and we use a number of adjectives to describe these persons – such as kind, hardworking, easily angered, empathetic, optimistic or confident. But what does it mean to say that someone has a 'kind' personality? To understand and study a psychological construct effectively, we must first define what we want to measure. In general conversation, people typically use the term 'personality' to mean characteristics of the person that are enduring, reflect the whole person, and are inherent to that person. Pervin and Cervone (2010) provided the following definition of personality: 'psychological qualities that contribute to an individual's enduring and distinctive patterns of feeling, thinking and behaving' (p. 8). This definition captures the important features of personality because it describes qualities of the person that are relatively consistent over time and across situations (enduring), includes features that differentiate one person from another (distinctive), and reflects all aspects of the person (feeling, thinking and behaving).

Models of personality structure

As humans we each possess an intrinsic desire to understand ourselves and the world around us. Why one person behaves differently to another in a similar situation has fascinated natural philosophers for millennia. Indeed, comprehensive

3

accounts of personality and personality structure can be found in the works of Hippocrates (460–370 BC) and Galen (AD 129–199), which were based on the understanding of the body and its workings at that time.

Allport

The modern conception of personality was driven largely by Gordon Allport (1897–1967) – the founding father of modern personality theory – who wrote many important works about the structure of personality. Before the work of Allport, there was much confusion surrounding personality and the term had several distinct meanings that clouded the interpretation of study findings. In his seminal book, *Personality: A psychological interpretation* (1937), Allport devoted an entire chapter to the definition of personality and even coined the term 'personality' to reflect its current meaning in everyday use. But perhaps Allport's most important contribution was his description of personality traits as being embedded within a hierarchical structure. This conceptualisation has been incorporated into most modern theories of personality.

Eysenck and Cattell

Two conceptual approaches dominated personality research during the twentieth century – those of Hans Eysenck (1916–1997) and Raymond Cattell (1905–1998). Eysenck (1947) originally proposed that all personality traits fall within two higher-order dimensions: *extraversion* (the degree to which people engage in interpersonal interactions) and *neuroticism* (the degree to which people are emotionally unstable), and he later added a third dimension: *psychoticism* (the degree to which people are aggressive and hostile). This framework became known as the PEN model of personality. The other conceptual approach was Cattell's (1943) 16-factor model. Cattell relied heavily on a new psychometric technique known as factor analysis to develop his model of personality, and building upon earlier work by Allport and Odbert (1936), he classified 4,504 personality adjectives within 16 primary personality dimensions. The framework became known as the 16PF model of personality.

The big five

Despite the many advances that were made using these frameworks, studies would often fail to replicate these dimensional structures and most researchers now agree that personality is best captured by five dimensions that overlap with the work of Cattell and Eysenck. The 'big five' model (as it is known) adopts extraversion and neuroticism from Eysenck's PEN model and also includes three other dimensions, termed *openness* (assessing an individual's tendency to seek out new experiences), *agreeableness* (assessing an individual's concern for cooperation and social harmony) and *conscientiousness* (assessing organisation and goal-directed behaviour). Costa and McCrae (1992) proposed that all personality traits can be classified within 30 lower-order personality facets that, in turn, can be classified within the five higher-order personality dimensions (see Table 1.1). These dimensions can be easily recalled using the acronyms OCEAN

Table 1.1 **The five dimensions of personality (Costa & McCrae, 1992)**

Dimension	Description
Neuroticism	Distinguishes those who possess emotional stability (calm, controlled and even-tempered) from those who are emotionally unstable (anxious, hostile and irritable)
Extraversion	Distinguishes between those who are introverted (unsociable, quiet and passive) and those who are extraverted (sociable, outgoing and active)
Openness	Distinguishes between those who are open to new experiences (curious, creative and imaginative) and those who like the familiar (conventional, uncreative and unimaginative)
Agreeableness	Distinguishes between those who are compassionate (good-natured, unselfish and forgiving) and those who tend to antagonise (cynical, rude and uncooperative)
Conscientiousness	Distinguishes those who are conscientious (organised, punctual and hardworking) from those who are lackadaisical (unreliable, lazy and careless)

or CANOE. The five-factor model has dominated personality research in the twenty-first century.

CRITICAL FOCUS

The broader approach to behaviour prediction

Personality theory can trace its origin to early philosophers such as Hippocrates and Galen. However, during the early part of the twentieth century psychologists had incompatible perspectives on the contribution of personality to behaviour. Four main approaches dominated: the *psychoanalytic* (where behaviour is considered a product of conscious and unconscious psychological interactions), the *behaviourist* (where behaviour is considered a product of external influences), the *humanistic* (where behaviour is considered personal and subjective), and *trait* (where behaviour is considered a product of dispositional traits that differ from person to person). The models described in this chapter each fall within the broader realm of trait theory. However, even though the theoretical focus is on people's underlying traits, all personality theorists recognise that behaviour is best predicted by an interaction between personality traits and the situation that a person finds themself in.

How is personality measured?

Psychological constructs can be measured using various techniques. These include observations, interviews and questionnaires. In personality research, questionnaire-based assessments have been the most common. Often, people are asked to complete a battery of questions about various behaviours and report whether the behaviour is typical of them. These self-report measures are sometimes accompanied by 'other-report' measures where a friend or family member completes a personality assessment about the target person's personality. This helps the researcher acquire a more complete understanding of the target person's personality, as self-report measures are sometimes skewed by response accuracy or social desirability (reporting higher scores on more favourable personality characteristics).

When measuring personality, we are exposed to type-based assessments and trait-based assessments. Type-based assessments classify people as one type or another (e.g. introvert or extravert), whereas trait-based assessments place people on a continuum from one extreme (e.g. highly extraverted) to the other (e.g. highly introverted). Because most people do not classify well as one type or another, trait-based assessments are preferred (McCrae & Costa, 1989). From a sport perspective, the Big Five Inventory (John, Naumann, & Soto, 2008), the NEO inventories (NEO-FFI and NEO-PI-R; Costa & McCrae, 1992) and the international personality item pool (Goldberg et al., 2006) have all been used among athletic samples and have shown evidence of internal reliability and predictive validity in these samples.

Test your knowledge

1.1 Describe two models of personality structure and outline the main conceptual differences between the two.

1.2 Provide a description of each of the five dimensions of personality within Costa and McCrae's (1992) 'big five' framework.

1.3 Outline how personality has been measured in athletic samples and describe some of the limitations with self-report measures.

Answers to these questions can be found on the companion website at: **www.pearsoned.col.uk/psychologyexpress**

Further reading Personality structure and measurement

Topic	Key reading
History of personality theory	Barenbaum, N. B., & Winter, D. G. (2008). History of modern personality theory and research. In O. P. John, R. W. Robins, & L. A. Pervin (Eds.), *Handbook of personality: Theory and research* (3rd ed., pp. 3–26). New York: Guilford Press.
The five factor model of personality	McCrae, R. R., & Costa, P. T. (2008). The five-factor theory of personality. In O. P. John, R. W. Robins, & L. A. Pervin (Eds.), *Handbook of personality: Theory and research* (3rd ed., pp. 159–181). New York: Guilford Press.
The measurement of personality	John, O. P., Naumann, L. P., & Soto, C. J. (2008). Paradigm shift to the integrative big five trait taxonomy: History, measurement, and conceptual issues. In O. P. John, R. W. Robins, & L. A. Pervin (Eds.), *Handbook of personality: Theory and research* (3rd ed., pp. 114–158). New York: Guilford Press.

Personality in sport

Personality and sport performance

The relationship between personality and sport performance has been under investigation for over 70 years. There is evidence that personality test scores taken in youth sport can predict whether athletes progress to professional sport seven years later (Aidman, 2007). Research has also shown that personality assessments can predict the number of goals, assists and total points scored over a 15-year period (Gee, Marshall, & King, 2010). Comparisons of more and less successful athletes have also shown differences in personality. There is evidence that athletes who are regular starters have higher levels of extraversion and lower levels of neuroticism than non-regular starters (Evans & Quarterman, 1983) and that athletes competing in national or international competitions have lower levels of neuroticism and higher levels of conscientiousness than athletes competing in club or regional competitions (Allen, Greenlees, & Jones, 2011). Taken together, these findings suggest that personality is related to long-term success in sport.

In addition to long-term success, research has also explored how personality relates to short-term behaviours. Athletes with higher levels of conscientiousness and/or lower levels of neuroticism show more desirable coping strategies (Allen, Frings, & Hunter, 2012), and perceive these coping strategies to be more effective for peak performance (Kaiseler, Polman, & Nicholls, 2012). Other research has shown that extraverted athletes will outperform introverted athletes in the presence of an audience but not when there is no audience present (Graydon & Murphy, 1995), and that certain emotions (such as anger) might be beneficial for athletes with particular personality characteristics (Woodman et al., 2009). These findings suggest that personality contributes to how athletes respond in various athletic situations.

KEY STUDY

Piedmont, Hill, & Blanco (1999): Predicting athletic performance using the five-factor model of personality

Though many researchers have explored the association between personality characteristics and athletic success, Piedmont and his colleagues were the first to apply the five-factor framework in a sporting population. In this study, Piedmont et al. explored women football players' self-report ratings of personality and compared these to performance ratings for a complete season. First, they compared the five dimensions of personality to coaches' ratings of player performance, such as work ethic, 'team playerness' and game performance. They also compared the five personality dimensions to season statistics such as goals scored, games played, number of assists and number of shots. The personality dimensions of neuroticism and conscientiousness predicted coaches' ratings of athletic performance, whereas conscientiousness was the only dimension of personality that predicted game statistics. The study demonstrated that athletes with higher levels of conscientiousness

▶

and lower levels of neuroticism are perceived by their coaches to have performed better during the season, and that athletes with greater levels of conscientiousness show more impressive game statistics.

Population-based differences

The most common objective in sport personality research has been to identify personality differences between different populations of athletes. A notable early study compared the personality test scores of 865 athletes and 697 non-athletes (Schurr, Ashley, & Joy, 1977). In addition to personality differences between athletes and non-athletes, personality differences were also observed between team sport athletes and individual sport athletes. But when personality scores were compared between particular sports (e.g. rugby and football), no personality differences were observed. Similar findings have been observed in more recent studies. They show that team sport athletes have higher levels of extraversion and lower levels of conscientiousness than individual sport athletes (Allen, Greenlees, & Jones, 2011), and that athletes in high-risk sports have higher levels of extraversion and openness, and lower levels of conscientiousness and neuroticism, than athletes in low-risk sports (Tok, 2011). Thus, personality test scores can differentiate between athletes competing in different *types* of sport but not between individual sports.

Some research has moved beyond comparing personality scores between sports and explored personality differences within sports. There is some evidence that athletes in more attacking positions have higher levels of extraversion than those in more defensive positions (Schurr, Ruble, Nisbet, & Wallace, 1984), although more recent research suggests this may not be the case (Cameron, Cameron, Dithurbide, & Lalonde, 2012). Personality differences have also been explored between men and women participating in sport. Women typically report higher levels of neuroticism, agreeableness and conscientiousness (Allen, Greenlees, & Jones, 2011), and these differences seem to mirror the gender differences observed in non-athletic populations. In short, there is good evidence that personality differs between different populations of athletes. However, the underlying causes of these group-based differences remain unknown and are an important direction for future sport psychology research.

Test your knowledge

1.4 Can personality predict behaviour in sport? And is personality related to long-term athletic success?

1.5 How useful are personality tests in discriminating between different populations of athletes?

1.6 What are the most important dimensions of personality that can discriminate between athletic samples?

Answers to these questions can be found on the companion website at: **www.pearsoned.col.uk/psychologyexpress**

Further reading Population-based differences

Topic	Key reading
Team and individual sports; men and women	Allen, M. S., Greenlees, I., & Jones, M. V. (2011). An investigation of the five-factor model of personality and coping behaviour in sport. *Journal of Sports Sciences, 29*, 841–850.
High- and low-risk sports	Castanier, C., Le Scanff, C., & Woodman, T. (2010). Who takes risks in high-risk sports? A typological personality approach. *Research Quarterly for Exercise and Sport, 81*, 478–485.
High- and low-risk sports	Tok, S. (2011). The big five personality traits and risky sport participation. *Social Behavior and Personality, 39*, 1105–1112.
Endurance athletes and non-athletes	Hughes, S. L., Case, H. S., Stuempfle, K. J., & Evans, D. S. (2003). Personality profiles of Iditasport ultra-marathon participants. *Journal of Applied Sport Psychology, 15*, 256–261.

Personality and participation in sport

The idea that sport participation might help to develop desirable personality characteristics has intrigued sport psychologists for decades. There is good evidence that participation in sport can help to develop important life skills such as discipline, fair-play, sportsmanship, cooperation and helping behaviour (Gould & Carson, 2008) and it is possible that these important life skills become embedded within the personality of the child or adolescent. Many studies have compared personality test scores of those who participate in sport and those who do not. The research shows clear personality differences, with sport participants showing higher levels of extraversion (and sometimes lower levels of neuroticism) than non-sport participants (Hughes, Case, Stuempfle, & Evans, 2003).

These personality differences could have emerged because people choose to take part in activities that suit their personality. Sport competitions involve considerable communication and social interaction, and are therefore likely to attract those who enjoy meeting and interacting with new people (i.e. extraverted individuals). However, it is also possible that taking part in sport, and being compelled to communicate and interact with others, helps to develop desirable personality characteristics such as extraversion. The direction of causality has yet to be subjected to critical tests, and therefore whether sport participation contributes to personality development remains unknown.

KEY STUDY

Rhodes & Smith (2006): Personality correlates of physical activity: A review and meta-analysis

Much research has explored whether personality can predict participation in physical activity and organised sport. Because studies had often produced conflicting findings, Rhodes and Smith pooled the data from 33 previously published studies into one single

▶

analysis (a meta-analysis). The data sample included a large number of participants and the authors were able to examine a number of potential moderator variables (e.g. sex, age, culture). The study showed that people with high levels of extraversion, high levels of conscientiousness and/or low levels of neuroticism were more likely to take part in sport or physical activity. Openness and agreeableness were not related to physical activity involvement. The study also showed little evidence that age, sex or culture moderates the relationship between personality and physical activity.

Critique of personality research

Personality development

A common argument for the inclusion of physical activity in school curriculums is that physical activity contributes to positive psychological development in children and adolescents. However, to appreciate the potential for sport and other activities to affect personality we need to consider how changeable personality can be. In our definitions, we defined 'personality' as characteristics of the person that are relatively enduring and consistent. It would therefore appear that personality is not subject to change (at least in the short term). Yet, most adults report that their personality has changed somewhat as they have become older. Critical studies in behavioural genetics show that personality develops as a product of a complex interaction between a person's genes and their unique environmental experiences. Thus, although personality has a strong genetic component, there is the *potential* for personality to be modified through our life experiences (such as sport).

CRITICAL FOCUS

Nature or nurture?

Studies of human personality show that between 40 and 60 per cent of an adult's personality traits (for each of the five dimensions) are genetically inherited. Studies also show that personality is unrelated to parental rearing style. Personality is relatively stable in adulthood (over the age of 30). However, in childhood and adolescence, personality is more variable, which is important to grasp because children and adolescents dedicate much of their spare time to practising and competing in sport. During this time, the sport environment might be shaping the personality of the child or adolescent.

Interpersonal relationships and group dynamics

Personality has an important role in athlete–athlete and coach–athlete relationships. Research in athletic dyads (e.g. doubles tennis) has shown that athletes are more committed to their athletic partnership if they (or their partner) have high levels of agreeableness, conscientiousness or openness (Jackson, Dimmock, Gucciardi, & Grove, 2010). Also, studies of coach–athlete relationships show that relationships are stronger (greater commitment and closeness) when either the coach or athlete has high levels of agreeableness, conscientiousness or extraversion; and that relationships are stronger when the athlete and coach have similar personalities – similar levels of extraversion or openness (Jackson, Dimmock, Gucciardi, & Grove, 2011).

One question that has intrigued sport psychologists is whether a team is more effective when made up of individuals with similar personalities or more effective when made up of individuals with many different personalities. Although research has yet to explore this idea in sport teams, evidence from non-sport settings shows that groups perform better and are more cohesive when composed of individuals with high levels of conscientiousness and agreeableness (and also when composed of individuals with *similar* levels of conscientiousness and agreeableness). Research also shows that a single disagreeable (low agreeableness) or apathetic (low conscientiousness) team member can affect the degree to which the group as a whole is cohesive and successful (Bell, 2007).

CRITICAL FOCUS

Solving problems in your team – beware of the narcissist

Many sport psychologists engage teams in group discussions. Sometimes these discussions are used to solve problems. At other times they conjure creative ideas for training and competition. But for many years, psychologists have examined the link between creativity and narcissism, suggesting that the most self-obsessed individuals may be more creative than the rest. A recent study suggests otherwise. Goncalo, Flynn and Kim (2010) examined the link between narcissism and creativity. They found that narcissists are not essentially more creative than others but they think they are and are skilled at persuading others to agree with them. Critically, they also reported a curvilinear effect: having more narcissists in a team does generate creative outcomes, but having too many narcissists reduces this effect.

Ethics and the application of personality research

For a long time it was thought that the study of personality had little practical application and that to use personality test scores as a selection tool is ethically questionable. These days it is recognised that personality can contribute to both short-term behaviours and long-term success, and also contribute to interpersonal relationships and group processes. If personality can predict performance in a given situation, there is no reason why personality assessments cannot contribute to the selection process.

Personality is just one of many factors that coaches may wish to consider when making team or competition selections, and finding the right balance of personalities for a team is often considered one of the most important roles of a coach (Summitt & Jenkins, 1998). Moreover, personality assessments can help identify 'at risk' populations who may need additional attention or support from sport psychology consultants. Indeed, if extraverted athletes outperform introverted athletes (of similar ability) in the presence of an audience (Graydon & Murphy, 1995), then different strategies might be used to introduce young athletes to high-performance settings (where audience levels can increase dramatically) depending on their personality scores. Further, personality assessments can be used to create awareness in 'at risk' populations. For example, when a new dyadic relationship is formed (e.g. an athlete acquires a new coach), personality tests could be used to identify those who are 'at risk' of personality clashes, and sport psychology consultants can then recommend intervention techniques to implement if such clashes arise.

Test your knowledge

1.7 Discuss the issue of causality in the relationship between personality and sport participation.

1.8 Describe why personality is important for new relationships in sport settings.

1.9 Critically discuss the practical advantages that can be gained from understanding personality effects in sport.

Answers to these questions can be found on the companion website at: **www.pearsoned.col.uk/psychologyexpress**

Chapter summary – pulling it all together

→ Can you tick all of the points from the revision checklist at the beginning of this chapter?

→ Attempt the sample question from the beginning of this chapter using the answer guidelines below.

→ Go to the companion website at www.pearsoned.co.uk/psychologyexpress to access more revision support online, including interactive quizzes, flashcards, You be the marker exercises as well as answer guidelines for the Test your knowledge and Sample questions from this chapter.

Further reading for Chapter 1

Allen, M. S., Greenlees, I., & Jones, M. V. (2013). Personality in sport: A comprehensive review. *International Review of Sport and Exercise Psychology*, 6,184–208.

John, O. P., Robins, R. W., & Pervin L. A. (2008). *Handbook of personality: Theory and research* (3rd ed.). New York: Guilford Press.

Answer guidelines

 Sample question   *Essay*

To what extent has our understanding of personality aided athletics success? Critically discuss with reference to empirical evidence and theoretical explanations.

Approaching the question

You can touch upon many topics when answering this question, so it would be sensible briefly to define 'personality' as you begin your answer. You might then wish to provide a brief outline of the most important model(s)of personality to help structure your discussion of personality effects in sport. One way of addressing this question is to focus on the research that has linked personality to specific behaviours (or performance) in sport and then for each point to outline a specific example of how this knowledge can be used to develop sport performance. You could then conclude your answer by bullet-pointing more generally the various ways personal and team performance benefit from an understanding of athlete personality (e.g. building interpersonal relationships, or identifying 'at risk' populations).

Important points to include

Much of the research on personality in sport was published in the 1960s and 1970s. Therefore, it is important to consider current research in the field that has used more up-to-date conceptual frameworks of personality. An examiner will be impressed that, in addition to the core concepts, you are also aware of contemporary literature that has examined new and interesting ideas (e.g. interpersonal relationships).

Make your answer stand out

When describing how personality can contribute to athletic success, try to outline the important personality dimensions. For instance, agreeableness has an important role in group performance but seems to be relatively unimportant for individual performance. This could help you describe how different personalities might be important in different performance settings.

Try to be critical of the literature. There is a lot of research that has shown personality differences between different populations of athletes (and between athletes and non-athletes), but very little research has addressed cause and effect. Does personality directly affect sport participation? And does sport participation contribute to personality development? Where possible, try to get hold of the original journal articles and describe the various methods that have been used in the studies.

Explore the accompanying website at www.pearsoned.co.uk/psychologyexpress

→ Prepare more effectively for exams and assignments using the answer guidelines for questions from this chapter.

→ Test your knowledge using multiple choice questions and flashcards.

→ Improve your essay skills by exploring the You be the marker exercises.

Notes

2

Motivation

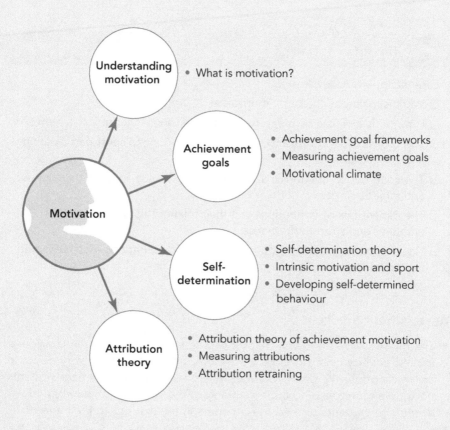

- **Understanding motivation**
  - What is motivation?

- **Motivation**

- **Achievement goals**
  - Achievement goal frameworks
  - Measuring achievement goals
  - Motivational climate

- **Self-determination**
  - Self-determination theory
  - Intrinsic motivation and sport
  - Developing self-determined behaviour

- **Attribution theory**
  - Attribution theory of achievement motivation
  - Measuring attributions
  - Attribution retraining

A printable version of this topic map is available from
www.pearsoned.co.uk/psychologyexpress

Introduction

Motivation to take part in activities such as sport varies considerably between individuals and within individuals (over time). The personal and environmental factors that drive our motivation are of particular interest to applied practitioners targeting sport and exercise participation and athletic success. This is because a person's motivation can have a powerful effect on their behaviour. For example, an athlete motivated by money is likely to show different behaviours to an athlete motivated by enjoyment and success. In this chapter we will explore a number of frameworks of motivation and their application to sport and physical activity. In particular, the key areas we cover are achievement goal theory, self-determination theory and attribution theory. How achievement goals, extrinsic motivation and causal judgements can be manipulated will form a central focus of this chapter.

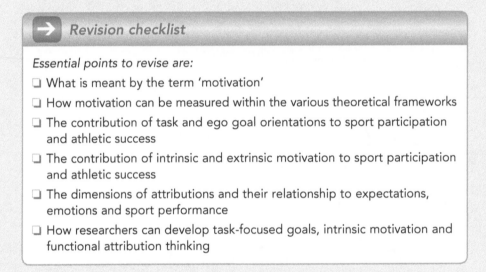

➡️ *Revision checklist*

Essential points to revise are:

❏ What is meant by the term 'motivation'

❏ How motivation can be measured within the various theoretical frameworks

❏ The contribution of task and ego goal orientations to sport participation and athletic success

❏ The contribution of intrinsic and extrinsic motivation to sport participation and athletic success

❏ The dimensions of attributions and their relationship to expectations, emotions and sport performance

❏ How researchers can develop task-focused goals, intrinsic motivation and functional attribution thinking

Assessment advice

- The models covered in this chapter can be fairly complex when considered in their entirety, and therefore we are only able to cover the very basics in our description. We offer a number of key readings that can help students develop a more detailed understanding of the various frameworks and we encourage students to read these papers in the lead-up to their exams.

- To pass your exam will require an understanding of the basic components of the theories. But, to achieve a high grade in your exam you will also need to know the research that has tested components of the theories, including how assessments were made, the design of the research, and whether hypotheses were supported.

- Theories of motivation have many practical applications. When outlining the theories, using examples to illustrate relationships will help you demonstrate to your examiners that you recognise how the theory can be applied in real-world settings.

Sample question

Could you answer this question? Below is a typical essay question that could arise on this topic.

 Sample question   *Essay*

> Outline two conceptual models of motivation. Critically discuss how the two models can be used to further our understanding of motivation in sport and exercise settings.

Guidelines on answering this question are included at the end of this chapter, whilst guidance on tackling other exam questions can be found on the companion website at **www.pearsoned.co.uk/psychologyexpress**

Understanding motivation

Motivation is something that affects us all in our day-to-day lives. We might feel motivated to save money for a holiday, we might feel a lack of motivation to train when attending a gym, or we might struggle for motivation to revise for our exams. We also hear about the motivation of others – religious motives to remove science from schools, politicians' motives to change society, or psychologists' motives to improve health and well-being. The term *motivation* is frequently used both in everyday conversation and in the research publications of psychologists. Therefore it is important to provide an accurate definition of the term.

What is motivation?

There are many definitions available in the literature to describe motivation. Roberts (2012) commented that definitions of motivation are sometimes so broad that they could incorporate almost the entire field of psychology, and at other times so narrow that it becomes almost useless as an organising construct. Most psychologists contend that motivation is not so much an entity (like emotion) but a process – in particular, a process that is reflected in the initiation, direction, magnitude and continuation of goal-directed behaviour (Elliot, 2006). There are many theories of motivation available that can help us understand sport and exercise behaviour, and three in particular have attracted a great deal of interest from sport and exercise psychologists. These are achievement goal theory, self-determination theory and attribution theory.

17

Achievement goals

Achievement goal theory is the name given to the collective body of theory and research into the kinds of goals (purposes, reasons) that direct achievement-related behaviour. The overall goal of action in any achievement setting (e.g. sport, academia) is assumed to be the desire to develop and demonstrate competence, and to avoid demonstrating incompetence (Nicholls, 1984). Thus, achievement goals are concerned largely with how people construe competence. Achievement goal theory is one of the few motivational frameworks developed within a sport/physical education context and over 300 published articles have explored achievement goal theories in sport and physical activity (Roberts, 2012).

Achievement goal frameworks

Achievement goal theory (e.g. Ames, 1984; Nicholls, 1984) contends that competence or ability can be evaluated using self- or other-referenced criteria. Specifically, people can be task-goal oriented or ego-goal oriented.

- *Task-goal orientation* is where success is evaluated in terms of task mastery or personal improvement.
- *Ego-goal orientation* is where success is evaluated in terms of demonstrating competence and superiority over others.

Task and ego goals refer to states that people experience in a given situation, but people also show a proneness to the two types of involvement (i.e. an orientation).

Task- and ego-goal orientations are relatively orthogonal, meaning that they do not correlate with each other – people can be high in both goals, low in both goals, or high in one and low in the other. Individuals who focus on task mastery or improvement (a high task-goal orientation) are more likely to persist in the face of failure, exert greater effort, set challenging goals and remain interested in the task. On the other hand, individuals concerned with demonstrating high ability and competence (a high ego-goal orientation) are more inclined to avoid difficult tasks, reduce persistence in the face of challenges, exert less effort and withdraw participation (Nicholls, 1989).

The dichotomous model of achievement goals (task- and ego-goal orientation) has been the most widely adopted achievement goal framework. However, recognising that motivation can also be approach or avoidance focused, Elliot (1999) proposed a 2×2 achievement goal model, where task and ego goals (which he labelled mastery and performance goals) can be either approach focused (goals directed towards approaching a desirable outcome) or avoidance focused (goals grounded in the avoidance of failure). *Mastery-approach goals* are focused on task-based competence (e.g. 'I want to learn as much as possible'), *mastery-avoidance goals* are focused on task-based incompetence (e.g. 'I am concerned I may not learn everything'), *performance-approach goals* are focused on normative competence (e.g. 'it is important that I do better than others'), and

Valence		Definition: Absolute (task)	Definition: Intrapersonal (self)	Definition: Interpersonal (other)
Valence	Positive (approaching success)	Task-approach goal	Self-approach goal	Other-approach goal
Valence	Negative (avoiding failure)	Task-avoidance goal	Self-avoidance goal	Other avoidance goal

Figure 2.1 The 3 × 2 achievement goal framework (Elliot et al., 2011)

performance-avoidance goals are focused on normative incompetence (e.g. 'my goal is to avoid performing poorly').

More recently, Elliot, Murayama and Pekrun (2011) extended the model to distinguish between mastery goals that are *task-based* (which reflect the absolute demands of the task) and those that are *self-based* (which reflect self-set standards). Both types of mastery goals, along with performance (other-based) goals can be approach or avoidance focused (Figure 2.1).

Measuring achievement goals

Achievement goals are usually measured via self-report questionnaires. The most commonly used measures are the Task and Ego Orientation in Sport Questionnaire (TEOSQ; Duda, & Nicholls, 1992) and the Perceptions of Success Questionnaire (POSQ; Roberts, Treasure, & Balague, 1998). Both of these questionnaires are based on the dichotomous achievement goal framework and provide separate scores for task and ego orientations. Another measure, the 2 × 2 Achievement Goal Questionnaire for Sport (AGQ-S; Conroy, Elliot, & Hofer, 2003) assesses both task and ego goals as they reflect approach and avoidance valence. Each of these measures has demonstrated evidence of validity and reliability in athletic samples and can be used to measure achievement goals accurately in sport and physical education settings.

Motivational climate

An important consideration in achievement goal research is the *motivational climate*. This refers to the situational goal structure operating in an achievement context (Ames, 1992). The motivational climate in a given situation can be task-involving (a mastery climate) or ego-involving (a performance climate). In a *mastery climate* the emphasis is on effort, personal improvement and skill development, whereas in a *performance climate* the emphasis is on normative comparison and public evaluation.

Physical education classes and sports clubs can differ dramatically in the emphasis placed on task mastery (e.g. teachers emphasising and rewarding personal improvement) and performance (e.g. teachers acknowledging and rewarding success and victory). The motivational climate within a sport club or physical education class can have a strong effect on sport participants. A climate that promotes task mastery is generally associated with a greater task-goal orientation and greater levels of effort and enjoyment, whereas a climate that promotes performance comparisons is generally associated with a greater ego-goal orientation and lower levels of effort, satisfaction and enjoyment (van de Pol, Kavussanu, & Ring, 2012).

CRITICAL FOCUS

Developing a mastery climate

Epstein (1989) outlined six factors that can help teachers organise classroom instruction and interaction. These are: Task, Authority, Recognition, Grouping, Evaluation and Time.

- *Task*. Teachers and instructors should make tasks challenging and diverse.
- *Authority*. Students should be given choices and leadership roles.
- *Recognition*. Learning should be private and based on individual progress.
- *Grouping*. Cooperative learning and peer interaction should be promoted.
- *Evaluation*. Teacher evaluation should be based on task mastery and learning.
- *Time*. Time requirements should be adjusted to personal capabilities.

These can be easily remembered by the acronym TARGET. By manipulating these six factors instructors can promote a mastery climate that should lead to greater effort and enjoyment for those taking part (Ntoumanis & Biddle, 1999).

Further reading Achievement goal theory

Topic	Key reading
Achievement goal theories	Harwood, C., Spray, C. M., & Keegan, R. (2008). Achievement goal theories in sport. In T. S. Horn (Ed.), *Advances in sport psychology* (3rd ed., pp. 157–185). Champaign, IL: Human Kinetics.
Measurement of achievement goals	Conroy, D. E., & Hyde, A. L. (2012). Achievement motivation processes. In G. Tenenbaum, R. C. Eklund, & A. Kamata (Eds.), *Measurement in sport and exercise psychology* (pp. 303–317). Champaign, IL: Human Kinetics.
Motivational climate	Ntoumanis, N., & Biddle, S. J. H. (1999). A review of motivational climate in physical activity. *Journal of Sports Sciences, 17,* 643–665.

Self-determination

Self-determination theory

Self-determination theory (Deci & Ryan, 1985; 2012) is a social cognitive theory of human motivation and personality that differentiates motivation in terms of being autonomous and controlled. Self-determination theory (SDT) assumes that people evolved to be inherently active, intrinsically motivated and oriented towards developing naturally through integrative processes. For these processes to operate effectively, people require particular psychological 'nutriments' (Deci & Ryan, 2012). SDT proposes that there are three *basic psychological needs* that are essential for optimal development and functioning – the need for competence, the need for autonomy and the need for relatedness.

- The need for *autonomy* reflects the degree to which individuals feel volitional and responsible for their own behaviour.
- The need for *competence* concerns the degree to which individuals experience opportunities to express their capabilities.
- The need for *relatedness* is the extent to which individuals feel a sense of connectedness to others in their social environment.

These three psychological needs motivate the individual to initiate behaviour (Figure 2.2).

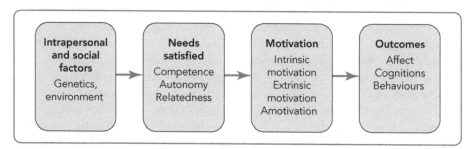

Figure 2.2 Self-determination theory (Deci & Ryan, 1985; 2012)

SDT considers three main types of motivation that have different behaviour outcomes. *Intrinsic motivation* is engagement in behaviour for enjoyment and pleasure with no discernible reinforcement or reward, whereas *extrinsic motivation* is engagement in behaviour for external reinforcements such as gaining rewards or avoiding punishments. For instance, a person may join a more successful sports team to increase their chances of winning trophies (extrinsic motivation) or because they enjoy new challenges (intrinsic motivation). SDT also considers *amotivation*, which refers to a lack of intention to perform the behaviour.

Extrinsic motivation can be further broken down into four distinct categories. These are *external regulation, introjected regulation, identified regulation* and *integrated regulation*. Along with intrinsic motivation, these can be placed on a continuum of autonomous (self-determined) behaviour (Table 2.1). These motivational states have different effects on regulations, goals, affect and behaviour (Deci & Ryan, 2012).

Table 2.1 **Types of motivation in self-determination theory**

Motivation type	Description
External regulation	Behaviour controlled by external means such as rewards or punishments
Introjected regulation	Engagement in behaviour to avoid external sources of disapproval, or for externally referenced approval
Identified regulation	Engagement in behaviour for personally held values or benefits from the activity
Integrated regulation	Engagement in behaviour to help reaffirm behaviour as integral to self-identity
Intrinsic motivation	Engagement in behaviour for enjoyment and pleasure, with no discernible reinforcement or reward

Note: Motivation types towards the lower end of the table represent more autonomous (self-determined) forms of behaviour.

Intrinsic motivation and sport

Many studies have tested components of SDT in sport and physical activity settings (Hagger & Chatzisarantis, 2007). There is good evidence that external rewards can, under certain circumstances, undermine intrinsic motivation. For example, in university athletes it has been demonstrated that those on scholarships show lower levels of intrinsic motivation than those not on scholarships (Ryan, 1980). The critical factor is the salience of the controlling and informational aspects of the external reward. A scholarship can often be perceived as controlling and can therefore lower athletes' perceptions of autonomy and, in turn, their intrinsic motivation.

In addition to extrinsic rewards, there is evidence that positive/negative feedback, competition (focus on winning) and intrapersonal events (goal orientations) can also affect autonomous behaviour (intrinsic motivation) through their effect on basic psychological needs.

Psychological needs and motivation types have been linked with a number of psychological and behaviour responses. There is evidence that psychological need thwarting (when needs are not met) is associated with lower perceived vitality and greater perceived exhaustion in youth sport (Bartholomew, Ntoumanis, Ryan, & Thøgersen-Ntoumani, 2011). Also, in physical education classes a needs-supporting environment is associated with greater levels of intrinsic motivation that, in turn, is associated with greater levels of concentration, positive emotions and perceptions of task challenge. On the other hand, a needs-unsupporting environment is associated with amotivation, which in turn is associated with greater feelings of unhappiness (Standage, Duda, & Ntoumanis, 2005).

Developing self-determined behaviour

Sport psychology consultants are interested in identifying ways to move people along the motivation continuum towards more autonomous types of behaviour. The most appropriate way to do this is to satisfy psychological needs. Rewards do not automatically undermine intrinsic motivation, and in practice it is appropriate to use small rewards that are *not too salient or controlling*, and these can be phased out as intrinsic motivation develops (Gill & Williams, 2008). Carefully chosen rewards can help develop a sense of competence and, in turn, intrinsic motivation. Coaches and physical education instructors should also provide positive feedback and reinforcement in a way that emphasises task mastery rather than outcomes. Developing a task-oriented motivational climate can help satisfy basic psychological needs and in turn foster intrinsic motivation.

KEY STUDY

Standage, Duda, & Ntoumanis (2003): Predicting motivational regulations in physical education

A number of studies have proposed possible links between achievement goal theory and self-determination theory. In particular, task-goal orientation (or a motivational climate that promotes task mastery) has been proposed to satisfy two of the three basic psychological needs (the need for autonomy and the need for competence) and therefore should facilitate self-determined motivation. Standage, Duda and Ntoumanis (2003) explored the relationship between goal orientations, perceptions of motivational climate and motivational styles proposed by self-determination theory in a sample of British secondary school students. The study showed that task-goal orientation and perceptions of a mastery climate were positively related to more self-determined types of motivation. The findings suggest that a useful approach to developing intrinsic motivation in physical education classes is to foster an environment that promotes and rewards task mastery rather than outcomes.

Test your knowledge

2.4 Describe basic psychological needs and how they relate to autonomous behaviour.

2.5 List and define the four types of extrinsic motivation.

2.6 In the context of satisfying basic psychological needs, describe how you would develop intrinsic motivation in youth sport.

Answers to these questions can be found on the companion website at: **www.pearsoned.col.uk/psychologyexpress**

Further reading Self-determination theory

Topic	Key reading
Overview of self-determination theory	Ryan, R. M., & Deci, E. L. (2007). Active human nature: Self-determination theory and the promotion and maintenance of sport, exercise and health. In M. S. Hagger, & N. L. D. Chatzisarantis (Eds.), *Intrinsic motivation and self-determination in exercise and sport* (pp. 1–19). Champaign, IL: Human Kinetics.
Self-determination in sport and physical education	Ntoumanis, N. (2012). A self-determination theory perspective on motivation in sport and physical education: Current trends and possible future directions. In G. C. Roberts & D. C. Treasure (Eds.), *Advances in motivation in sport and exercise* (3rd ed., pp. 91–128). Champaign, IL: Human Kinetics.

Attribution theory

Attribution theory refers to the collective body of theory and research on the psychology of explanation. Attributions are the explanations people give for an event related to either themselves or others. For example, a sport performer might *attribute* their success in competition to several weeks of intense training or to a lucky penny found on the day of competition.

The field was pioneered by the Australian psychologist Fritz Heider (1896–1988), whose seminal book – *The psychology of interpersonal relations* (1958) – incorporated his most influential ideas about how people perceive causes. People generally attribute behaviour in one of two ways – as resulting from *internal* dispositions (e.g. personality, attitudes) or resulting from *external* sources (e.g. social pressure, random chance). Heider (1958) described what is now termed the *fundamental attribution error* – an overreliance on dispositional factors, rather than situational factors, when attributing the behaviour of others. This pioneering work provided a platform for further research into attribution patterns and over 30 different attribution biases have now been identified.

The most common attribution bias observed in sport settings is the *self-serving bias*. This refers to a tendency to attribute positive outcomes to the self (e.g. high ability, effort) and negative outcomes to external factors (e.g. poor officials, difficult playing conditions). This attribution bias is a robust phenomenon and is proposed to occur as a mechanism to enhance or protect personal self-esteem (Miller & Ross, 1975). In sport, the self-serving bias is more common among younger athletes, male athletes and inexperienced athletes, and following important or close outcomes (Allen, 2012).

Attribution theory of achievement motivation

The attribution theory of achievement motivation (ATAM; Weiner, 1985; 2012) has been the most widely adopted attribution framework in sport. This model predicts that following important or unexpected outcomes, people either publicly or privately seek to understand why the outcome has occurred. The attributions that people identify influence their emotions, expectations, decisions and behaviours.

The ATAM model extended the internal–external dimensional structure and proposed that all attributions made in an achievement context can be classified within the dimensions of locus of causality, stability and controllability.

- *Locus of causality* distinguishes between factors that reside within the person (e.g. ability and effort) and those that reside outside of the person (e.g. task difficulty and luck).

- *Stability* distinguishes between factors that are relatively stable over time (e.g. ability and task difficulty) and those that are relatively unstable (e.g. effort and luck).

- *Controllability* distinguishes between factors that are under the person's volitional control (e.g. effort) and those that the individual has no control over (e.g. natural ability, luck).

It is the degree to which attributions fall along these three dimensions that influences emotions, expectations and behaviours (Figure 2.3).

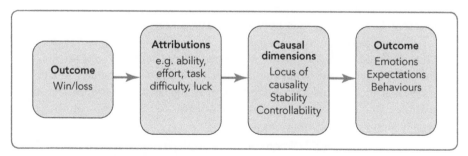

Figure 2.3 The attribution theory of achievement motivation (Weiner, 1985; 2012)

Research in sport has shown support for the main components of the model. Generally, athletes show greater confidence and expectations for the future when they attribute their successes to stable rather than unstable factors (e.g. personal ability) and when they attribute their failures to unstable rather than stable factors (e.g. poor strategy). Also, people experience greater levels of pride and self-esteem when they attribute their successes to internal factors (e.g. effort) and experience greater levels of anger and frustration when they attribute their failures to factors under the control of others (e.g. poor decisions by officials). The attributions made following competition outcomes can also affect behaviour and performances in subsequent competitions. Following failure, athletes are able to maintain their performance levels when attributions are made to controllable and unstable factors (e.g. wrong strategy), but when attributions are made to uncontrollable and stable factors (e.g. poor ability) subsequent performance levels go down (Coffee & Rees, 2011).

CRITICAL FOCUS

Attribution dimensions

Most research in sport has explored attributions as classified within the three dimensions proposed by Weiner (1985) – locus of causality, stability and controllability. However, Rees, Ingledew and Hardy (2005) proposed that research in sport would benefit by focusing on a broader range of generalisability dimensions – in addition to stability, assessing the globality and universality of attributions. *Globality* is the degree to which the cause is perceived to generalise across people, and *universality* is the degree to which the cause is perceived to generalise across situations. Rees, Ingledew and Hardy (2005) recommend assessing the four dimensions of controllability, stability, globality and universality, and exploring how attributions as classified within these four dimensions contribute to people's expectations, emotions and behaviours. Research has shown that following competition success, attributions classified as stable, global and/or non-universal are associated with increased confidence in sport performers (Coffee & Rees, 2008).

Measuring attributions

Early attribution research often focused on the four most commonly identified attributions – ability, effort, task difficulty and luck. However, problems can arise when researchers attempt to classify athlete attributions along causal dimensions. Although many people might identify ability as a stable factor, others might perceive ability as changing over time. Similarly, most people would see luck as an unstable property, but others might perceive this as a stable characteristic of the individual (lucky or unlucky). Therefore, most researchers recognise that the most appropriate assessment method is for athletes to classify their attributions personally along causal dimensions.

In sport, the Revised Causal Dimension Scale (McAuley, Duncan, & Russell, 1992) and the Controllability, Stability, Globality and Universality questionnaire (Coffee

& Rees, 2008) each require athletes to identify the most important cause of the outcome and then rate that cause along attribution dimensions (e.g. from very stable to very unstable). Both questionnaires have demonstrated evidence of validity and reliability in adult sport populations.

Attribution retraining

Attribution retraining is the process by which a coach or sport psychology consultant attempts to modify a person's attributions. When athletes show undesirable attribution patterns (e.g. attributing poor performance to stable and uncontrollable causes, such as poor ability), it is appropriate to encourage athletes to reflect on other (more controllable and unstable) factors that could have contributed to poor performance (e.g. employing the wrong strategy). Research has shown that it is possible to modify athletes' attributions through verbal persuasion methods, and that such attribution retraining leads to greater levels of confidence and expectations for the future, greater levels of effort and persistence, and overall better performance in future competitions (Le Foll, Rascle, & Higgins, 2008).

Test your knowledge

2.7 Using examples from sport, define attributions and outline the self-serving bias.

2.8 Describe the main components of Weiner's (1985) attribution theory and the general support for this model in athletic settings.

2.9 Outline how you would develop functional attributions in sport performers.

Answers to these questions can be found on the companion website at: **www.pearsoned.col.uk/psychologyexpress**

Further reading Attribution theory

Topic	Key reading
The ATAM model of attribution	Weiner, B. (1985). An attributional theory of achievement motivation and emotion. *Psychological Review, 92*, 548–573.
Overview of attributions in sport	Biddle, S. J. H., Hanrahan, S. J., & Sellars, C. N. (2001). Attributions: Past, present, and future. In R. N. Singer, H. A. Hausenblas, & C. M. Janelle (Eds.), *Handbook of sport psychology* (2nd ed., pp. 444–471). New York: Wiley.
Contemporary research in sport	Rees, T., Ingledew, D. K., & Hardy, L. (2005). Attribution in sport psychology: Seeking congruence between theory, research and practice. *Psychology of Sport and Exercise, 14*, 189–204.

Chapter summary – pulling it all together

→ Can you tick all of the points from the revision checklist at the beginning of this chapter?

→ Attempt the sample question from the beginning of this chapter using the answer guidelines below.

→ Go to the companion website at www.pearsoned.co.uk/psychologyexpress to access more revision support online, including interactive quizzes, flashcards, You be the marker exercises as well as answer guidelines for the Test your knowledge and Sample questions from this chapter.

Further reading for Chapter 2

Roberts, G. C., & Treasure, D. C. (2012). *Advances in motivation in sport and exercise* (3rd ed.). Champaign, IL: Human Kinetics.

Van Lange, P. A. M., Kruglanski, A. W., & Higgins E. T. (2012). *Handbook of theories of social psychology* (Vol. 1). London: Sage.

Answer guidelines

 Sample question   *Essay*

Outline two conceptual models of motivation. Critically discuss how the two models can be used to further our understanding of motivation in sport and exercise settings.

Approaching the question

The question asks you to critically review two of the three models outlined in this chapter. Therefore, it is worthwhile reading about each of the models before selecting the two you feel most comfortable describing. When you begin your answer it can be useful to start with a definition of motivation and why it is an important topic of inquiry in sport and exercise. This will set you up nicely to describe the basic components of each of the theories you have chosen, being careful to provide accurate definitions of important terms and the relationships between model components. In addition to describing the main components of the models, try to outline their relevance for sport and exercise settings. A useful way to end your answer is to describe, using examples, how the theory can be applied in real-world settings.

Important points to include

The important points to include will depend on the topics you have selected in your answer. For achievement goal theory, make sure you provide accurate definitions of task- and ego-goal orientations and how each is proposed to affect thoughts, affect and actions. Better answers will describe how the dichotomous achievement goal framework can be extended to include approach–avoidance valence. Make sure you include a description of motivational climate and practical suggestions for developing a task-goal orientation. For achievement goal theory, you need to provide accurate definitions of the three psychological needs and how these can affect self-determined behaviour. Provide good definitions of intrinsic motivation, extrinsic motivation and amotivation. Better answers will describe the four types of extrinsic motivation as they fall on a continuum of self-determined motivation. Be sure to describe the sport-based research that has tested components of this model and, using examples, outline how you would attempt to foster intrinsic motivation in sport and exercise settings. For attribution theory, it would be useful to provide a definition of attributions and the self-serving bias before describing the main components of the ATAM model. Outline the three dimensions of attributions, and use examples to illustrate how specific causes classify within these dimensions. Be sure to describe the sport-based research that has explored the effect of attributions on emotions, expectations and subsequent performance, and detail how attribution retaining can be used to develop desirable attributions and better performances in athletic populations.

Make your answer stand out

These models can seem fairly complex for those new to the area of motivation. The best way to achieve a good grade in your exam is to be accurate and specific in your descriptions and definitions. But don't forget to outline the application to sport and the relative support of the models in sport and physical activity settings. A good way to impress your examiner is to identify contemporary research in the area and provide an outline of that research, including the study sample, methods, main findings and practical relevance of the findings. Describing research in this way will demonstrate to your examiner that you have read critically into the area.

Explore the accompanying website at www.pearsoned.co.uk/psychologyexpress
→ Prepare more effectively for exams and assignments using the answer guidelines for questions from this chapter.
→ Test your knowledge using multiple choice questions and flashcards.
→ Improve your essay skills by exploring the You be the marker exercises.

Notes

3

Emotion

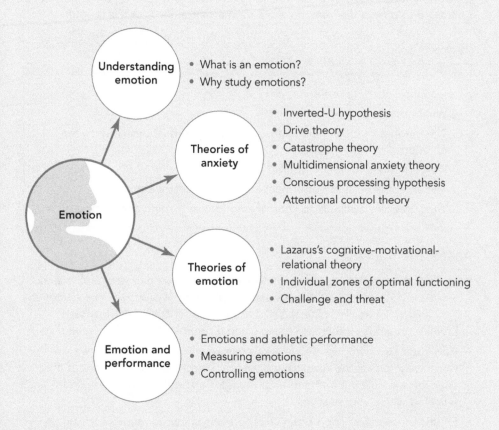

Understanding emotion
- What is an emotion?
- Why study emotions?

Theories of anxiety
- Inverted-U hypothesis
- Drive theory
- Catastrophe theory
- Multidimensional anxiety theory
- Conscious processing hypothesis
- Attentional control theory

Emotion

Theories of emotion
- Lazarus's cognitive-motivational-relational theory
- Individual zones of optimal functioning
- Challenge and threat

Emotion and performance
- Emotions and athletic performance
- Measuring emotions
- Controlling emotions

A printable version of this topic map is available from
www.pearsoned.co.uk/psychologyexpress

Introduction

The emotions that people experience before and during important events are thought to have an important influence on behaviour. Throughout competitions, athletes' emotions are drawn out, strained and occasionally eviscerated at the time they most need to retain control. Those athletes better able to retain control over their emotions should therefore have an advantage over those who lose control. To understand how athletes might control their natural emotional responses, we need to understand more about emotions in general and identify the emotions that have the greatest influence on performance. In this chapter we consider what emotions are, where they come from, and how different emotions might help or hinder performance. We also look further into the different, and sometimes contrasting, predictions of various anxiety and emotion theories. How athletes can be trained to control their emotions will form a central focus of this chapter.

> **→ Revision checklist**
>
> *Essential points to revise are:*
> - ❏ What emotions are
> - ❏ The theories that can help us to understand the relationship between emotions and performance
> - ❏ How emotions can be measured
> - ❏ The antecedents and performance consequences of emotion
> - ❏ The strategies available to control emotions in training and competition

Assessment advice

- Much of the emotion research in sport settings has examined negatively toned emotions (e.g. anxiety) but there is some exploration of positively toned emotions (e.g. enjoyment and happiness). We shall offer a brief outline of the most prominent theories within the literature and recommend some further reading.

- How sport psychologists define and measure emotions affects the way in which we interpret the research we read. It is necessary to be aware of the difficulties in defining and measuring emotions and this knowledge could be reflected within your answers.

- Emotion research in sport often incorporates various correlates such as personality, motivation and group processes. Keep these links in mind when answering questions about emotion in sport.

- Undergraduate programmes in sport psychology continually emphasise the application of sport psychology research to the real world. Hence, applied research should form part of your reading on this topic and you can weave this knowledge into your answers.

Sample question

Could you answer this question? Below is a typical essay question that could arise on this topic.

 Sample question   *Essay*

Critically compare and contrast theories of anxiety and emotion. Consider how these models can be used by applied sport psychologists.

Guidelines on answering this question are included at the end of this chapter, whilst guidance on tackling other exam questions can be found on the companion website at **www.pearsoned.co.uk/psychologyexpress**

Understanding emotion

To study emotion effectively, we have to overcome a challenging paradox. Scholars begin their research on emotions by searching for conceptual clarity and precise definitions. But in an age of science, it is more important to understand a particular process deeply before proper definitions materialise (Oatley, Keltner, & Jenkins, 2006). Scholars, therefore, operate within changing boundaries, balancing the definitions and conceptual models proposed by different theorists whilst presenting their research on a particular topic. And because those interested in studying emotion emerge from psychology, sociology, philosophy, neuroscience, psychiatry, biology and anthropology, it is impossible to be exhaustive on this topic. Despite these challenges, we need to establish a foothold within the research so we begin by exploring what is an emotion.

What is an emotion?

William James posed this exact question in a paper in 1884. Curiously, scholars have yet to agree on a precise definition of an emotion. Many theorists have offered definitions (e.g. Ekman, 1992; Lazarus, 1991) while others (e.g. Griffiths, 1997; Mandler, 1984) have argued that emotion is too heterogeneous to define. What can be established, however, is the existence of emotional components such as expression in facial movements, posture and gesture as well as physiological responses (e.g. increase heart rate) and specific action tendencies (e.g. to run and hide or stay and fight). The following definition (from Deci, 1980) can help us to begin our understanding of emotion:

> An emotion is a reaction to a stimulus event (either actual or imagined). It involves change in the viscera and musculature of the person, is experienced subjectively in characteristic ways, is expressed through such means as facial changes and action tendencies, and may mediate and energize subsequent behaviours. (p. 85)

Why study emotions?

Though several theorists have added to our understanding of emotion, the scope of this chapter precludes an exhaustive review of these theories and models. What is feasible is an inspection of prominent theories that emerge consistently within the sport psychology literature. Though the nature of positively valenced (e.g. happiness, enjoyment) and negatively valenced (e.g. anxiety, aggression) emotions has been examined in sport and exercise psychology, the research spotlight has shone most strongly on negatively valenced emotions. This makes sense intuitively not only because most athletes recall the fear, anxiety or aggression they experienced before or during competition (and attribute their inert performance to the experience of those emotions), but also because they compete in stressful and unpredictable environments. We begin our discussion with arousal, stress and anxiety before exploring more generally how other (positively toned) emotions contribute to performance in sport.

Theories of anxiety

The terms 'anxiety', 'stress' and 'arousal' sometimes appear interchangeably. However, there are distinct definitions that distinguish these constructs.

- *Arousal* refers to physiological and psychological activation that varies on a continuum from deep sleep to high alertness.
- *Anxiety* is an emotional label for a specific type of arousal experience. It is an emotional state characterised by worry, feelings of apprehension and bodily tension.
- *Stress* is an on-going process that involves making appraisals of situational demands and personal resources to cope with those demands.

Defining terms is important to the research process but it also raises some questions. A counterintuitive question raised in the literature harboured much debate: can anxiety ever be helpful to sport performers?

The inverted-U hypothesis

Yerkes and Dodson (1908) presented one of the first models to help understand the association between sensory stimulation (arousal) and human performance. The basic premise argued that arousal and performance vary systematically in the form of an inverted-U function. This means that a low level of arousal or stimulation improves task performance but performance is likely to be low. As the level of arousal increases, so too does performance. But eventually, the level of arousal will rise too high and hinder the athlete's performance. At this point, heightened arousal will gradually hamper performance so that it decreases constantly. This is known as the Yerkes–Dodson law. Though it received empirical support, it is also criticised forcefully because the simple inverted-U hypothesis does not present the complexity in relations between arousal and performance. One detail that is often ignored is that these researchers did not use humans in their research – they used mice. What Yerkes and Dodson did contribute to the literature was that there is a relationship between arousal and performance and this relationship is curvilinear.

Drive theory

Emerging from the pioneering work of Triplett (1898) on social facilitation, drive theory proposed a positive linear relationship between arousal level and performance (Spence & Spence, 1966). As arousal levels increase, performance on physical and simple tasks should improve. In practice, however, many athletes can become overly aroused and perform poorly or miss specific cues (e.g. making false starts in track sprints). Researchers have posed questions about the shape of the arousal curve and where exactly optimal arousal occurs (Hardy, 1990).

Catastrophe theory

In the cusp catastrophe theory of anxiety, performance depends on a complex interaction of arousal and anxiety (Hardy, 1990). Anxiety is considered a multidimensional construct comprising a cognitive component and a physiological arousal component. Within this model, it is predicted that physiological arousal relates to performance as indicated by the inverted-U curve, but only when an athlete experiences low cognitive anxiety. When cognitive anxiety is high, increases in arousal improve performance up to a point, after which increases may produce a dramatic decline in performance (a 'catastrophe'). This decline contrasts with the gradual decline in the inverted-U hypothesis. Though some scientific support exists for the model, it has been difficult to test empirically (Woodman & Hardy, 2001a).

Multidimensional anxiety theory

Multidimensional anxiety theory (Martens, Vealey, & Burton, 1990) contends that anxiety can be divided into two primary components: cognitive and somatic.

- *Cognitive anxiety* is the mental component of anxiety and reflects feelings of worry.
- *Somatic anxiety* is the physiological component of anxiety and reflects negative perceptions of physiological symptoms.

Somatic anxiety differs somewhat from physiological arousal as it reflects a perception of physiological symptoms rather than the physiological symptoms themselves. The model proposes that each anxiety component relates differently to athletic performance. Cognitive anxiety is negatively associated with performance (i.e. increases in cognitive anxiety produce decreases in performance), while somatic anxiety is related to performance in an inverted-U manner (i.e. increases in somatic anxiety help performance up to a point, after

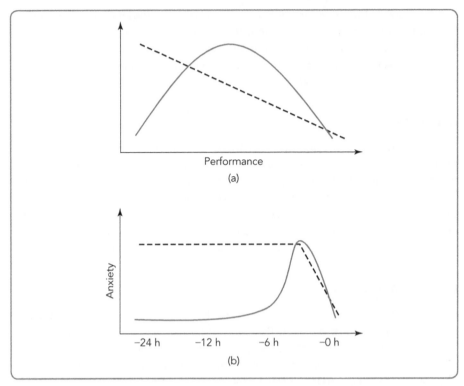

Figure 3.1 (a) The relationship of cognitive anxiety (dashed line) and somatic anxiety (solid line) to sport performance, and (b) how these anxiety components change in the hours leading up to competition (based on Martens, Vealey, & Burton, 1990)

which, further increases in somatic anxiety cause performance to deteriorate). The model also proposes that each anxiety component changes during the lead-up to competition. Cognitive anxiety remains high throughout the days before competition and reduces once the competition starts, whereas somatic anxiety remains low throughout the days before competition, increases rapidly immediately prior to the start of competition, and then reduces once the competition starts (Figure 3.1(b)). Research has supported the changing of cognitive and somatic anxiety in this manner during the lead-up to competition (Hanton, Thomas, & Maynard, 2004), but the negative linear relationship of cognitive anxiety, and the inverted-U relationship of somatic anxiety to athletic performance has not been fully supported (Craft, Magyar, Becker, & Feltz, 2003; Woodman & Hardy, 2003).

Conscious processing hypothesis

The conscious processing (or reinvestment) hypothesis (Masters & Maxwell, 2008) explores what happens to skilled action when people become aware of task-related movements as they perform them. If a golfer, for example, were to bring to mind the mechanics of his chipping stroke while preparing to chip, a breakdown in normal skill execution is likely. The conscious processing (or reinvestment) hypothesis proposes that anxious individuals attempt to guarantee task success by consciously monitoring their performance. This attempt to consciously monitor action means that individuals are likely to interfere with their normal, covert, automatic task processing and assume unsuitable control strategies based upon explicit knowledge. There is good evidence that conscious processing leads to a decline in performance and that anxiety contributes to conscious processing (Masters & Maxwell, 2008).

Attentional control theory

Attentional control theory (ACT; Eysenck, Derakshan, Santos & Calvo, 2007) predicts that anxious individuals are more susceptible to reduced skilled performance because they focus more frequently on potential threats in the environment. This occurs because anxiety impairs the *shifting function* (the ability to shift attention optimally within and between tasks) and the *inhibition function* (the ability to resist disruption from task-irrelevant stimuli) of the attention system (Eysenck, Derakshan, Santos & Calvo, 2007). ACT contends that anxiety affects processing efficiency (the relationship between the effectiveness of performance and the effort spent on the task) rather than performance effectiveness. Therefore, increases in anxiety may not lead to a decrease in performance provided the performer can draw on additional cognitive resources (i.e. additional effort). Only when additional resources (effort) are unavailable will anxiety lead to decreases in performance. Research has supported the main predictions of ACT using eye-tracking technology and has shown that anxious sport performers fixate more frequently on threatening or irrelevant stimuli in the environment (Moran, Byrne, & McGlade, 2002; Wilson, Wood, & Vine, 2009).

KEY STUDY

Wilson, Smith, & Holmes (2007): The role of effort in influencing the effect of anxiety on performance

This study tested the contrasting predictions of attentional control theory and the conscious processing hypothesis. In a sample of 18 golfers, Wilson et al. explored golfers' anxiety, mental effort and putting performance. Over a series of 20 putts, they found that high performance could be maintained through increased levels of anxiety by increasing levels of effort (a reduction in processing efficiency). Because high performance was maintained through high-anxiety situations, the study showed greater support for the predictions of attentional control theory than for the conscious processing hypothesis.

Further reading Anxiety in sport

Topic	Key reading
Theories of anxiety	Woodman, T., & Hardy, L. (2001a). Stress and anxiety. In R. N. Singer, H. A. Hausenblas & C. M. Janelle (Eds.), *Handbook of sport psychology* (pp. 290–318). New York: Wiley.
Conscious processing hypothesis	Masters, R., & Maxwell, J. (2008). The theory of reinvestment. *International Review of Sport and Exercise Psychology, 1,* 160–183.
Attentional control theory in sport	Wilson, M. (2008). From processing efficiency to attentional control: A mechanistic account of the anxiety–performance relationship. *International Review of Sport and Exercise Psychology, 1,* 184–201.

Theories of emotion

Anxiety has been the most frequently examined emotion in sport. However, it is also recognised that other negative emotions (e.g. anger, dejection) and positive emotions (e.g. enjoyment, happiness, excitement) can also contribute to athletic behaviour. For example, Scanlan and her colleagues (Scanlan & Simons, 1992; Scanlan, Carpenter, Lobel, & Simons, 1993) examined the sources of enjoyment among youth and elite sport performers and established that enjoyment is gained from learning, mastering and demonstrating sport skills, competitive excitement, affiliation with peers and positive parental involvement. Further research also established that the enjoyment needs of children change as they continue their involvement in sport (McCarthy, Jones, & Clark-Carter, 2008). The role of both positive and negative emotions is recognised in current research (e.g. Woodman et al., 2009) and this burgeoning research has much to offer the field of sport psychology. We will now briefly describe three general models of emotion that have been researched in sport.

Lazarus's cognitive-motivational-relational theory

One theory of emotion that is applicable to the sport domain is Lazarus's (1991) cognitive-motivational-relational theory. This theory has been used to inform research in sport and has received support for some of its tenets (e.g. Uphill & Jones, 2007). According to Lazarus's theory, two key processes are involved in the generation and regulation of emotions: cognitive appraisal and coping. In sport and other domains, the appraisal of a situation, rather than the situation itself, is what influences the emotional response. From a cognitive-motivational-relational perspective, situations encompass primary and secondary appraisals.

- Primary appraisals determine the relevance of the event or situation for the athlete and comprise three components: goal relevance, goal congruence and type of ego involvement.
- Secondary appraisal is an evaluation of (a) coping options, (b) individual responsibility and (c) future expectations. Briefly, it is an evaluation of what action might prevent harm, moderate it, or produce additional harm or benefit.

Lazarus's theory provides a valuable framework for studying emotion in sport, especially considering the value placed on individual differences in motivation and how personal resources and the environment combine to produce personal meaning and emotion.

Individual zones of optimal functioning

The Individual Zone of Optimal Functioning (IZOF) model postulates the functional relation among emotions and optimal performance. It aims to predict the quality of forthcoming performances based on the performer's emotional state before the performance (Kamata, Tenenbaum, & Hanin, 2002). Hanin (2000) argued that emotional patterns of successful performances can be distinguished from those of less successful performances. To illustrate, when an athlete's pre-competitive anxiety is within or near their personal 'optimal zone', their performance is successful (Figure 3.2). However, when it is outside their optimal zone, performance wanes. A meta-analysis of 19 studies conducted between

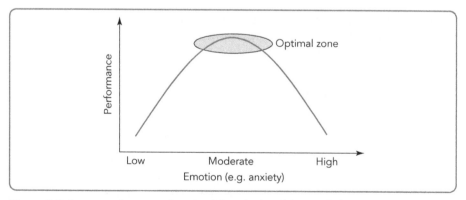

Figure 3.2 An example zone of optimal functioning (blue oval) for an athlete. For different athletes the zone may be shifted left or right, or be narrow or wide

1978 and 1997 examined the validity of such in–out zones. Those athletes who were within their optimal zones had performances that were almost one-half a standard deviation better than those who were outside their zones (Kamata, Tenenbaum, & Hanin, 2002).

Challenge and threat

The theory of challenge and threat states in athletes (Jones, Meijen, McCarthy, & Sheffield, 2009) integrates research on the appraisal, emotional response, arousal and performance consequences of competition. The model contends that people perceive competitive situations as either a challenge (positively) or a threat (negatively). A threat state occurs when the demands of competition outweigh the resources available to cope with those demands, and a challenge state occurs when resources meet or exceed demands. Resources include factors such as high self-confidence and perceptions of control (Jones, Meijen, McCarthy, & Sheffield, 2009). In a challenge state, athletes are proposed to experience more positive emotions and are more likely to perceive emotions (whether positive or negative) as helpful to performance. In a threat state, athletes are proposed to experience more negative emotions and are more likely to perceive emotions as unhelpful to performance. Some research has supported a link between anxiety and a threat response (Meijen, Jones, McCarthy, Sheffield, & Allen, 2013), but other research exploring physiological markers of challenge and threat suggest that these states are not strongly linked to either positive or negative emotions (Turner, Jones, Sheffield, & Cross, 2012).

Test your knowledge

3.4 Why are researchers interested in understanding positive emotions in sport?

3.5 Outline the main components of the IZOF model.

3.6 Explain how challenge and threat relate to emotions in sport and the supporting evidence.

Answers to these questions can be found on the companion website at: **www.pearsoned.col.uk/psychologyexpress**

Further reading Emotions in sport

Topic	Key reading
Positive emotion in sport	McCarthy, P. J. (2011). Positive emotion in sport performance: Current status and future directions. *International Review of Sport and Exercise Psychology, 4*, 50–69.
Theories of emotion	Hanin Y. L. (2000). *Emotions in sport.* Champaign, IL: Human Kinetics.

Topic	Key reading
Challenge and threat states in sport	Jones, M. V., Meijen, C., McCarthy, P. J., & Sheffield, D. (2009). A theory of challenge and threat states in athletes. *International Review of Sport and Exercise Psychology, 2,*161–180.

Emotion and performance

Emotions and athletic performance

Positive emotions do not necessarily have positive effects on sport performance, and negative emotions do not necessarily have negative effects on sport performance (Jones, 2012). The relationship between anxiety and sport performance can be complex, as characterised by the models we have discussed, and two comprehensive meta-analyses of 29 (Craft, Magyar, Becker, & Feltz, 2003) and 48 (Woodman & Hardy, 2003) published studies showed that self-reported anxiety is not strongly related to performance outcomes. Generally, the anxiety models that have received the greatest support in sport settings are the conscious processing hypothesis (Masters & Maxwell, 2008) and the attentional control theory (Eysenck, Derakshan, Santos, & Calvo, 2007), neither of which posits a straightforward negative association of anxiety and performance.

Emotions may have either positive or negative consequences depending on the characteristics of the task. For power sports that require high arousal (e.g. boxing, rugby), negative emotions such as anger and anxiety may benefit performance, but for sports requiring fine motor skills (e.g. archery, snooker) these emotions may harm performance (Woodman et al., 2009). Although emotions will have different effects depending on the nature of the task, most sports involve some level of coordination and motor control, and therefore some emotions may have similar effects across sports. Indeed, a meta-analysis of 16 published studies (Beedie, Terry, & Lane, 2000) showed that self-reported tension (anxiety), depression and anger had medium negative associations with performance outcomes in sport. However, many scholars might contest the findings of such research syntheses as self-report emotion scales have often struggled to pass basic tests of validity and reliability.

Measuring emotions

The emotional states of athletes are most commonly measured using self-report questionnaires. For example, the Competitive State Anxiety Inventory-2 (Martens, Vealey, & Burton, 1990) has been the most commonly used assessment of anxiety. The most common assessment measures of other emotions are the Positive and Negative Affect Schedule (Watson, Clark, & Tellegen, 1988) and the Profile of Mood States (McNair, Lorr, & Droppelman, 1971). Although such measures have been used frequently, concerns have been raised regarding the validity and reliability of each of these instruments in athletic populations. More recently, a sport-specific measure was developed that assesses five basic emotions: anxiety, dejection, excitement, happiness and anger (Jones, Lane, Bray, Uphill, & Catlin, 2005).

Though self-report measures represent the dominant form of recording emotional experience among sport performers, other measures are circulating. For example, Fenz and Epstein (1967) assessed patterns of heart rate, respiration rate and skin conductance during a jump sequence for experienced and inexperienced parachutists. Although such physiological markers have been known to predict performance, it is not always clear which emotion the physiological activity is accompanying (e.g. anxiety or excitement). More recently, researchers have begun to measure emotions using observer ratings, and measures of vocal, facial and brain activity (e.g. Davis et al., 2008). These assessment methods may provide useful additions to the self-report questionnaires commonly used with sport performers.

KEY STUDY

Lane, Sewell, Terry, Bartram, & Nesti (1999): Confirmatory factor analysis of the Competitive State Anxiety Inventory-2

The study by Lane et al. used a statistical technique known as factor analysis to assess the validity of the CSAI-2 (Martens, Vealey, & Burton, 1990). A large cohort of volunteers ($n = 1,213$) completed the questionnaire within one hour of competition. The general finding of the study was that the factor structure proposed by Martens et al. is flawed. In particular, the researchers raised concerns regarding many of the items used to assess cognitive anxiety. Most items in the questionnaire assess anxiety using the term 'concerned'. Lane, Sewell, Terry, Bartram and Nesti (1999) argued that the term 'concern' may not always be interpreted as anxiety by all persons, but rather the participants may simply be acknowledging the importance and difficulty of the challenge ahead. They recommended that researchers do not use the CSAI-2 to assess anxiety in sport performers.

Controlling emotions

The ability to regulate emotions is central to athletic success (Jones, 2012). A number of strategies have been proposed to help athletes regulate or control their emotions before and during competition. Five strategies have been outlined as particularly useful in sport settings:

1 The replacement of negative self-statements with positive or neutral self-statements.

2 Personal goals grounded in approaching success rather than the avoidance of failure (losses).

3 Creating images (in the mind) of the targeted emotional state.

4 Relaxation techniques such as controlled breathing or targeted muscle tension and relaxation.

5 Reinterpreting a stimulus in such a way as to change its emotional 'punch' (e.g. seeing officiating errors as random rather than biased).

Each of these strategies (self-talk, goal setting, imagery, relaxation and reappraisal) has been identified as useful for emotion regulation in sport (Jones, 2012). But emotion regulation can have costs in addition to benefits. Emerging evidence suggests that the suppression of emotions may cause people to perform worse on cognitive tasks and that the exaggeration of emotions may reduce working memory resources. Therefore, coaches need to be mindful of the potential disadvantages that could materialise by changing athletes' emotions dramatically (Jones, 2012).

CRITICAL FOCUS

A touching story

Many people are unaware of the influence of tactile communication or physical touch in our lives. In sport, we witness high fives and fist bumps, but did you ever wonder whether such apparently casual behaviour could affect whether a team wins or loses? Research suggests that physical touch promotes cooperation, communicates distinct emotions and soothes when stress abounds. Kraus, Huang and Keltner (2010) suggested that physical touch would lead to increases in individual and group performance. In their ethological study (i.e. study of human behaviour in social contexts), they coded the touch behaviour of players from the National Basketball Association during the 2008–09 seasons. Early season touch predicted greater performance for individuals and teams later in the season. Touch predicted improved performance even after the researchers accounted for pre-season expectations, early season performance and player status.

Test your knowledge

3.7 Is there good support for the notion that emotions influence sport performance?

3.8 Describe the various ways in which psychologists can measure emotion.

3.9 Outline a training plan to improve the emotional control of high-level athletes.

Answers to these questions can be found on the companion website at: **www.pearsoned.col.uk/psychologyexpress**

Chapter summary – pulling it all together

→ Can you tick all of the points from the revision checklist at the beginning of this chapter?

→ Attempt the sample question from the beginning of this chapter using the answer guidelines below.

→ Go to the companion website at **www.pearsoned.co.uk/psychologyexpress** to access more revision support online, including interactive quizzes, flashcards, You be the marker exercises as well as answer guidelines for the Test your knowledge and Sample questions from this chapter.

Further reading for Chapter 3

Jones, M. V. (2012). Emotion regulation and sport performance. In S. M. Murphy (Ed.), *The Oxford handbook of sport and performance psychology* (pp. 154–172). New York: Oxford University Press.

Answer guidelines

 Sample question **Essay**

Critically compare and contrast theories of anxiety and emotion. Consider how these models can be used by applied sport psychologists.

Approaching the question

Because this question asks you to compare and contrast the conceptual models of emotion, it gives you some scope to choose among the models. Remember that when you choose these models, you ought to ensure that they incorporate positive and negative emotions. You may wish to outline one or two models of anxiety before considering the more general frameworks of emotion. The second part of the question explores the application of these models to research and applied practice in sport. Although this element of the question gives you a chance to discuss various topics, you might wish to focus your answer on a few topics such as measurement and the emotion–performance relationship. Again, with extensive research available, it would be worth demonstrating your knowledge, understanding and critical analysis of classic research articles and current applications of these theories/models.

Important points to include

It is sensible to present a definition of emotion and a basic outline of the models you wish to discuss. Remember that this question has two parts and the second part seeks critical analysis and synthesis of the literature examining these models. Therefore, it is better to devote more time towards the second part of this question focusing upon a critical in-depth discussion. The authors who developed these models should be recognised with suitable references in your answer. Where possible, give an illustration of the research emerging from the models within the literature and the significance of these contributions, especially when recommendations are suggested to revise current theoretical understanding.

Make your answer stand out

Well-written answers follow a logical structure. Open your answer with a brief description of what will follow for the reader. This allows the reader to follow your argument, flowing carefully from one key point to the next. Watch for non sequiturs in your writing. These are arguments in which the conclusion does not follow from its premises. You can demonstrate your knowledge of the chosen models/theories by presenting examples of recent studies that have tested components of these models. It can be useful to describe the sample used in the study, the general procedures used, and the main findings. A brief description of a study might only take a few lines of text but it will demonstrate to an examiner that you have read critically into the area.

Explore the accompanying website at www.pearsoned.co.uk/psychologyexpress

→ Prepare more effectively for exams and assignments using the answer guidelines for questions from this chapter.

→ Test your knowledge using multiple choice questions and flashcards.

→ Improve your essay skills by exploring the You be the marker exercises.

Notes

Notes

4

Self-confidence

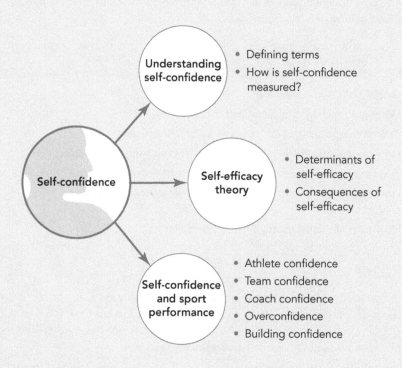

- **Self-confidence**
  - **Understanding self-confidence**
    - Defining terms
    - How is self-confidence measured?
  - **Self-efficacy theory**
    - Determinants of self-efficacy
    - Consequences of self-efficacy
  - **Self-confidence and sport performance**
    - Athlete confidence
    - Team confidence
    - Coach confidence
    - Overconfidence
    - Building confidence

A printable version of this topic map is available from
www.pearsoned.co.uk/psychologyexpress

Introduction

The US athlete Carl Lewis once said, 'If you don't have confidence, you'll always find a way not to win'. As this quotation illustrates, most professional athletes recognise that to be successful in sport you must have exceptional self-belief. Self-confidence is something that varies considerably within people (across situations) and between people. It is therefore unsurprising that self-confidence has been one of the most heavily researched topics in the social psychology of sport. This chapter considers the various factors that might affect a person's self-confidence and how self-confidence can affect the way we feel, think and behave when approaching and participating in motivated performance situations. The key areas we cover are self-efficacy theory, psychological skills to develop or control self-confidence, the relative importance of self-confidence for peak performance, self-confidence among team sport athletes, self-confidence among sport coaches, and how overconfidence might on occasions lead to negative performance consequences.

> ### → Revision checklist
>
> *Essential points to revise are:*
> ❏ What is meant by the term 'self-efficacy'
> ❏ The antecedents and consequences of self-efficacy
> ❏ How we can measure self-confidence and self-efficacy in sport
> ❏ The reciprocal nature of the confidence–performance relationship
> ❏ How collective efficacy and coaching efficacy can affect sport performance
> ❏ How to build self-efficacy in sport performers

Assessment advice

- Self-confidence represents a major field of research inquiry in sport. Therefore, we are only able to cover the basics in this chapter. If a particular topic or relationship that you think is important has not been described here, make sure you follow up on the suggested readings.

- Although it is important to have an understanding of the four determinants of self-efficacy, you also need to be aware of the relative importance of each one, be able to define each one with examples, and be able to describe how several techniques can be used to manipulate each one.

- Be aware that research showing a significant relationship between self-confidence and performance will not necessarily address causality. Although it may be confidence affecting sport performance, it could just as easily be performances affecting self-confidence.

- When outlining the research on confidence and sport performance it can be useful to describe how athlete confidence, coaching confidence and team confidence can each have different effects on performance, and to provide examples to illustrate your points.

Sample question

Could you answer this question? Below is a typical essay question that could arise on this topic.

 Sample question   *Essay*

To what extent has self-efficacy theory advanced our understanding of sport performance? Critically discuss with reference to theoretical models and empirical evidence.

Guidelines on answering this question are included at the end of this chapter, whilst guidance on tackling other exam questions can be found on the companion website at **www.pearsoned.co.uk/psychologyexpress**

Understanding self-confidence

Confidence is something that is familiar to us all. We have all been in situations where we have felt unprepared and unconfident as well as situations where we have felt relaxed and very confident. When people talk about confidence they will often use terms such as self-belief, self-control, high expectations and even self-efficacy. However, in psychological circles different terms can often have different meanings and therefore it is important to be aware how one term differs from another.

Defining terms

Students are often unclear about how self-confidence differs from another commonly used term – *self-efficacy*. According to Bandura (1997), 'perceived self-efficacy refers to beliefs in one's capabilities to organise and execute the courses of action required to produce given attainments' (p. 3). To most people, this definition would appear to be describing what laypeople refer to as self-confidence. Bandura (1997) does attempt to distinguish self-efficacy from self-confidence by describing self-confidence as a 'strength of belief but does not necessarily specify what that certainty is about' (p. 382). However, this definition of self-confidence does not reflect how people typically use the term and is not widely accepted among researchers. Most researchers consider self-efficacy and self-confidence as the same construct; however, 'confidence is a catchword used in sports rather than a construct embedded in a theoretical system' (Bandura, 1997, p. 382). Because sport-based research is often grounded within *self-efficacy theory*, researchers will often use the term 'self-efficacy' in place of 'self-confidence'. Nevertheless, conceptually the two terms are interchangeable.

Perceived self-efficacy should, however, be distinguished from other constructs such as *self-esteem* and *outcome expectations*. Perceived self-efficacy is a judgement of capability and self-esteem is a judgement of self-worth. They are entirely different phenomena. Self-efficacy also differs from performance expectations. Self-efficacy is a judgement of capability to execute given types of performance, whereas outcome expectations are judgements about the outcomes that are likely to flow from such performances. However, the outcomes that people anticipate depend largely on their judgements of how well they will be able to perform in given situations (Bandura, 2006). Therefore a person's expectations and self-efficacy beliefs are strongly related.

How is self-confidence measured?

There are a number of assessment methods available to researchers to quantify a person's self-confidence. Self-report measures are the most common, given the difficulties in judging another person's self-confidence, but these are heavily influenced by social desirability effects. That is, sport performers are often reluctant to report that they have low self-confidence, particularly before an important competition. Despite this limitation, self-report measures are generally deemed more accurate than other-report measures or observation techniques.

A number of questionnaire assessments have been used to assess confidence in sport. The CSAI-2 (Martens et al., 1990), CSAI-2R (Cox, Martens, & Russell, 2003) and State Sport Confidence Inventory (Vealey, 1986) assess general competition self-confidence, and include questions such as 'I am confident about performing well' that are rated on a scale from 1 (not at all) to 4 (very much so). Although the specificity of efficacy measures depends upon the level the researcher wishes to generalise (Bandura, 1997), sport-specific measures are generally preferred to general measures of confidence and show greater predictive validity in athletic samples.

Bandura (2006) outlined that self-efficacy varies in *level, generality* and *strength*. People can differ in the difficulty of tasks that they believe they are capable in performing (level), efficacy beliefs associated with one activity can be generalised to similar ones within the same activity domain (generality), and people can differ in their confidence in attaining a given level of performance (strength). Measures of efficacy strength are most common in sport and exercise research. Self-efficacy strength is usually measured as a percentage and will often focus on a number of performance qualities essential for success in a given sport. For instance, a self-efficacy measure in golf might include an assessment of confidence in the following areas: driving off the tee, recovering from mistakes, putting, pitching/chipping, maintaining concentration, escaping from bunkers, approach shots to green and emotional control.

Further reading Measuring self-efficacy

Topic	Key reading
Measuring efficacy beliefs	Bandura, A. (2006). Guide for constructing self-efficacy scales. In F. Pajares & T. Urdan (Eds.), *Self-efficacy beliefs of adolescents* (Vol. 5, pp. 307–337). Greenwich, CT: Information Age Publishing.
Example of a self-efficacy measure in sport	Treasure, D. C., Monson, J., & Lox, C. L. (1996). Relationship between self-efficacy, wrestling performance, and affect prior to competition. *The Sport Psychologist, 10*, 73–83.

Test your knowledge

4.1 Define 'self-efficacy' and explain how it differs from other commonly used terms in sport.

4.2 Describe the various ways in which self-efficacy can be measured in sport settings.

4.3 Based on Bandura's (2006) guidelines, develop a self-efficacy measure for use in tennis.

Answers to these questions can be found on the companion website at: **www.pearsoned.col.uk/psychologyexpress**

Self-efficacy theory

Self-efficacy theory falls within the broader framework of social cognitive theory (Bandura, 1986; 2012). Social cognitive theory not only considers how people acquire knowledge and competencies, but also considers how they motivate and regulate their behaviour and create social systems that help structure their lives. The *social* portion of the title acknowledges social origins of thoughts and actions, and the *cognitive* portion of the title acknowledges the contribution of cognitive processes to person motivation, affect and action (Bandura, 2012). Self-efficacy forms a central component of this theory and is illustrated in Figure 4.1.

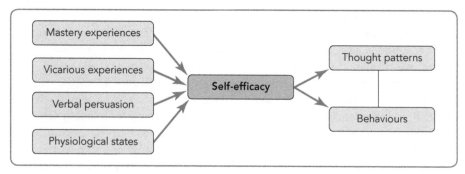

Figure 4.1 **Self-efficacy theory (Bandura, 1977)**

Determinants of self-efficacy

According to Bandura (1977), there are four main sources of information that contribute to a person's self-efficacy beliefs.

Mastery experiences

Mastery experiences refer to a person's past performance accomplishments and are the strongest source of self-efficacy information. Generally, if the task has been successfully accomplished in the past then people with have high efficacy beliefs that the task can be accomplished in the future. For inexperienced performers, a loss may be detrimental to self-efficacy. However, once an elevated sense of efficacy has been achieved through experience, a loss may not have much of an influence (Bandura, 1977). In sport, it has been shown that *imagined past experiences* (imagery) can also affect self-efficacy. For example, Jones, Mace, Bray, MacRae and Stockbridge (2002) found that imagining oneself climbing successfully (known as 'motivational general mastery' imagery) could help build self-efficacy in novice climbers, and Callow and Waters (2005) found that images involving the feeling of movement (known as 'kinaesthetic imagery') were effective in building confidence in flat-race horse jockeys (also see Chapter 10).

Vicarious experience

The second source of efficacy information is vicarious experience (also known as modelling). Watching others perform a given behaviour can provide information about one's own capabilities. Watching others perform the behaviour successfully is more likely to build efficacy beliefs when the model is similar to the self – for example, in age and experience (Bandura, 1997). In sport, video modelling (watching others' successful performances) has been identified as an effective efficacy-building strategy (Starek & McCullagh, 1999). Because model similarity is important for efficacy beliefs, many researchers have advocated the self-as-a-model approach. Watching past personal performances on video (with unsuccessful instances edited out) has also been identified in some studies as an effective efficacy-building strategy (McCullagh, Law, & Ste-Marie, 2012).

Verbal persuasion

The third source of efficacy information is verbal persuasion. Social influence is a strong determinant of self-efficacy beliefs (Bandura, 1997) and the social support given to athletes has been shown to have a strong effect on their personal efficacy beliefs (Freeman & Rees, 2010). In addition, positive *self-persuasion* (also known as self-talk) has also been identified as an effective efficacy-building strategy. For example, Hatzigeorgiadis, Zourbanos, Goltsios and Theodorakis (2008) found that motivational self-talk was a useful strategy for building self-efficacy in junior tennis players, and Weinberg, Miller and Horn (2012) found that both motivational and instructional self-talk were useful for improving performance in cross-country running, which they suggest may reflect changes in self-efficacy (also see Chapter 10).

Physiological states

The final source of efficacy information is a person's physiological state. Physiological and emotional states influence self-efficacy when people learn to associate poor performance with negative physiological arousal and successful performance with pleasant feeling states. In sport settings, self-efficacy has often shown a negative association with the appraisal of physiological states (Craft, Magyar, Becker, & Feltz, 2003; Woodman & Hardy, 2003) and some emerging evidence suggests that the suppression of physiological arousal might be an effective method of building self-efficacy in sport performers (Karimian, Kashefolhagh, Dadashi, & Chharbaghi, 2010).

Consequences of self-efficacy

Self-efficacy beliefs can have a meaningful effect on thoughts, affect and actions (Bandura, 1997). When faced with stressful stimuli, low-efficacy individuals tend to give up, attribute failure internally and experience greater anxiety or depression, whereas, high-efficacy individuals tend to seek out new challenges, try hard and persist (Bandura, 1986). In sport settings, research has shown that people with high efficacy beliefs set more challenging goals than those with either low or medium efficacy beliefs (Boyce & Bingham, 1997). It has also been demonstrated in sporting tasks that people with high efficacy beliefs sustain their maximum heart rate (effort) for a longer duration than people with low efficacy beliefs (Greenlees, Graydon, & Maynard, 1999). The tendency for highly efficacious individuals to put forth more effort and set more challenging goals should have a positive effect on athletic performance outcomes.

Further reading Self-efficacy

Topic	Key reading
Social cognitive theory	Bandura, A. (2012). Social cognitive theory. In P. A. M. Van Lange, A. W. Kruglanski, & E. T. Higgins (Eds.), *Handbook of theories of social psychology* (Vol. 1, pp. 349–373). London: Sage.
Self-efficacy theory	Bandura, A. (1977). Self-efficacy: Towards a unifying theory of behavioral change. *Psychological Review, 84*, 191–215.

Test your knowledge

4.4 Describe the basic ingredients of social cognitive theory.

4.5 Using examples, outline the four sources of self-efficacy information.

4.6 Using examples, describe how self-efficacy can influence athlete thought patterns and behaviours.

Answers to these questions can be found on the companion website at: **www.pearsoned.col.uk/psychologyexpress**

Self-confidence and sport performance

The factor that most consistently distinguishes highly successful athletes from less successful athletes is self-confidence (Feltz, Short, & Sullivan, 2008).

Athlete confidence

The relationship between self-confidence (self-efficacy) and athletic performance has been explored in a number of studies. In nearly all cases, it has been shown that self-confidence has a positive correlation with success (Craft, Magyar, Becker, & Feltz, 2003; Moritz, Feltz, Fahrbach, & Mack, 2000; Woodman & Hardy, 2003). Several factors have been shown to affect the magnitude of this relationship. The study by Woodman and Hardy (2003) showed that self-confidence is important for success for both men and women, but that confidence was slightly more important for men. Also, self-confidence is more important in sports involving open skills (e.g. tennis) than closed skills (e.g. archery), and more important in individual sports than in team sports (Craft, Magyar, Becker, & Feltz, 2003). How self-confidence is measured is also important. General measures of self-confidence such as the CSAI-2 are not as strong in predicting athletic success as sport-specific measures (Moritz, Feltz, Fahrbach, & Mack, 2000; Woodman & Hardy, 2003). In particular, Woodman and Hardy (2003) found that the self-confidence dimension of the CSAI-2 showed a small effect size in predicting sport performance, whereas domain- (sport-) specific measures showed a medium to large effect size in predicting sport performance.

CRITICAL FOCUS

The reciprocal nature of the performance–self-efficacy relationship

The relationship between self-efficacy and performance is hypothesised as bi-directional (Bandura, 1997). Performance (i.e. mastery experiences) is thought to shape self-efficacy beliefs, and self-efficacy is proposed to influence performance through its effect on thoughts, affect and actions. An important study of novice golfers tested this hypothesis directly. Over a series of eight trials, Beattie, Lief, Adamoulas and Oliver (2011) found that putting performance had a strong effect on subsequent self-efficacy, predicting (at best) 49 per cent of the variability. But self-efficacy had no effect on subsequent putting performance, predicting (at best) 2.7 per cent of the variability. This suggests that, at least in novice/inexperienced athletes, performance has a stronger effect on self-efficacy than has self-efficacy on performance.

KEY STUDY

Woodman, Akehurst, Hardy, & Beattie (2010): Self-confidence and performance: A little self-doubt helps

There is a large body of research documenting the positive effects of a high level of self-confidence in sport. However, Woodman et al. were interested in whether lowering

▶

self-confidence on a simple task (a little self-doubt) could motivate people to try harder and improve task performance.

They randomly allocated 28 participants to either an experimental or a control group. After a warm-up and verbal instructions, all participants completed measures of self-confidence and were required to complete a one-minute skipping challenge (with a grey skipping rope). They were then told that they would be required to complete the same skipping challenge and that there was a £25 prize for the person performing the most skips. However, those in the experimental group received additional information. They were instructed that the new (white) rope would be more difficult to use and might interfere with performance due to differences in weight, length and stiffness. In reality the two skipping ropes were identical. The aim was to induce doubt into the participants' ability to skip with the new rope to reduce self-confidence. All participants then completed another measure of self-confidence and repeated the one-minute skipping challenge.

The study was successful in lowering self-confidence in the experimental group, with no change shown in the control group. Interestingly, the performance in the control group remained unchanged, whereas for those in the experimental group (whose confidence had been lowered) performance was significantly improved.

In short, the study showed that performance improved when self-confidence decreased and supported the view that a little self-doubt might, *under certain circumstances*, be beneficial to performers.

Team confidence

Often sport performers are involved in team competitions rather than individual competitions and in such instances team confidence (judgements of collective capabilities) becomes more important than self-confidence. Team confidence is often referred to as *collective efficacy*. Bandura (1997) defined collective efficacy as 'a group's shared belief in its conjoint capabilities to organise and execute the courses of action required to produce given levels of attainments' (p. 477). The determinants of efficacy beliefs operate in much the same way at the team level as they do at the individual level. *Mastery experiences* (past team performances), *vicarious experiences* (modelling on other teams), *verbal persuasion* and *physiological states* are all proposed to influence collective efficacy (Bandura, 1986). Collective efficacy should also influence thoughts, affect and actions in a similar manner to self-efficacy. In team sport settings, it has been demonstrated that highly efficacious teams tend to set more challenging group goals (Greenlees, Graydon, & Maynard, 2000), put forth greater effort (Greenlees, Graydon, & Maynard, 1999) and show better team performances (Myers, Feltz, & Short, 2004).

Coach confidence

The confidence a coach has in their ability to effectively coach their athletes (termed *coaching efficacy*) can affect coaches' thoughts, feelings and behaviours, and, in turn, the learning and performances of their athlete(s). The sources and

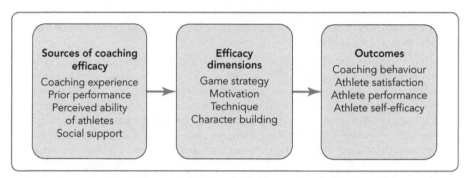

Figure 4.2 Conceptual model of coaching efficacy (Feltz, Chase, Moritz, & Sullivan, 1999)

outcomes of coaching efficacy are outlined in Figure 4.2. Coaches with high levels of coaching efficacy demonstrate more effective tactical skills, use more effective motivational and corrective feedback techniques, demonstrate more commitment and give more time to coaching, have athletes who are more satisfied with their coach, and lead their teams to more successful performances (Feltz, Chase, Moritz, & Sullivan, 1999). Another important factor in the coach–athlete relationship is *proxy efficacy*. Proxy efficacy is defined as 'one's confidence in the skills and abilities of a third party or parties to function effectively on one's behalf' (Bray, Gyurcsik, Culos-Reed, Dawson, & Martin, 2001, p. 426). An athlete's confidence in his or her coach's ability (proxy efficacy) may be especially important when learning a new skill and can influence the allocation of responsibility for successes and failures, and how often athletes turn to their coach for assistance (Bray & Shields, 2007).

CRITICAL FOCUS

Can I lower my opponents' confidence?

One potential way to gain an advantage in competitions is not only by building your own self-confidence but also by lowering your opponents' confidence. In a novel experiment by Greenlees, Buscombe, Thelwell, Holder, & Rimmer (2005), male tennis players watched video clips of a target tennis player warming up and rated their impressions of that player. However, a quarter of the tennis players viewed the target player showing positive body language (e.g. head held high) and wearing sport-specific clothing, another quarter viewed the target player showing positive body language and wearing general clothing, another quarter viewed the target player showing negative body language (e.g. head down) and wearing sport-specific clothing, and the last quarter viewed the target player showing negative body language and wearing general clothing. The results showed that tennis players were much less confident of success against the target player when the target player was showing positive body language. Type of clothing had no effect on impressions. Therefore, to lower your opponents' self-confidence it is important to demonstrate positive body language.

Overconfidence

It is often assumed that high levels of confidence will benefit performance. However, problems can arise not only when an athlete has too little confidence but also when they are overconfident. Overconfidence can be problematic as athletes may not put forth the required effort to achieve success. Optimal self-confidence means being convinced that you can achieve success but at the point where you remain motivated to put forth all the required effort to achieve that success. Research has demonstrated that *slightly* overestimating one's ability has the most positive effect on performance (Bandura, 1986).

Building confidence

There are many ways to build self-efficacy in sport performers and these generally involve manipulating one or more of the four sources of information that shape a person's efficacy beliefs. Positive mental rehearsal (imagery) is one of the most common methods advocated by sport psychology consultants. Provided the images are positive (for example, imagining oneself successfully defeating an opponent), self-efficacy beliefs should improve. Another commonly advocated technique is positive self-persuasion (self-talk). Athlete self-talk is common in sports such as tennis and badminton, and provided the self-statements are positive and instructional (e.g. 'be strong, attack the net, win') self-efficacy can be maintained and improved. Video modelling has also been advocated as an effective efficacy-building strategy. Because model similarity is particularly important in modelling interventions (Bandura, 1997), the self-as-a-model approach has been one of the most widely used in sport. This involves recording and editing video footage of the target athlete so that only positive video clips are shown. By encouraging athletes to view the most successful components of their past performances, their beliefs in their personal capabilities can improve.

Further reading	Confidence in sport
Topic	*Key reading*
Self-modelling	Ram, N., & McCullagh, P. (2003). Self-modeling: Does watching yourself performance influence physical and psychological performance? *The Sport Psychologist, 17*, 220–232.
Collective efficacy	Greenlees, I., Graydon, J., & Maynard, I. (1999). The impact of collective efficacy beliefs on effort and persistence in a group task. *Journal of Sports Sciences, 17*, 151–158.
Coaching efficacy	Feltz, D. L., Chase, M. A., Moritz, S. E., & Sullivan, P. J. (1999). A conceptual model of coaching efficacy: Preliminary investigation and instrument development. *Journal of Educational Psychology, 91*, 675–776.

4.7 Using examples, distinguish between self-efficacy, collective efficacy, coaching efficacy and proxy efficacy.

4.8 What factors can affect the magnitude of the relationship between self-confidence and athletic performance?

4.9 Drawing on self-efficacy theory, design an intervention to build efficacy beliefs of coaches, athletes or teams.

Answers to these questions can be found on the companion website at:
www.pearsoned.col.uk/psychologyexpress

Chapter summary – pulling it all together

→ Can you tick all of the points from the revision checklist at the beginning of this chapter?

→ Attempt the sample question from the beginning of this chapter using the answer guidelines below.

→ Go to the companion website at www.pearsoned.co.uk/psychologyexpress to access more revision support online, including interactive quizzes, flashcards, You be the marker exercises as well as answer guidelines for the Test your knowledge and Sample questions from this chapter.

Further reading for Chapter 4

Feltz, D. L., Short, S. E., & Sullivan, P. J. (2008). *Self-efficacy in sport: Research and strategies for working with athletes, teams, and coaches.* Champaign, IL: Human Kinetics.

Answer guidelines

 Sample question   *Essay*

To what extent has self-efficacy theory advanced our understanding of sport performance? Critically discuss with reference to theoretical models and empirical evidence.

Approaching the question

The question asks how self-efficacy theory has advanced our understanding of sport performance. Therefore it would be useful to begin your answer by providing a definition of self-efficacy and an outline of the main components (antecedents and consequences) of self-efficacy theory. You will need to consider the applicability of this theory to sport performance and therefore you should outline the research that has attempted to manipulate the sources of self-efficacy information (e.g. imagery and self-talk interventions) and the research that has explored how self-efficacy relates to sport performance. When outlining your answer, try to use examples to illustrate causal relationships – how manipulation of one factor should cause changes in another. Be sure to detail how the research can be used to create more effective performances in real-world settings.

Important points to include

The key points to get across are that (1) self-efficacy varies within and between competitions and is therefore open to manipulation, (2) by manipulating the four sources of efficacy, information self-efficacy can be developed, and (3) high levels of self-efficacy should (in most instances) help improve sport performance through its effect on decisions, goals, affect, effort and persistence. Good answers will draw on specific research examples to illustrate how manipulation of the sources of efficacy information (through well-known psychological techniques such as imagery and self-talk) can help build self-efficacy beliefs. Good answers will also discuss the various factors that can affect the magnitude of the relationship between self-efficacy and sport performance (e.g. gender, type of sport). In your answer it would be useful to describe how self-efficacy theory can be applied not only to athletes but also to coaches (coaching efficacy) and sports teams (collective efficacy).

Make your answer stand out

The best way to make your answer stand out is to incorporate a blend of classic theoretical papers and recent research findings into your answer. Demonstrate to the examiner that you understand how a study was conducted by providing a brief outline of the researchers' methods and main findings. This is a very useful way to seize a few extra exam points. Good answers will also provide a detailed definition (perhaps direct quotations) of the different efficacy constructs (e.g. self-efficacy, proxy efficacy) and how each falls within the broader social cognitive theory. Consideration of measurement issues is another way to demonstrate critical thinking. Outline how different measurements of self-efficacy (broad or sport specific) can affect study findings and provide suggestions (and perhaps an example of a good self-efficacy questionnaire) based on Bandura's (2006) guidelines for useful approaches to measuring self-efficacy.

Explore the accompanying website at www.pearsoned.co.uk/psychologyexpress

→ Prepare more effectively for exams and assignments using the answer guidelines for questions from this chapter.

→ Test your knowledge using multiple choice questions and flashcards.

→ Improve your essay skills by exploring the You be the marker exercises.

Notes

5

Concentration

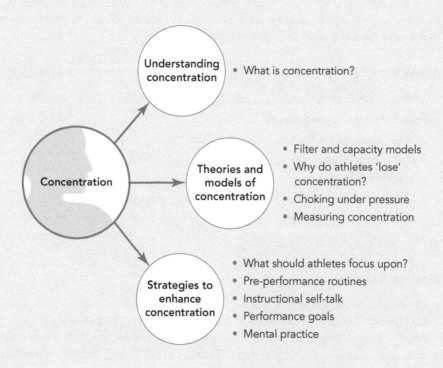

- **Understanding concentration**
  - What is concentration?

- **Theories and models of concentration**
  - Filter and capacity models
  - Why do athletes 'lose' concentration?
  - Choking under pressure
  - Measuring concentration

- **Concentration**

- **Strategies to enhance concentration**
  - What should athletes focus upon?
  - Pre-performance routines
  - Instructional self-talk
  - Performance goals
  - Mental practice

A printable version of this topic map is available from
www.pearsoned.co.uk/psychologyexpress

Introduction

Every now and then, athletes perform in a mental cocoon: a state of mind where they think, feel and do only what is necessary to accomplish what they are doing without dwelling on what has happened or speculating about what might happen. Within these 'peak experiences' or 'flow states', athletes become absorbed in the task at hand – so absorbed that time often appears to slow down, and each movement begins and ends gracefully with predestined precision. This coveted state remains mysterious and often elusive, especially when athletes need it most. Indeed, unwanted thoughts and feelings can often invade athletes' minds, rendering their plans and strategies ineffective, often with disastrous outcomes. But why do athletes' minds drift towards unwanted thoughts, feelings and actions? What mechanism can explain why athletes 'choke' when they most want to succeed? We shall briefly explore these questions with reference to theories and models of attention. We shall then examine ways in which concentration could be measured alongside interventions to improve concentration skills in athletes.

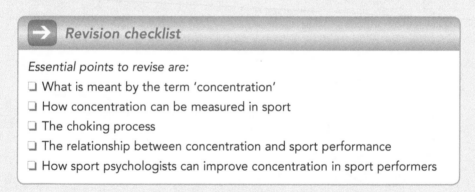

Revision checklist

Essential points to revise are:
- ❏ What is meant by the term 'concentration'
- ❏ How concentration can be measured in sport
- ❏ The choking process
- ❏ The relationship between concentration and sport performance
- ❏ How sport psychologists can improve concentration in sport performers

Assessment advice

- Concentration and attention are significant research topics in sport psychology but particularly in cognitive psychology and cognitive neuroscience. Textbooks on cognitive psychology normally include one or two chapters on attention and are worth reading to understand its history, models, constraints and limitations.
- Several models have been proposed to understand the attention system within and outside sport contexts. You should be aware of the relative importance of each one and its associated strengths and weaknesses.
- Although athletes acknowledge the importance of concentration to perform well, many gaps remain in our knowledge about concentration among sport performers. Be aware of the gaps in the literature and do not be afraid to draw attention to these gaps when detailing the research on concentration.

Sample question

Could you answer this question? Below is a typical essay question that could arise on this topic.

 Sample question   *Essay*

Consider the role of concentration in sport performance and outline practical strategies that can help athletes concentrate in pressure situations.

Guidelines on answering this question are included at the end of this chapter, whilst guidance on tackling other exam questions can be found on the companion website at **www.pearsoned.co.uk/psychologyexpress**

Understanding concentration

To prevent undue confusion about the terms 'concentration' and 'attention', it seems sensible to begin by explaining the distinction between them because these terms are used interchangeably in the literature. Most sports people use the term 'concentration' in conversations, commentaries and interviews, though it represents only one component of the tri-dimensional construct of attention. Attention refers to 'the process of exerting mental effort on specific features of the environment or on certain thoughts or activities' (Goldstein, 2008, p. 100).

What is concentration?

Concentration is one of three facets that fall within the broader construct of attention. Attention encompasses (1) a perceptual skill to focus selectively on task-relevant information while ignoring distractions, (2) an ability to divide attention between two or more tasks at the same time, and (3) concentration or 'the ability to focus effectively on the task at hand while ignoring distractions' (Moran, 2012a, p. 128). In the literature, these three elements are represented by selective attention, divided attention and concentration.

Theories and models of concentration

Filter and capacity models

The cognitive revolution of the 1950s established a view of the mind as an information-processing system with limited capacity. Within this central idea, three metaphors emerged to describe the attention system: as a filter, as a spotlight and as a resource.

63

The filter model

The metaphor of attention as a 'filter' established itself when Broadbent (1958) attempted to explain the 'cocktail party' problem – the ability of people at a party to pay attention to just one conversation even though many conversations are taking place around them. Cherry (1953) mimicked this real-life experience in the laboratory by asking people to listen to different messages played on headphones in their two ears. The participants were requested to repeat aloud the message arriving at one ear while ignoring the message arriving at the other ear. The participants recalled correctly the content of the message repeated aloud (or shadowed) but little of the message presented at the unattended ear, prompting Cherry's conclusion that when people do not attend to auditory information, little of it is processed. In other words, as Broadbent (1958) explained, when people pay auditory attention, they filter out other stimuli, allowing them to focus solely on the auditory information.

The spotlight model

Although people value what they hear in everyday life, they often rely more on what they see. Researchers took this lead and explored visual processing of information, which created the 'spotlight' metaphor (e.g. Posner, 1980). Attention as a mental spotlight captures the notion that our minds gather information by directing a beam of light towards particular stimuli. Rather than attention being a rigid 'filter', it was now regarded as a flexible 'mental spotlight' for perceptual analysis of stimuli. This metaphor percolated attention research over the past 30 years but has faltered upon two unknowns: who or what directs the spotlight and what lies outside the mental spotlight of our concentration (e.g. unconscious factors).

The resource model

Many sport performers can execute two skills at once. A competent basketball player can dribble a basketball whilst scanning among his team mates to deliver a decisive pass. But what can explain our ability to do two or more things at once? Resource theorists (e.g. Kahneman, 1973) argued that one's attention reflects a limited pool of attention that is flexibly distributed to the needs of the task. Spare attentional capacity increases, for instance, according to one's motivation, arousal and practice, but difficult tasks reduce it. The skills and exploits of sport performers are restricted by available mental resources, especially those allocated to working memory – a mental system allowing us to store and manage information for a limited time (Lavallee, Kremer, Moran, & Williams, 2012).

Why do athletes 'lose' concentration?

Filter and capacity models represent useful metaphors for understanding the workings of the mind. However, they are somewhat limited in their focus on information flowing from the outside world inwards but not from the other direction: long-term memory to short-term (working) memory (Moran, 2012a). In practice, many athletes become distracted by unwanted thoughts and feelings, often ruminating over something that happened or speculating about what to do next. To understanding losing concentration, we must understand what concentration means and whether concentration is 'lost' or 'misdirected'. We have already explained that concentration represents 'the ability to focus effectively on the task at hand while ignoring distractions' (Moran, 2012a, p. 128). Such distractions can be categorised as internal or external.

- *Internal distractions* include such things as thoughts, feelings and bodily sensations.
- *External distractions* include things such as weather conditions (e.g. heat), noise (e.g. a camera clicking) and gamesmanship.

Many external distractions are unavoidable and impress upon the competitor the need to deal with such distractions (e.g. wind, noise). Internal distractions, however, are self-generated and emerge from our thoughts and feelings, such as regretting a missed opportunity to score or wondering what might pass in the future.

Ironic processes and attentional control

To understand why athletes lose concentration we can consider two emotion-related models. In Chapter 3 we discussed *attentional control theory* (ACT; Eysenck, Derakshan, Santos, & Calvo, 2007). This model contends that anxiety disrupts the attention system in such a way that sport performers have greater difficulty shifting their attention optimally between and within tasks and resisting disruption from task-irrelevant cues (see Chapter 3). There is good support for anxiety affecting attention in this manner in sport performers (Moran, Byrne, & McGlade, 2002; Wilson, Wood, & Vine, 2009).

The other conceptual model, termed the *ironic processes model*, explains that our mind wanders because we try to control it (Wegner, 1994). This ironic theory of mental control suggests that when we are anxious or tired, trying not to think about something increases the chances that we will think about it. Wegner (1994) argued that the intention to suppress a thought activates a search for that thought to determine whether the act of suppression was successful. Under normal conditions, the conscious intentional system dominates the unconscious monitoring system but under stress or fatigue, the unconscious monitoring system prevails and the unwanted thought emerges. Although few research efforts have explored this model in detail, there is some evidence for its effects in sport performance situations (Wegner, Ansfield, & Pilloff, 1998; Woodman & Davis, 2008).

KEY STUDY

Bell & Hardy (2009): Effects of attentional focus on skilled performance in golf

Bell and Hardy (2009) examined the effectiveness of three different attentional foci for peak performance in sport. Thirty-three male golfers were assigned to one of the three attentional groups and completed five blocks of ten pitch shots (two in anxious conditions

▶

and three in neutral conditions). The three attention groups were: *internal focus* (a focus on the arms during the swing), *proximal external focus* (a focus on the position of the clubface during the swing) and *distal external focus* (a focus on the flight of the ball after it had left the clubface). The study showed that regardless of anxiety condition, those assigned to the distal external focus of attention performed the most accurate pitch shots and those assigned to an internal focus of attention performed the least accurate pitch shots.

Test your knowledge

5.1 What three facets comprise the construct of attention?

5.2 Describe the filter and capacity models of attention.

5.3 How can we explain why athletes lose concentration?

Answers to these questions can be found on the companion website at:
www.pearsoned.col.uk/psychologyexpress

Further reading Models of concentration

Topic	Key reading
Filter and capacity models	Moran, A. (2012b). Concentration: Attention and performance. In S. M. Murphy (Ed.), *The Oxford handbook of sport and performance psychology* (pp. 117–130). New York: Oxford University Press.
Attentional control theory in sport	Wilson, M. (2008). From processing efficiency to attentional control: A mechanistic account of the anxiety-performance relationship. *International Review of Sport and Exercise Psychology*, 1, 184–201.
Ironic processes model	Wegner, D. M., Ansfield, M., & Pilloff, D. (1998). The putt and the pendulum: Ironic effects of the mental control of action. *Psychological Science*, 9, 196–199.

Choking under pressure

An athlete whose performance falls suddenly and significantly under conditions of perceived pressure is suggested to have 'choked'. During the 2011 US Masters, Irish golfer Rory McIlroy held a four-shot lead going into the final day of the competition, but dropped six shots in three holes on the back nine to finish outside the top ten. Choking can be defined as 'performance decrements under pressure situations' (Baumeister, 1984, p. 610) and more specifically as 'the occurrence of inferior performance despite striving and incentives for superior performance' (Baumeister & Showers, 1986, p. 361).

Two different theories have been proposed to explain why athletes choke under pressure. *Distraction theories* propose that in high-pressure situations, an individual's attention is diverted to task-irrelevant thoughts, such as worries about the situation (Beilock & Carr, 2001). The attention an athlete needs to execute the task at hand competes with the situation-related worries, creating a dual-task environment. *Explicit monitoring* or skill-focus theories, on the other hand, suggest that pressure increases an individual's self-consciousness to perform a skill correctly.

Distraction

According to incentive-based, or over-motivation, theories, reduced performance arises from excessive arousal in basic reward pathways that incur a cost in one's working memory or attention (Short & Sorrentino, 1986). With greater arousal, attention narrows and our ability to see the 'whole picture' and make decisions reduces. For example, Mobbs et al. (2009) investigated whether large reward contingencies impair performance and if these were associated with a shift in activity from prefrontal areas to more impulsive brain systems. The participants chased an artificial prey around a computerised maze and received either a large (£5.00) or small (£0.50) amount of money for capturing the prey. Performance decrements and near-misses induced by high rewards were strongly correlated with increased midbrain activity. Such findings support an incentive-based explanation of choking. More recent research, however, has suggested that self-presentation concerns (i.e. trying hard to impress others) may be more important than rewards for choking in sport (Mesagno, Harvey, & Jannelle, 2011).

Explicit monitoring

According to explicit monitoring, or skill-focused, theories, people choke because competition pressure causes athletes to attend closely to skill processes in a manner that disrupts skill execution. In particular, allocating attention to execute a skill in a step-by-step process is thought to disrupt the learning and execution of proceduralised processes that usually operate outside conscious awareness (DeCaro, Thomas, Albert, & Beilock, 2011). In sport, the conscious processing hypothesis, and the more general 'reinvestment theory' (Masters & Maxwell, 2008), has received the greatest experimental attention. Research has shown that arousal, and more specifically anxiety, contributes to athletes over-thinking their movements and leads to a decline in performance (see Chapter 3).

CRITICAL FOCUS

Clutch performances

If we dwell upon choking under pressure, we might forget how often athletes perform in the clutch. Otten (2009) defined a 'clutch performance' as any performance increment or superior performance that occurs under pressure circumstances. Sport fans witness these clutch performances much more often than they see athletes choke under pressure. The feats of Roger Federer in tennis and Tiger Woods in golf exemplify this phenomenon. But what could explain why some performers excel under pressure? Otten (2009) identified perceived control as the critical factor associated with a clutch performance. Another intriguing possibility is that individual differences in narcissism predict performance. Wallace and Baumeister (2002) showed that the performance of narcissists rises and falls with perceived opportunity for glory. Using various tasks and manipulations of self-enhancement, they found that narcissists performed better in conditions that provided an opportunity for self-enhancement.

Test your knowledge

5.4 Describe choking in sport.

5.5 Describe distraction theories and explicit monitoring theories of choking.

5.6 What is a clutch performance?

Answers to these questions can be found on the companion website at:
www.pearsoned.col.uk/psychologyexpress

Further reading Choking in sport

Topic	Key reading
Attention under pressure	Oudejans, R. R. D., Kuijpers, W., Kooijman, C. C. & Bakker, F. C. (2011). Thoughts and attention of athletes under pressure: Skill focus or performance worries? *Anxiety, Stress, & Coping*, 24, 59–73.
Alleviating choking	Mesagno, C., Marchant, D., & Morris, T. (2009). Alleviating choking: The sounds of distraction. *Journal of Applied Sport Psychology*, 20, 131–147.
Explanations of choking	Wilson, M., Chattington, M., Marple-Horvat, D. E., & Smith, N. C. (2007). A comparison of self-focus versus attentional explanations of choking. *Journal of Sport & Exercise Psychology*, 29, 439–456.
Choking in sport	Hill, D. M., Hanton, S., Matthews, N., & Fleming, S. (2010). Choking in sport: A review. *International Review of Sport and Exercise Psychology*, 3, 24–39.

Measuring concentration

As we have seen, the ability to concentrate on the task at hand is a prerequisite for competitive sport performers. We can measure attentional processes using psychometric instruments (for example, the TAIS; Nideffer, 1976), neuroscientific instruments (e.g. functional magnetic resonance imaging, fMRI) and experimental methods (e.g. testing the dual-task paradigm).

Self-report

For applied sport psychologists, psychometric instruments offer a simple and practical method to measure concentration processes but these instruments also have drawbacks. The two measures that have been most frequently used are the Test of Attentional and Interpersonal Style (TAIS; Nideffer, 1976) and the Thought Occurrence Questionnaire for Sport (TOQS; Hatzigeorgiadis & Biddle, 2000). The TAIS has demonstrated face validity (the extent to which the content of the measure appears to represent the required construct) and construct validity (the extent to which the measure taps into the required construct). However, Boutcher (2008) has questioned its predictive validity (the extent to which scores on the measure predict behaviour on a criterion measure in the future) in athletic samples, as theTAIS was originally developed to measure attentional processes in everyday experiences rather than issues specific to sport. The TOQS assesses self-preoccupied thinking, including components of worry about performance, and comprises three subscales: performance worries (e.g. 'that I am not going to win this competition'), situation-irrelevant thoughts (e.g. 'about what I'm going to do when I get home') and thoughts of escape (e.g. 'that I am fed up with it'). This measure has shown evidence of face, construct and predictive validity in adult and youth sport populations (Lane, Harwood, & Nevill, 2005). However, the measure suffers from the same limitations as all self-report instruments, such as acquiescence (a tendency to agree or disagree with questions, regardless of the content), social desirability (a tendency to endorse items on the basis of how socially desirable they are) and response distortion (a tendency to manipulate scores by answering in a certain way).

Direct observation

An exciting field of research exploring attentional processes is captured within cognitive neuroscience. Cognitive neuroscience is the scientific study of biological substrates underlying mental processes. Cognitive neuroscientists use techniques such as electroencephalography (EEG), positron emission tomography (PET scanning) and functional magnetic resonance imaging (fMRI). EEG technology is used to measure electrical activity at one's scalp emerging from the electrical activity of neurons in the underlying brain region. In PET scanning, a radioactive substance is administered to the participant. Active areas of the brain look brighter on the image than less active areas. fMRI scanning relies on the different magnetic properties of oxygenated haemoglobin (in the blood) compared to deoxygenated haemoglobin. Milton, Solodkin, Hlustik and Small (2007) examined motor planning (i.e. pre-shot routine) in expert and novice female golfers. Expert golfers demonstrated fundamentally different brain activation in their pre-shot routine compared with novice golfers. In particular, novice golfers had difficulties filtering the relevant information needed to plan a successful golf shot.

Strategies to enhance concentration

Sport psychologists encounter a considerable challenge when they work with athletes to enhance their concentration. The challenge arises because some of the strategies purported to improve concentration lack a plausible theoretical rationale or sufficient evidence of empirical validity. One example, the 'concentration grid' exercise (Figure 5.1), requires participants to scan digits within a limited time on a grid divided into 100 randomly numbered, equal-sized squares (from 00 to 99). The participant marks off as many consecutive numbers as they can within a limited time under different levels of distraction (from silence to verbal abuse). Greenlees, Thelwell and Holder (2006) examined the efficacy of the concentration grid as a concentration enhancement exercise among 28 soccer players and reported that it lacked the efficacy credited to it within the literature.

84	27	51	78	59	52	13	85	61	55
28	60	92	04	97	90	31	57	29	33
32	96	65	39	80	77	49	86	18	70
76	87	71	95	98	81	01	46	88	00
48	82	89	47	35	17	10	42	62	34
44	67	93	11	07	43	72	94	69	56
53	79	05	22	54	74	58	14	91	02
06	68	99	75	26	15	41	66	20	40
50	09	64	08	38	30	36	45	83	24
03	73	21	23	16	37	25	19	12	63

Figure 5.1 The concentration grid. For this exercise, athletes are required to mark off as many consecutive numbers as possible within a one-minute period (Harris & Harris, 1984)

A second concentration exercise, known as 'simulation training', proposes that athletes can learn to concentrate better in competitive situations by simulating such conditions in practice. A plausible rationale for this exercise exists within the encoding specificity principle of learning. Research has shown that information recall is helped when the conditions in which people recall resemble those in which the original encoding occurred.

What should athletes focus upon?

Coaches often advise athletes to 'let it flow' and 'stop trying too hard' when faced with pressure situations. Though the advice might be borne out of good intentions, it does not help a golfer (for example) to cope with a problem of movement execution. Researchers have only recently begun to manipulate attentional focus (via instruction, secondary tasks or pressure) and measure the influence on movement quality. Gray (2004) asked skilled baseball players to perform a simulated hitting task under baseline and pressure conditions. In the pressure condition, baseball players executed fewer hits and showed greater variability in the timing of the different stages of their swings, relative to baseline performance. It appears that skilled batters were able to monitor the direction of the bat under pressure, attending to the step-by-step elements of skill execution. This attention to a well-learned task prompted adjustments to the skill and, therefore, an increased kinematic variability.

Pre-performance routines

Pre-performance routines are preferred action sequences and/or repetitive behaviours preceding self-paced skills (Cotterill, 2010). They are a familiar part of sport performances – whether it is a golfer practising his or her putting stroke before a putt or a tennis player bouncing the ball three times before a serve, these action sequences are favoured by these athletes. Theoretically, pre-performance routines can aid concentration because athletes get an opportunity to focus solely upon task-relevant information to execute the skill. In particular, they are able to play in the 'present' rather than regretting what has passed or predicting what might happen. Finally, routines might help athletes to execute the skill automatically rather than consciously controlling the well-learned skill. This is important because over-thinking the mechanics of a well-learned automated closed skill (e.g. golf swing) can disrupt movement and performance (Masters & Maxwell, 2008).

Instructional self-talk

Instructional self-talk (or trigger words) are short phrases to help an athlete to focus upon a specific action. For example, a golfer might remind himself to take the club back 'smooth and low' to create a wide take-away on his backswing. These statements remind the athlete what to focus upon rather than what to avoid. To date, no published research has demonstrated whether instructional self-statements can improve athletes' concentration. However, qualitative reports show that instructional self-talk is often adopted by athletes in a direct attempt to aid their focus or concentration (Hardy, Gammage, & Hall, 2001).

Performance goals

Within the goal-setting literature, researchers have distinguished among three types of goal: outcome goals (the result of a competition), performance goals (short-term targets that remain within the athlete's control) and process goals (specific actions to achieve a goal). There is evidence that setting either performance goals or process goals can help direct attention. For example, Kingston and Hardy (1997) randomly assigned 37 male golfers to one of two goal-setting training programmes – process-related goals or performance-related goals. There was also a third group that did not participate in the goal-setting programme. They found that golfers who were trained to use more performance-related goals reported better concentration than those assigned to use process goals and those receiving no goal training. This seems to support the idea that goal setting can facilitate concentration skills in athletes.

Mental practice

Mental practice refers to the systematic use of mental imagery to rehearse physical actions. The argument that visual mental rehearsal could aid concentration among sport performers remains equivocal because few studies have explored this possibility directly. Anecdotal accounts from professional athletes appear to support the idea that imagery use can aid concentration (Moran, 2012a), but this possibility has so far not been subjected to critical scientific study.

CRITICAL FOCUS

Associative or dissociative attention strategy

During endurance events, sport performers are said to adopt one of two association strategies. An *associative attention strategy* involves monitoring (deliberately focusing on) bodily functions such as heart rate, muscle tension, breathing and pain. A *dissociative attention strategy*, on the other hand, involves tuning out or distracting oneself from internal bodily functions (Morgan & Pollock, 1977). Research has shown that elite and non-elite athletes have different attention preferences. Elite athletes tend to use an associative attention strategy whereas non-elite athletes tend to use a dissociative attention strategy (Morgan & Pollock, 1977). Interestingly, elite athletes have been found to use a dissociative attention strategy in training and an associative attention strategy in competitions and there is some evidence that an associative strategy is correlated with better performances in competition (Masters & Ogles, 1998).

More recently, Wulf, Höß and Prinz (1998) have considered an *internal focus* of attention that is directed at the performer's own body movements and an *external focus* of attention that is directed at the effects that his or her movements have on the environment. Research has shown that an external focus of attention can be advantageous as it speeds up the learning process and enhances movement effectiveness and efficiency (Wulf & Lewthwaite, 2010).

Test your knowledge

5.7 Describe the evidence linking simulation training and concentration training exercises (e.g. the concentration grid) to improving concentration in sport.

5.8 Outline the concentration techniques that may help improve concentration in athletes.

5.9 Describe the various ways you could measure concentration processes in athletes.

Answers to these questions can be found on the companion website at:
www.pearsoned.col.uk/psychologyexpress

Chapter summary – pulling it all together

→ Can you tick all of the points from the revision checklist at the beginning of this chapter?

→ Attempt the sample question from the beginning of this chapter using the answer guidelines below.

→ Go to the companion website at www.pearsoned.co.uk/psychologyexpress to access more revision support online, including interactive quizzes, flashcards, You be the marker exercises as well as answer guidelines for the Test your knowledge and Sample questions from this chapter.

Further reading for Chapter 5

Moran, A. (2012b). Concentration: Attention and performance. In S. M. Murphy (Ed.), *The Oxford handbook of sport and performance psychology* (pp. 117–130). New York: Oxford University Press.

Answer guidelines

 Sample question   *Essay*

Consider the role of concentration in sport performance and outline practical strategies that can help athletes concentrate in pressure situations.

Approaching the question

As with most essay questions, it is sensible to define the construct you are about to explore before proceeding with your answer. Definitions help the reader grasp your knowledge and understanding of the topic. Once you have written your definition, you can create a scaffold for your answer by describing the models that researchers use to understand concentration processes in sport. In this chapter, we have discussed four techniques suggested to improve concentration skills: pre-performance routines, instructional self-talk, performance goals and mental practice. You should indicate in your answer whether evidence is available to support the efficacy of each of the techniques in terms of improving concentration. If there are gaps that exist in this literature, you should also highlight this contrast. Demonstrate your knowledge of contemporary research by outlining one or two recent studies in each area you are describing.

Important points to include

Once you have outlined and defined the construct of concentration, it could be worthwhile outlining the various factors that cause athletes to lose concentration (e.g. crowd noise, bodily sensations). This will help you progress your answer towards more detailed accounts of why concentration can be lost (e.g. Wegner, 1994). Good answers will draw upon the 'choking in sport' literature, providing appropriate definitions (use direct quotations if necessary), an overview of the various theoretical models, and specific research examples to illustrate key points. Your answer should progress naturally towards the various techniques that can be used to help improve concentration in athletes. Outline the efficacy of standard concentration exercises such as the concentration grid exercise, drawing upon important research to support your conclusions, and provide a critical analysis of each of the four applied techniques that can be adopted before and during competitions.

Make your answer stand out

A useful way to earn additional marks in an exam is to provide in-depth research examples in key areas. Demonstrate to your examiner that you have read the study in detail by describing the basic procedures and conclusions outlined in the paper. Another useful way to pick up extra marks is to consider the various ways in which concentration can be measured and provide an outline of the strengths and weaknesses of both self-report and EEG technology methods. You can also pick up additional marks by describing, where appropriate, concentration styles such as associative and dissociative strategies and discussing practical applications. Where there are gaps in the literature, don't be afraid to point this out and describe potential studies that could be conducted in the future to address these research gaps.

Explore the accompanying website at www.pearsoned.co.uk/psychologyexpress

→ Prepare more effectively for exams and assignments using the answer guidelines for questions from this chapter.
→ Test your knowledge using multiple choice questions and flashcards.
→ Improve your essay skills by exploring the You be the marker exercises.

Notes

6

Coping

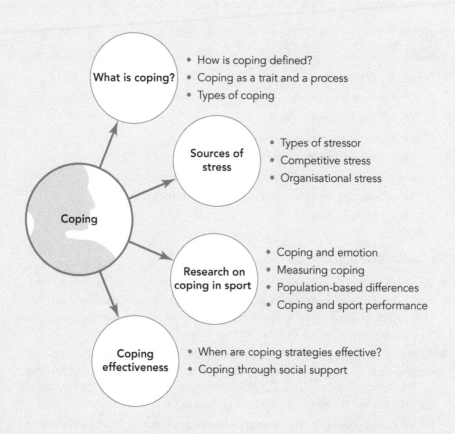

- **What is coping?**
  - How is coping defined?
  - Coping as a trait and a process
  - Types of coping

- **Sources of stress**
  - Types of stressor
  - Competitive stress
  - Organisational stress

- **Coping**

- **Research on coping in sport**
  - Coping and emotion
  - Measuring coping
  - Population-based differences
  - Coping and sport performance

- **Coping effectiveness**
  - When are coping strategies effective?
  - Coping through social support

A printable version of this topic map is available from
www.pearsoned.co.uk/psychologyexpress

Introduction

Coping with challenging circumstances is something that everybody is familiar with, including professional athletes. Throughout competitions, athletes face numerous environmental stressors: golfers struggle to escape from bunkers, ice-skaters fall, racing drivers stall their engines, and canoeists hit gates. The manner in which athletes respond to such stressors can have a profound influence on both their short-term and long-term success (Lazarus, 2000). Our goal in this chapter is to define the coping construct and understand how coping might contribute to sport performers' success and well-being. We shall explore the types of stressors that athletes face, the types of coping strategy available to athletes, the different approaches to researching and measuring coping in sport, and how athletes might be trained to cope more effectively in stressful situations.

> → *Revision checklist*
>
> *Essential points to revise are:*
> ❏ What is meant by the term 'coping'
> ❏ The various types of coping
> ❏ The sources of stress experienced by athletes
> ❏ The measurement of coping
> ❏ How social support might help athletes perform under stress
> ❏ The relationship between coping and performance in sport
> ❏ Coping effectiveness

Assessment advice

- Research on coping considers many demographic variables (e.g. sex, age) and psychological variables (e.g. anxiety). For this reason, we have briefly described some of these associations, but recommend students read further to broaden and deepen their understanding of coping in sport.

- Students should be mindful of studies that have explored specific coping strategies (e.g. social support) and those that have grouped such strategies within dimensions (e.g. emotion-focused coping) and the implications this might have for developing intervention techniques.

- When considering the relationship between coping and sport performance, students should consider not only the coping strategy but also the perceived effectiveness of the strategy. Even though some coping strategies might seem, in principle, a good idea, this might not be the case for all athletes.

- There is much research on the coping strategies used by different populations of athletes. When outlining such research, students would do well to outline the real-world application of findings using examples where appropriate.

Sample question

Could you answer this question? Below is a typical essay question that could arise on this topic.

 Sample question **Essay**

To what extent has our understanding of coping contributed to sporting success? Critically discuss with reference to contemporary research and theory.

Guidelines on answering this question are included at the end of this chapter, whilst guidance on tackling other exam questions can be found on the companion website at **www.pearsoned.co.uk/psychologyexpress**

What is coping?

How is coping defined?

There are many different approaches to researching and understanding coping, and many definitions are available to us. The most often cited definition of coping comes from the work of Lazarus and Folkman (1984). These authors published a number of important works on stress, appraisal and coping, which fall within the more encompassing cognitive-motivational-relational theory of stress and emotion (see Chapter 3). These authors define coping as 'constantly changing cognitive and behavioural efforts to manage specific external or internal demands that are appraised as taking or exceeding resources of the person' (Lazarus & Folkman, 1984, p. 141). In this view, coping is a dynamic and recursive process involving the person's internal environments (i.e. beliefs about the self, goals and values) and external environments (e.g. weather conditions) (Lazarus, 1999). However, people have also been known to display a specific coping 'style' that remains relatively consistent across situations.

Coping as a trait and a process

Research on coping has typically been explored by two approaches: *coping style* and *coping process*. Coping style refers to the strategies that remain relatively consistent over time and circumstances, whereas the coping process reflects the effort to manage psychological stress in a given situation. In Nicholls and Polman's (2007) systematic review of the coping literature in sport, it was found that most research had adopted the process approach to coping (46 studies), but a number of studies had supported the contention that athletes show some consistency in coping styles across competitions (11 studies). The authors concluded that coping in sport is best viewed as a dynamic process based upon athletes' appraisal of the situation and previous coping attempts.

Types of coping

As there are an infinite number of strategies that people might use to cope in a given situation, researchers have found it useful to develop classifications of coping strategies to help shape the development of theoretical models. The most common classification scheme for coping responses was developed by Folkman and Lazarus (1988), who considered two main types: problem-focused and emotion-focused.

- *Problem-focused coping* reflects coping directed towards resolving the problem itself, such as altering an aspect of the environment or changing the situation.
- *Emotion-focused coping* reflects coping by managing emotions, such as cognitively reinterpreting the situation or not thinking about the stressor.

For example, if a right-handed boxer were stressed about competing against a left-handed boxer, he or she might choose a problem-focused coping strategy such as spending more time training against a left-handed boxer. In contrast, the boxer might choose an emotion-focused coping strategy such as focusing upon a breathing technique to reduce arousal levels and his or her anxiety. Sometimes, researchers include a third type of coping termed *avoidance coping*. This category reflects mental or physical efforts to avoid dealing with the stressor (e.g. alcohol, avoiding training).

Because specific coping strategies do not always categorise neatly as one type or another (for example, seeking emotional support could be viewed as problem-focused or emotion-focused) recent research has started to move away from these traditional classification schemes. For example, in sport settings athletes have been shown to use a number of discrete coping strategies including thought control, mental imagery, relaxation, effort expenditure, logical analysis, seeking support and expressing emotions (Gaudreau & Blondin, 2002). The advantage of assessing discrete coping strategies over broad coping dimensions is that applied sport psychologists can tailor their interventions towards more specific targets (e.g. a particular coping strategy).

Test your knowledge

6.1 What do psychologists mean by the term 'coping'?

6.2 Should we view coping as a dynamic or static process?

6.3 Using examples, outline the different ways in which researchers can classify coping strategies.

Answers to these questions can be found on the companion website at: **www.pearsoned.col.uk/psychologyexpress**

Further reading Understanding coping in sport

Topic	Key reading
Defining and understanding coping	Lazarus, R.S., & Folkman, S. (1984). *Stress, appraisal and coping*. New York: Springer.
Coping as a process or a trait	Nicholls, A. R., & Polman, R. C. J. (2007). Coping in sport: A systematic review. *Journal of Sports Sciences, 25*, 11–31.
Dimensions of coping in sport	Nicholls, A. R., & Thelwell, R. C. (2010). Coping conceptualised and unravelled. In A. R. Nicholls (Ed.), *Coping in sport: Theory, methods, and related constructs* (pp. 3–14). Hauppauge, NY: Nova.

Sources of stress

Types of stressor

There are many stressors that athletes are required to cope with in their training and competitions. Because stress-related cognitions and behaviours abound, researchers have sought an appropriate classification scheme to differentiate among them. The most common classification scheme is separation of stressors that are competitive and those that are organisational (Hanton, Fletcher, & Coughlan, 2005).

- *Competitive stress* refers to 'an on-going transaction between an individual and the environmental demands associated primarily and directly with competitive performance' (Hanton, Fletcher, & Coughlan, 2005, p. 1130).

- *Organisational stress* refers to 'an on-going transaction between an individual and the environmental demands associated primarily and directly with the organisation within which he or she is operating' (Hanton, Fletcher, & Coughlan, 2005, p. 1130).

An example of competitive stress is competing against an opponent with a higher national ranking. An example of organisational stress is having to perform well to secure a new club contract. A third category, *personal stress*, is sometimes included to reflect individual and environmental demands from one's personal life (McKay, Niven, Lavallee, & White, 2008). This might include the stress of having to balance time demands of a family with training for competitions.

Competitive stress

Several researchers have explored the sources of competitive stress among sport performers. In one notable study, Scanlan, Stein and Ravizza (1991) examined the sources of stress among 26 former elite figure skaters. Five major sources of stress emerged from the data:

- Negative aspects of competition (e.g. experiencing competition worries)
- Negative significant-other relationships (e.g. failing to meet others' expectations)
- Demands or costs of skating (e.g. dealing with family's financial sacrifice)
- Personal struggles (e.g. perfectionism)
- Traumatic experiences (e.g. death).

It was clear from the data that the sources of stress in sport performers emerge from both competition and non-competition sources. Many other studies have since examined the sources of stress in various sports and age groups. Research in golf, for example (Giacobbi, Foore, & Weinberg, 2004; Nicholls & Polman, 2008), has shown that sources of stress fall into two broad categories: *personal* (e.g. competitive stress, physical and mental errors) and *environmental* (e.g. weather conditions, opponents playing well).

Organisational stress

A number of studies have also explored organisational stress in athletes. In a case study of organisational stress in elite sport, Woodman and Hardy (2001b) identified four major organisational stress issues: environmental, personal, leadership and team.

- *Environmental issues* included selection, finances and the training environment.
- *Personal issues* involved nutrition, injury, goals and expectations.
- *Leadership issues* included coaches and coaching styles.
- *Team issues* were team atmosphere, roles, communication and support network.

Fletcher and Hanton (2003) complemented and extended this research line by interviewing 14 international male and female performers from several sports. Similar sources of organisational stress emerged but these were classified into different higher-order themes: (1) accommodation, (2) travel and (3) the competition environment.

 Sample question   *Essay*

Critically describe the research on the sources of stress among sport performers.

KEY STUDY

Thatcher & Day (2008): Re-appraising stress appraisals: The underlying properties of stress in sport

Much research has explored the sources of stress in sport and many have been identified that are specific to the population being studied. The study by Thatcher and Day (2008) sought to explore more generally whether the sources of stress proposed by Lazarus and Folkman (1984), presumed to be representative of all situations and populations, could be identified in an athletic sample. They interviewed 16 national-level trampolinists about their most stressful competitive experience. Using a deductive content analysis (theory driven), they identified the eight sources of stress identified by Lazarus and Folkman in addition to two further sources of stress. The ten sources of stress identified were novelty (something not experienced before), predictability (when expectations are not met), event uncertainty (not knowing), imminence (awareness of the imminence of competition), duration (the time during the event), temporal uncertainty (not knowing when an event will happen), ambiguity (when required information is unclear), timing in relation to the life cycle (other stressful events in one's life), self and other comparison (comparisons with other people), and inadequate preparation (not being prepared for competition). The authors recommended that further research explore the transferability of these ten sources to other sporting populations.

Research on coping in sport

Coping and emotion

In Chapter 3 we introduced two theories of emotion that form larger, more general frameworks of stress, appraisal, coping and emotion. These are Lazarus's (1999) cognitive-motivational-relational theory (CMRT), and the theory of challenge and threat states in athletes (TCTSA; Jones, Meijen, McCarthy, & Sheffield, 2009).

Cognitive-motivational-relational theory

To recap briefly, the CMRT contends that two key processes are involved in the generation and regulation of emotions: cognitive appraisal and coping. This model suggests that the appraisal of a situation, rather than the situation itself, is what influences the emotional response. The appraisal process involves two steps: a *primary appraisal* and a *secondary appraisal*. Primary appraisal is the relevance of a situation to a person's well-being in terms of his or her goals, whereas secondary appraisal focuses on the options for coping. It is the combination of elements within primary and secondary appraisal that explains how emotions arise. No emotions will arise if the athlete appraises an encounter as unimportant. However, when an event is perceived as relevant to athlete goals, the coping options available to the athlete (secondary appraisal) will determine the occurrence of positive and negative emotions.

Theory of challenge and threat states in athletes

The theory of challenge and threat states in athletes (TCTSA; Jones, Meijen, McCarthy, & Sheffield, 2009) also incorporates elements of appraisal, coping and emotion. When sport performers are actively engaged in competition, their evaluation of competition demands and resources determines whether psychological states of challenge or threat are experienced. A challenge state occurs when evaluated resources meet or exceed evaluated demands (i.e. the athlete can cope with competition demands) and a threat state occurs when demands exceed resources (i.e. the athlete cannot cope with competition demands). In a challenge state, athletes are proposed to experience more positive emotions and are more likely to perceive emotions (whether positive or negative) as helpful to performance. In a threat state, athletes are proposed to experience more negative emotions and are more likely to perceive emotions as unhelpful to performance.

Research on coping and emotion

Only a few studies have explored the relationship between coping and emotion in sport. In a study of university athletes, Ntoumanis and Biddle (1998) found that problem-focused coping predicted the occurrence of positive emotions whereas emotion-focused coping predicted the occurrence of negative emotions. However, in a study of Olympic athletes, Pensgaard and Duda (2003) found no relationship between discrete coping strategies and athlete emotions. Both studies, however, found that perceived coping effectiveness (judgements of the relative success of coping strategies) was positively correlated with positive emotions.

Measuring coping

Coping in sport has been measured using both qualitative and quantitative methods. Semi-structured interviews paint an informative picture of the coping process in sport, but there is often a delay, sometimes of several months, between the actual event and recalling that event. This delay might affect the accuracy of the account one provides about coping with a stressor (Smith, Leffingwell, & Ptacek, 1999). A number of questionnaire-based measures have also been developed to assess sport-specific coping, with some focusing on coping strategies used in a particular situation and others assessing the typical coping responses of athletes. Commonly used questionnaires include:

- Coping Strategies in Sport Competition inventory (Gaudreau & Blondin, 2002)
- M-COPE inventory (Crocker & Graham, 1995)
- Ways of Coping in Sport scale (Madden, Kirkby, & McDonald, 1989)
- Coping Function Questionnaire (Kowalski & Crocker, 2001).

These inventories are continually being developed and refined, but none of the questionnaires hasbeen validated across all sport populations. For example, the Coping Function Questionnaire has been validated in youth sport but not in adult sport populations, and the Coping Strategies in Sport Competition Inventory has been validated in adult populations but not youth sport populations. Validation is an on-going process, but each of these questionnaires has shown evidence of validity and reliability in some athletic populations.

Population-based differences

The coping strategies that athletes use in competition can be predicted, at least to some extent, by levels of mental toughness (see Chapter 9) and also by general personality scores (see Chapter 1). Research has also explored how other individual and group-based differences (e.g. age, ethnicity, gender, sport) might predict athletes' reported coping styles.

One line of research has explored the coping strategies used by individual and team sport athletes. It has been found that team sport athletes use a greater range of coping strategies than individual sport athletes and this may reflect the greater number of coping strategies available to those participating in team competitions (Holt & Dunn, 2004). Athlete coping responses might also differ in terms of gender and age. There is evidence that older athletes cope more effectively with stress but the literature on gender differences is more inconclusive (Nicholls & Polman, 2007). Older athletes may cope more effectively with competition demands because older athletes typically have greater experience of those demands. It is less clear why male and female athletes would cope differently, but this may reflect the different competition demands across men's and women's sports. Alternatively, the finding that women are more likely to use particular coping strategies (e.g. seeking emotional support) might reflect the different personality characteristics of men and women (see Chapter 1).

Coping and sport performance

The strategies used to cope with task demands have been shown to have a meaningful effect on athletic performance. For example, Gaudreau, Nicholls and Levy (2010) explored the coping strategies used by golfers over six consecutive rounds of golf. They found that when golfers used more task-oriented coping strategies (e.g. expending more effort, cognitive reappraisal) their achievement levels were higher than when they used disengagement-oriented coping strategies (e.g. denial, venting emotions). These findings appear to support the general body of literature linking coping strategies to achievement in sport. However, researchers have also suggested that the perceived effectiveness of coping strategies may be more important than the coping strategies themselves. We explore this possibility in the next section.

CRITICAL FOCUS

Coping with retirement

Retirement from sport can be a particularly traumatic time for many athletes. This is because athletes develop a sense of loss of their athletic identity. A systematic review by Park, Lavallee and Tod (2013) identified 32 studies that had explored coping with retirement from sport. The review found that the most common method of coping with retirement from sport was seeking support from others and trying to keep busy. No one coping strategy was identified as more effective than others, with the exception of searching for new careers or interests. This finding suggests that athletes might do well to formulate a plan of action in the later stages of their career to help the transition from athlete to non-athlete.

Test your knowledge

6.4 Outline how coping strategies might contribute to the emotional states of athletes.

6.5 Describe how you could measure the coping responses of athletes.

6.6 Do different populations of athletes show different coping styles?

Answers to these questions can be found on the companion website at:
www.pearsoned.col.uk/psychologyexpress

Further reading Coping and sport performance

Topic	Key reading
Coping and emotion in sport	Thatcher, J., Jones, M., & Lavallee, D. (2011). *Coping and emotion in sport* (2nd ed.). Abingdon, UK: Routledge.
Measuring coping in sport	Nicholls, A. R., & Ntoumanis, N. (2010). Traditional and new methods of assessing coping in sport. In A. R. Nicholls (Ed.), *Coping in sport: Theory, methods, and related constructs* (pp. 35–51). New York: Nova.
Population-based differences	Nicholls, A. R., & Polman, R. C. J. (2007). Coping in sport: A systematic review. *Journal of Sports Sciences, 25*, 11–31.
Coping and sport performance	Nicholls, A. R. (2010). Coping in sport: Theory, methods, and related constructs. New York: Nova.

Coping effectiveness

Coping effectiveness refers to the extent to which a coping strategy, or combination of strategies, is successful in alleviating the negative emotions caused by stressors (Nicholls & Polman, 2007). Even though some strategies might seem particularly helpful (such as seeking social support) and others particularly harmful (such as alcohol), the effectiveness of specific coping strategies is not always clear. Psychologists need to be aware of the perceived effectiveness of the coping strategies that athletes routinely employ.

When are coping strategies effective?

We explained that athletes use various problem-focused and emotion-focused coping strategies in response to stressors. The extent to which problem- and emotion-focused coping strategies work depends on the encounter and this notion is neatly encapsulated in the *goodness-of-fit model* (Folkman, 1991). To explain, when the athlete has the potential for personal control, problem-focused coping will be more effective. However, emotion-focused coping is more effective in those encounters when the athlete has less control. The sport literature has offered support for this model. For example, Anshel and Kaissidis (1997) demonstrated a positive link between a high level of control and problem-focused coping. When athletes had less perceived control, they used more emotion-focused coping. Research has begun to explore the efficacy of coping effectiveness training for coping effectiveness and athletic performance. This was the focus of a study by Reeves, Nicholls and McKenna (2011). Over a series of weeks, footballers were trained in how to deal with controllable and uncontrollable stressors. The authors found that during and after the intervention there was an improvement in reported coping effectiveness and subjective performance ratings. This suggests that athletes can be trained to cope more effectively and that this can aid athletic performance.

CRITICAL FOCUS

Self-control

Some people appear to have enough will power to achieve their goals while others are thwarted by temptations and distractions along the way. However, research by Muraven (2010) suggested that our capacity for self-control resembles a muscle – it can be strengthened by regular exercise. In their study, participants who practised self-control by cutting back on sweets or squeezing a handgrip significantly improved on a concentration task requiring significant self-control compared with those who practised tasks that did not require self-control. These findings suggest that self-control may be improved by regularly practising small acts of self-control.

Coping through social support

Research has illustrated that athletes in supportive relationships (e.g. with a coach) experience favourable outcomes such as positive mental health and well-being (Cohen & Wills, 1985; Cohen, Underwood, & Gottlieb, 2000). This realisation prompted sport researchers to examine more specifically whether the support offered to athletes contributes to athlete cognitions, such as self-confidence, and objective performance outcomes (Rees & Freeman, 2010). For example, Rees and Freeman (2007) explored athlete perceptions of the support they received and how it related to levels of stress and self-confidence in the days going into competition. They found that greater social support was associated with lower levels of stress and greater levels of confidence going into the competition. A further study by Rees and Freeman (2010) found that, in addition to greater confidence, athletes receiving greater social support reported fewer task-irrelevant thoughts and showed better performances. Thus, social support would appear a very useful strategy for coping with the demands of competition.

CRITICAL FOCUS

The benefits of smiling

Throughout the lifespan, people with positive emotions feel happier, have more stable personalities and marriages, and display better cognitive and interpersonal skills than those with negative emotions (Abel & Kruger, 2010). It seems that positive emotions

▶

have many benefits in our lives. One way we can assess the emotions of others is through facial expressions that vary in form and intensity. Researchers have reported that positive emotions inferred from smile intensity in childhood photos and college yearbooks correlated with marriage stability and satisfaction (Harker & Keltner, 2001). In sport, Abel and Kruger (2010) examined the smile intensity of Major League Baseball (MLB) players alongside detailed statistics (e.g. career length, marital status) and their association to longevity. For those who had died, longevity ranged from an average of 72.9 years for players with no smiles, to 75 years for players with partial smiles, to 79.9 years for players with Duchenne smiles (big smiles). This suggests that smiling regularly may be a useful way of coping with daily life stress.

Test your knowledge

6.7 How do problem- and emotion-focused coping relate to coping effectiveness?

6.8 Is there a link between coping effectiveness and performance in competition?

6.9 Has seeking social support been identified as an effective coping strategy?

Answers to these questions can be found on the companion website at:
www.pearsoned.col.uk/psychologyexpress

Further reading Coping effectiveness

Topic	Key reading
Goodness of fit model in sport	Poliseo, J. M., & McDonough, M. H. (2012). Coping effectiveness in competitive sport: Linking goodness of fit and coping outcomes. *Sport, Exercise, and Performance Psychology, 1*, 106–119.
Coping effectiveness in sport	Nicholls, A., Polman, R., Morley, D., & Taylor, N. J. (2009). Coping and coping effectiveness in relation to a competitive sport event: Pubertal status, chronological age, and gender among adolescent athletes. *Journal of Sport & Exercise Psychology, 31*, 299–317.
Coping through social support	Rees, T., & Freeman, P. (2012). Coping in sport through social support. In J. Thatcher, M. Jones, & D. Lavallee (Eds.), *Coping and emotion in sport* (2nd ed., pp. 102–117). Abingdon, UK: Routledge.

Chapter summary – pulling it all together

→ Can you tick all of the points from the revision checklist at the beginning of this chapter?

→ Attempt the sample question from the beginning of this chapter using the answer guidelines below.

→ Go to the companion website at www.pearsoned.co.uk/psychologyexpress to access more revision support online, including interactive quizzes, flashcards, You be the marker exercises as well as answer guidelines for the Test your knowledge and Sample questions from this chapter.

Further reading for Chapter 6

Nicholls, A. R. (2010). *Coping in sport: Theory, methods, and related constructs.* New York: Nova.

Answer guidelines

 Sample question   **Essay**

To what extent has our understanding of coping contributed to sporting success? Critically discuss with reference to contemporary research and theory.

Approaching the question

The question is extremely broad and allows you to explore a number of areas of coping in sport. It would be useful to start your answer by providing a definition of coping and how it can be thought of as both a process and a trait. You should outline the sources of stress that athletes experience in sport and describe the different ways in which athletes might cope with such stressors (i.e. problem- and emotion-focused coping). You could then describe how coping strategies might differ between different populations and the implications this has for applied practice. This will set you up nicely to answer the question directly about the role of coping in sport performance. You should describe how different coping strategies might relate to success in sport and more specifically the role of coping effectiveness. You could end your essay by describing the interventions that applied practitioners might use to help athletes cope in sport (e.g. social support).

Important points to include

Important points to include are a definition of coping and the different types of coping strategy used by athletes. You should outline the two main sources of stress in sport (competitive and organisation), using research and practical examples, outline the different ways in which researchers can measure coping in sport, and describe the research on population-based differences(and possible explanations). Make sure you directly answer the question by describing the research on coping and performance in sport, including coping effectiveness.

Make your answer stand out

The best answers will have a clear introduction, well-supported coverage of different arguments and critical evaluation throughout, and a logical conclusion. Research examples that outline procedures and main findings (with a brief citation) will help you cement your conclusions. To impress your examiner you need to demonstrate that you have read critically into the area. You could do this by outlining strengths and weaknesses in the field or current areas of debate (e.g. classifying specific coping dimensions into broad coping dimensions). Moreover, your examiner will be impressed if you can demonstrate an understanding of contemporary research in the area (i.e. research published during the current or previous year).

Explore the accompanying website at www.pearsoned.co.uk/psychologyexpress

→ Prepare more effectively for exams and assignments using the answer guidelines for questions from this chapter.

→ Test your knowledge using multiple choice questions and flashcards.

→ Improve your essay skills by exploring the You be the marker exercises.

Notes

7

Group processes

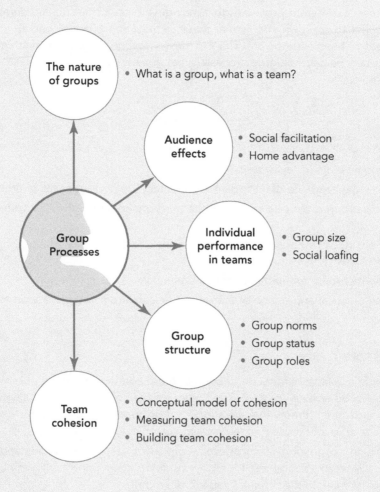

The nature of groups
- What is a group, what is a team?

Audience effects
- Social facilitation
- Home advantage

Group Processes

Individual performance in teams
- Group size
- Social loafing

Group structure
- Group norms
- Group status
- Group roles

Team cohesion
- Conceptual model of cohesion
- Measuring team cohesion
- Building team cohesion

A printable version of this topic map is available from
www.pearsoned.co.uk/psychologyexpress

Introduction

When Chelsea FC won the 2012 UEFA Champions League final, it was described as an outstanding team effort and the team were praised for their overall resilience and their ability to work as a cohesive unit. But what makes an effective team? Is a group more than the sum of its individual components? In sport psychology, it is not possible to explore the psychological processes that govern success without also considering the processes that operate in groups. In the preceding chapters we have encountered a number of personal and social factors that can affect how people behave in stressful and uncertain performance situations. In group settings, there are different ways of measuring performance, different processes that may govern performance, and different approaches to improving performance. Since most sports are played in competitive team settings, this chapter moves beyond the individual athlete to consider the psychological processes that govern success in organised team sport.

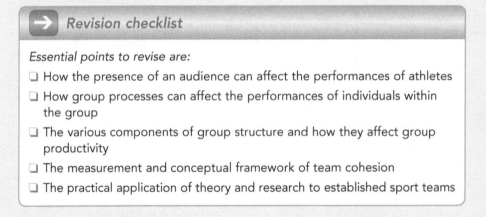

→ Revision checklist

Essential points to revise are:
- ❏ How the presence of an audience can affect the performances of athletes
- ❏ How group processes can affect the performances of individuals within the group
- ❏ The various components of group structure and how they affect group productivity
- ❏ The measurement and conceptual framework of team cohesion
- ❏ The practical application of theory and research to established sport teams

Assessment advice

- Provide a comprehensive description of the theoretical models, but remember that a good answer will go beyond mere description to critically evaluate the elements of the theory that are supported by research (including how they were tested) and those that remain simple conjecture.
- Measuring psychological constructs accurately is essential to understanding group research. Therefore, it is always useful to outline how variables have been assessed in the research you are describing.
- The topic of group processes represents a diverse collection of theoretical approaches, methodological designs and real-world applications. Therefore, it is useful when constructing your answers to outline the practical implications of the theories and research.

Sample question

Could you answer this question? Below is a typical essay question that could arise on this topic.

 Sample question   *Essay*

> Critically review how group processes can affect the performances of sport teams. Discuss with reference to contemporary theory and research, and make practical suggestions for applied sport psychology consultants.

Guidelines on answering this question are included at the end of this chapter, whilst guidance on tackling other exam questions can be found on the companion website at **www.pearsoned.co.uk/psychologyexpress**

The nature of groups

The need for interpersonal attachments is a fundamental motivational characteristic of humans (Baumeister & Leary, 1995). Because the need to belong is fundamental, people typically seek out social situations that satisfy this need. One of the most popular social situations is organised team sport.

What is a group, what is a team?

There are many definitions of groups available in the psychology literature, but one simple characteristic that is shared by all groups, whether large or small, structured or unstructured, is simple interdependence (Lewin, 1948). Other definitions of groups will often include features such as shared experiences or social structure, but the definition most often adopted is the following one by Brown (1988): 'a group exists when two or more people define themselves as members of it and when its existence is recognised by at least one other' (pp. 2–3). This definition is useful because, in addition to interdependence, it includes another important feature of groups – shared awareness.

In general conversation, people use the terms 'team' and 'group' interchangeably. However, the two terms do have distinct meanings. Like groups, teams show interdependence and shared awareness, but they are also defined by structure, cohesiveness, social identity, group norms and common goals (Carron & Eys, 2012). Thus, all teams are groups but not all groups are teams.

CRITICAL FOCUS

A general framework for group productivity

Much of the early research in group dynamics focused on losses to productivity arising from individual performance errors. One of the best-known frameworks is Steiner's

(1972) conceptual model of process losses, which can be written as an equation:

actual group performance = potential productivity – process losses

Potential productivity is the performance that might be obtained based upon the resources of the group (e.g. ability, knowledge) and losses due to faulty processes can occur through communication, coordination and interaction. Steiner's equation has received some criticism for its exclusive focus on performance reduction and it has been suggested that the equation should be modified to include *process gains* (Shaw, 1976). It is also relatively difficult to test, since a group's potential productivity is unstable and therefore difficult to estimate.

Audience effects

Competitive sport is among the most watched forms of entertainment on television and the finals of major competitions (e.g. FIFA World Cup, UEFA Champions League, NFL Super Bowl) often attract a global audience in the hundreds of millions. Many athletes are affected when they have to perform in front of an audience and there are a number of theories that detail the processes through which an audience contributes to performance gains and losses.

Social facilitation

Norman Triplett (1861–1931) is often credited with having performed the first study in social psychology (and sport psychology). In this research, Triplett (1898) conducted an archival study of professional cycling races and found that times were faster for individuals when they raced against others. An experimental study in children also demonstrated better performance times when they were being watched. He concluded that the mere presence of an audience is enough to enhance task performance, and he termed this effect *social facilitation*. Following this pioneering research, a number of independent researchers performed similar studies that would often produce conflicting or confusing results. Some studies observed performance gains and others performance losses.

The contradictory findings were addressed somewhat in the work of Zajonc (1965) and Cottrell (1972). When people perform in the presence of an audience, they automatically assume they are being evaluated and this leads to feelings of apprehension. Evaluation apprehension can lead to physiological arousal that triggers the *dominant response tendency*. In other words, the presence of an audience increases the tendency to perform dominant responses and decreases the tendency to perform non-dominant responses. If the dominant response is the most appropriate in a given situation (usually simple tasks) then social facilitation effects will occur – the audience will enhance performance. However, if the non-dominant response is the most appropriate (usually with complex tasks) then an audience will interfere with performance.

So, we can see that the methods employed in early research (the use of simple or complex tasks) could account for the contradictory findings we observe.

Home advantage

A more familiar concept that most people can recognise is the case of the home advantage. The home advantage refers to the consistent finding that home teams in sport competitions win over 50 per cent of the games played under a balanced home and away schedule (Courneya & Carron, 1992). The home advantage is a robust phenomenon, and a recent meta-analysis (an overall analysis of 87 independent samples from new and published data), which included over a quarter of a million games, showed that home teams win, on average, 60.4 per cent of the time (Jamieson, 2010).

To help understand this phenomenon, Courneya and Carron (1992) developed a framework of game location factors. In this framework, four game location factors (the influence of the crowd, travel effects, location familiarity and competition rules) feed into the psychological states of competitors, coaches and officials, and, in turn, influence the behaviour of these individuals, resulting in an advantage for the home team. The main components of this model have generally been supported. There is evidence that crowd size and crowd noise can influence the decision making of referees in a manner that favours the home team (e.g. Unkelbach & Memmert, 2010). There is also evidence that performance deteriorates with greater distance travelled to competitions (e.g. Recht, Lew, & Schwartz, 1995) and when home teams move to a new stadium (e.g. Pollard, 2002). Taken together, research findings have shown support for three of the four game location factors (crowd, travel and familiarity) contributing to the home advantage in sport.

The home advantage has been shown to be more prevalent in some populations than in others. The home advantage is greater in games contested before 1950 than after 1950 and is greater in sports with a shorter season (Jamieson, 2010). Clear differences in the magnitude of the home advantage can also be observed between different sports. These differences may reflect the differing levels of interdependence between sports.

CRITICAL FOCUS

A home disadvantage?

In Chapter 5 we discussed the choking process in sport – in particular, that greater pressure can sometimes lead to a critical drop in performance. Because a home crowd can create additional pressure on athletes, it had been hypothesised that there should be a home disadvantage (Baumeister & Steinhilber, 1984). Research in sport, however, has produced conflicting findings regarding this phenomenon (Tauer, Guenther, & Rozek, 2009; Wallace, Baumeister, & Vohs, 2005). This discrepancy in study findings may reflect the differing in-game circumstances under which pressure leads to choking. In a recent study of professional ice-hockey shootouts, McEwan, Martin Ginis and Bray (2012)

▶

found evidence for a *home advantage* in loss-imminent situations (when a team needed to score to avoid a loss) and evidence for a *home disadvantage* in win-imminent situations (when a team was shooting to win). This suggests that a home disadvantage can be observed in sport under specific circumstances.

Further reading Audience effects

Topic	Key reading
Social facilitation and home advantage	Jones, M. V., Bray, S. R., & Lavallee, D. (2007). All the World's a stage: Impact of an audience on sport performance. In S. Jowett & D. Lavallee (Eds.), *Social Psychology in Sport* (pp. 103–113). Champaign, IL: Human Kinetics.
Conceptual model of the home advantage	Carron, A. V., Loughead, T. M., & Bray, S. R. (2005). The home advantage in sport competitions: Courneya and Carron's (1992) conceptual framework a decade later. *Journal of Sports Sciences, 23*, 395–407.

Test your knowledge

7.1 What is a group and why is it important to consider group processes in sport?

7.2 Describe social facilitation and how it can differ across complex and simple tasks.

7.3 Why do you think the magnitude of the home advantage differs between sports? Try to use examples and draw upon psychological theory (Courneya & Carron, 1992) in your answer.

Answers to these questions can be found on the companion website at:
www.pearsoned.col.uk/psychologyexpress

Individual performance in teams

Group size

During his tenure as manager of Chelsea FC, it was widely reported that Jose Mourinho would limit his squad size to 24 players even though most clubs at the time had a squad size of over 30. So, is there an optimal group size? And what advantages might be gained by increasing or decreasing the number of athletes in a team?

For many sport clubs, an excessive squad size might lead to problems such as player dissatisfaction, crowding and a reduction in adequate instruction and feedback (Carron & Eys, 2012). Researchers have had differing perspectives on the optimal number of people in a group. However, Thelan (1949) advocated the principle of *least group size* – the group should be just large enough to carry out its activities effectively. In sport situations, the principle of least group size will vary between groups and also between sports. Carron, Widmeyer and Brawley (1989) identified the ideal squad size of various sports (as reported by athletes) and found that squad sizes approximately 25 per cent above or 25 per cent below the ideal were perceived by athletes to have undesirable performance consequences.

CRITICAL FOCUS

Group size and team productivity: the more the merrier?

The relationship between group size and team performance can be understood within Steiner's (1972) framework of group productivity. In Steiner's model, as the number of group members increases, the potential for that group to be productive also increases. But . . . this occurs at a decelerating rate. Once the number of group members necessary to perform a given task is reached, the inclusion of additional members will not increase the group's potential productivity but will contribute to process losses. Therefore, actual group performance will decrease with the addition of members past this critical point.

Social loafing

Approximately 100 years ago Maximilien Ringelmann (1861–1931) performed an experiment that quantified process losses that occur through increases in group size. Using individual productivity as a baseline measure, Ringelmann (1913) computed maximal strength scores on a rope-pulling task (tug-of-war fashion). Assuming an individual works at 100 per cent efficiency, two-person groups were shown to work at 93 per cent of their potential, three-person groups at 85 per cent of their potential, four person groups at 77 per cent of their potential and eight-person groups at 49 per cent of their potential. The study showed that as group size increases, an individual's performance becomes increasingly worse (now known as the *Ringelmann effect*).

According to Ringelmann (1913), groups fail to reach their full potential because various interpersonal processes (loss of motivation and/or loss of coordination) detract from the group's overall proficiency. In particular, Ringelmann felt that motivational losses occur because group members tend to rely more heavily on other group members as group size increases (this is now known as *social loafing*). Social impact theory (Latané, Williams, & Harkins, 1979) outlines more explicitly the causes of social loafing among group members. According to Latané et al., as the number of group members increases, the social pressure on each person decreases and their individual contributions become disguised by the overall group effect. When personal contributions become unrecognisable, individuals may become lost or deliberately hide in the crowd (the free-rider effect). Social loafing can also occur in response to group members making incorrect judgements about how labour is divided and adjusting their personal effort accordingly. Although social loafing is less evident in sport teams than in other group settings (e.g. academia and organisations), its effects are still observed at both the amateur and professional level (Høigaard et al., 2010).

Test your knowledge

7.4 Drawing on psychological theory, outline how squad size can affect the performances of individuals and groups.

7.5 Describe the Ringelmann effect and its potential causes.

7.6 What do you think are some of the limitations with self-report measures of social loafing?

Answers to these questions can be found on the companion website at: www.pearsoned.col.uk/psychologyexpress

---

Group structure

When a new group is formed, individual team members begin to interact and communicate, and the psychological structure of the group starts to form. Accepted and unaccepted behaviours quickly become apparent (group norms), some individuals become instrumental to the group (achieve high status) and others assert their personal responsibilities (roles).

Group norms

Norms represent the standards for behaviour in a group. They are not formally adopted by the group but emerge naturally in response to behaviour changes until a consensus is reached in the group. They develop slowly over time and are very resistant to change (Carron & Eys, 2012). In sport teams there are four distinct situations that can have different norms: during competitions, during practice, in social situations and during the off-season (Munroe, Estabrooks, Dennis, & Carron, 1999). Although norms differ in each situation, attendance and punctuality are frequently reported as important group norms across situations (Munroe, Estabrooks, Dennis, & Carron, 1999). Behaviour that challenges the norms and expectations of the group is often referred to as deviant. *Ingroup deviance* (as it is known) tends to have negative consequences for the deviant but can have positive effects for the group. When norms are violated, efforts are typically undertaken to re-establish appropriate conduct. This is often accomplished by downgrading those who challenge the group's norms and upgrading those who support them. In this way, group expectations are communicated and enforced, and the positivity and distinctiveness of the group is protected (Eidelman, Silvia, & Biernat, 2006).

Group status

In society, a number of personal and situational characteristics contribute to a person's status. These include social class, occupation, income, marital status, ethnic background, religion and clothing, among others. Interestingly, participation in sport and physical activity can also afford an individual a higher social status – particularly in children and adolescents.

A person's status differs within and between the different groups to which they belong. Jacob and Carron (1996) identified 17 factors that afforded a person status in sports teams. These included age, experience, role in the group, skill/ability, playing position, social class, language, income, marital status and religion. Generally, factors that had been achieved by the person (e.g. skill/ability) held the greatest importance for status, and athletic experience was identified as the *most important factor* affecting status. Understanding the sources of status is important because status can influence the dynamics of the group. In particular, people with a higher social status are given greater authority and power (Carron & Eys, 2012). For example, persons with higher status tend to provide and receive a greater number of communications and such communications are given greater credibility within the group.

Group roles

In sports teams, there are two general categorisations of roles: *formal roles*, which are established by the group or organisation, and *informal roles*, which evolve from the interactions between group members. An example of a formal role is team captain and an example of an informal role is mentor. Roles can also be thought of as either *task based* (concerned with leadership and organisation) or *social based* (concerned with producing greater harmony and cohesion).

There are a number of factors that can affect how well an athlete performs his or her role responsibilities (Figure 7.1). *Role clarity* (also known as role ambiguity) is one such important factor. When athletes are unclear about their role in the team, they show greater levels of anxiety, lower satisfaction, an increased occurrence of social loafing and poor role performance. Also, teams that show greater role clarity (among group members) tend to have better communication within the team and greater levels of team cohesion

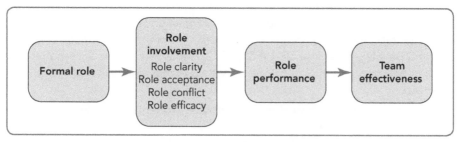

Figure 7.1 The relationship between group roles and team effectiveness (Carron & Eys, 2012)

(Carron & Eys, 2012). Another important factor is *role acceptance*. This refers to the degree to which an athlete is satisfied with his or her role in the team. When team members are not satisfied with their role (e.g. non-regular starter) they tend to show greater social loafing and a reduction in role performance (Carron & Eys, 2012).

Role conflict occurs when an athlete does not have sufficient ability, motivation or time to complete their role responsibilities. Conflict within and between roles has been linked to lower levels of satisfaction, lower levels of role efficacy and greater levels of athlete burnout. *Role efficacy* is similar to self-efficacy (see Chapter 4) and refers to an athlete's belief in his or her capability to perform role responsibilities. When athletes have high levels of role clarity and low levels of role conflict, they tend to show high levels of role efficacy. As with self-efficacy, greater role efficacy is linked to greater role performance (Carron & Eys, 2012).

KEY STUDY

Høigaard et al. (2010): Role satisfaction mediates the relationship between role ambiguity and social loafing among elite women handball players

The relationship between role clarity and role performance is well established. However, Høigaard et al. (2010) were interested in whether role clarity could predict the occurrence of social loafing and the mechanisms through which this occurs. Using a cross-sectional research design, 110 senior handball players from ten teams completed self-report measures of role clarity, role satisfaction and social loafing. Their data showed that when athletes were unclear about their role responsibilities, they reported lower levels of role satisfaction and greater levels of social loafing. Moreover, role clarity did not have a direct effect on social loafing but only an indirect effect through the variance shared with role satisfaction.

Team cohesion

Conceptual model of cohesion

Team cohesion can be defined as 'a dynamic process which is reflected in the tendency for a group to stick together and remain united in the pursuit of its instrumental objectives and/or for the satisfaction of member affective needs' (Carron, Brawley, & Widmeyer, 1998, p. 213). Most researchers accept that team cohesion is a multidimensional construct comprising task and social elements.

- *Task cohesion* is the degree to which group members work together to achieve common goals.
- *Social cohesion* is the degree to which group members like each other and enjoy each other's company.

Carron, Brawley, & Widmeyer (1998) proposed that four main factors affect task and social cohesion within a group: (1) *organisational factors* such as contractual obligations, (2) *leadership factors* such as greater support from coaches, (3) *personal factors* such as athlete personality and coach–athlete personality compatibility, and (4) *team factors* such as group norms and status.

Both task and social cohesion can affect a number of processes essential for group success. Members of highly cohesive teams tend to show reduced levels of social loafing, greater levels of collective efficacy (see Chapter 4), a greater use of team-serving attributions (the tendency to credit success to the team), and more successful team performances.

The relationship between team cohesion and team performance is thought to be bi-directional. That is, a high level of cohesion can facilitate team performance, and successful team performances can help develop team cohesion. A meta-analysis that analysed data from 46 published studies showed that both task and social cohesion contribute to team performance, and that team performance contributes to both task and social cohesion (Carron, Colman, Wheeler, & Stevens, 2002).

Measuring team cohesion

Measuring psychological variables in group settings provides additional challenges to researchers. This is because group members often have differing views on the variables under assessment. One method is to approach the group as a whole (e.g. a focus group interview) so that group members can discuss the variables of interest (in this case, cohesion) and come to an overall agreement. The disadvantage of this method is that one or two group members often take control of the discussion and social pressure may prevent other group members from suggesting alternative perspectives (this phenomenon is termed *groupthink*). Most researchers now recommend that data are collected from each team member independently. This allows researchers to explore whether the average perception of the group's cohesion is related to (for example) team performance, and also whether the level of agreement/disagreement between group members (about the group's cohesiveness) is related to team performance.

From a sport perspective, the Group Environment Questionnaire (Carron, Widmeyer, & Brawley, 1985), the Youth Sport Environment Questionnaire (Eys, Loughead, Bray, & Carron, 2009) and the Child Sport Environment Questionnaire (Martin, Carron, Eys, & Loughead, 2012) have all been used to measure cohesion in athletic samples. Each of these questionnaires assesses task and social components of cohesion and each has shown evidence of content and predictive validity in athletic samples.

Building team cohesion

Team building is one of the most important roles of a coach when forming a new team. To build team cohesion, Prapavessis, Carron and Spink (1996) recommend that sport psychology consultants target the development of cooperation, sacrifice and team goals. This can be achieved through manipulating elements of group structure (e.g. norms, roles) and the group environment (e.g. distinctiveness). For example, team uniforms are one way to develop team distinctiveness and this should help foster a sense of unity among group members (social cohesion). Martin, Carron and Burke (2009) conducted a systematic review of 17 team-building interventions in sport and found that goalsetting was the most effective team-building technique, and that interventions shorter than two weeks were not effective for teambuilding. They recommend using team goal setting and adventure programme techniques that are in excess of 20 weeks to develop cohesion and team performance.

Test your knowledge

7.7 Describe how group roles can affect individual performance in teams.

7.8 Outline Carron, Brawley and Widmeyer's (1998) conceptual model of cohesion and describe how you would assess task and social cohesion in sport teams.

7.9 Based on current theory and research, create a programme to develop team cohesion in youth sport.

Further reading Group processes

Topic	Key reading
Social loafing in sport	Woodman, T., Roberts, R., Hardy, L., Callow, N., & Rogers, C. H. (2011). There is an I in TEAM: Narcissism and social loafing. *Research Quarterly for Exercise and Sport, 82*, 285–290.
Group roles and team performance	Beauchamp, M. R., Bray, S. R., Eys, M. A., & Carron, A. V. (2002). Role ambiguity, role efficacy, and role performance: Multidimensional and mediational relationships within interdependent sport teams. Group Dynamics: *Theory, Research, and Practice, 6*, 229–242.
Team cohesion in team sport	Rovio, E., Eskola, J., Kozub, S. A., Duda, J. L., & Lintunen, T. (2009). Can high group cohesion be harmful? A case study of a junior ice-hockey team. *Small Group Research, 40*, 421–435.

Chapter summary – pulling it all together

→ Can you tick all of the points from the revision checklist at the beginning of this chapter?

→ Attempt the sample question from the beginning of this chapter using the answer guidelines below.

→ Go to the companion website at www.pearsoned.co.uk/psychologyexpress to access more revision support online, including interactive quizzes, flashcards, You be the marker exercises as well as answer guidelines for the Test your knowledge and Sample questions from this chapter.

Further reading for Chapter 7

Carron, A. V., & Eys, M. A. (2012). *Group dynamics in sport* (4th ed.). Morgantown, WV: Fitness Information Technology.

Answer guidelines

 Sample question Essay

Critically review how group processes can affect the performances of sport teams. Discuss with reference to contemporary theory and research, and make practical suggestions for applied sport psychology consultants.

Approaching the question

The question asks how group processes can affect team performance. Because this question is very broad, it would be useful to begin your answer by defining what a group is before critically evaluating the various conceptual models. You will need to consider how both external (e.g. audience) and internal (e.g. group roles) factors can affect group members and how group processes can affect the performance of the group as a whole. There is a lot of good research available and it might be worthwhile focusing your answer on one or two specific areas rather than trying to cover everything you have read in this chapter. Try to use a blend of classic research articles and modern applications of theory to illustrate your points. Be sure to detail how the theories can be used to create a more effective team in real-world settings.

Important points to include

Once you have outlined and defined the concept of a group, make sure you provide good definitions of the constructs that you are discussing. In this instance it might be wise to use direct quotations (although direct quotations should be avoided in most instances). Once constructs such as team cohesion and role efficacy (for example) have been defined, make sure you outline the full theoretical models, being careful to specify the causal relationships within these models. Avoid spreading your answer too thin– you can achieve a better grade by focusing on one or two areas and providing a more critical and in-depth discussion of these areas. A discussion of the practical application of the research is always a useful way to pick up additional marks and a nice way to conclude your answer. We have not gone into much detail on the practical side in this chapter, but for each theoretical relationship outlined here there is opportunity for intervention. For example, if a greater squad size can increase social loafing and disrupt team cohesion, then a practical application of this knowledge would be to encourage managers to limit their squad size as much as is practically possible (the principle of least group size).

Make your answer stand out

Make sure that your answer has structure. You can begin by providing definitions of the constructs you are to discuss and the general areas you are going to cover. Then provide detailed descriptions of conceptual models and be sure to include the research that has supported or refuted elements of the model (and relationships as yet untested). You can then conclude by outlining practical suggestions (based on the research you have outlined) and how future research into some of the untested relationships might lead to further practical applications of the theory.

Demonstrate your knowledge of contemporary research by outlining one or two recent studies in each area you are describing. This outline can simply include the sample that was used in the study, the experimental protocols and the main findings. A simple description of a study might only take a few lines of text but it will demonstrate to an examiner that you have read critically into the area.

Explore the accompanying website at www.pearsoned.co.uk/psychologyexpress

→ Prepare more effectively for exams and assignments using the answer guidelines for questions from this chapter.

→ Test your knowledge using multiple choice questions and flashcards.

→ Improve your essay skills by exploring the You be the marker exercises.

Notes

Notes

Notes

8

Judgement and decision making

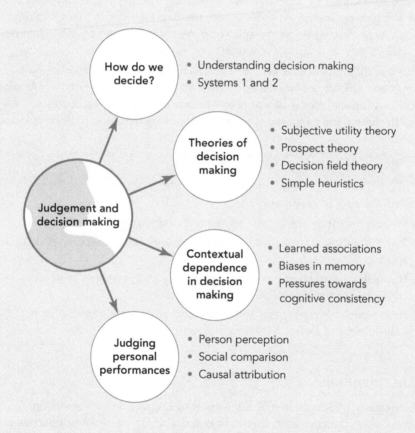

- **How do we decide?**
  - Understanding decision making
  - Systems 1 and 2

- **Theories of decision making**
  - Subjective utility theory
  - Prospect theory
  - Decision field theory
  - Simple heuristics

- **Judgement and decision making**

- **Contextual dependence in decision making**
  - Learned associations
  - Biases in memory
  - Pressures towards cognitive consistency

- **Judging personal performances**
  - Person perception
  - Social comparison
  - Causal attribution

A printable version of this topic map is available from
www.pearsoned.co.uk/psychologyexpress

Introduction

The razor's edge that divides success and failure in sport is finely balanced on good judgement and decision making. Imagine for a moment that you are a football referee officiating at a future World Cup final between England and Spain. You are drenched in sweat, and drained physically and mentally from the last 91 minutes of play, but you know that only two minutes remain before you blow the final whistle in normal play. The score is 1–1. Just then, Wayne Rooney goes down in the penalty area. You blow your whistle because you think it is a penalty, but for a moment, you're not convinced that he was tripped because of the way he landed. You begin to think – Did he dive? Would he dive? Did I see it correctly or am I mistaken? The noise from the stands gets louder and you are surrounded by Spanish players shouting 'He dived!' Do you point to the spot and give a penalty? As you can see, making decisions in these settings is difficult, especially when we consider how we are influenced by other people, the environment and our own thoughts and feelings.

Within this chapter, we shall explore decision making in sport, especially how athletes and officials are influenced by prior knowledge and a limited information-processing capacity. We shall also present some decision-making theories, research studies and suggestions to cope with decision-making challenges in sport.

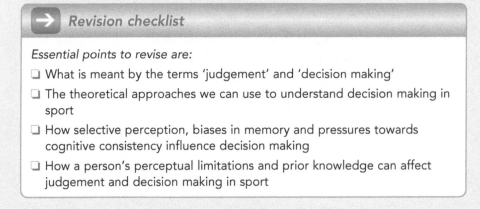

→ *Revision checklist*

Essential points to revise are:
- ❏ What is meant by the terms 'judgement' and 'decision making'
- ❏ The theoretical approaches we can use to understand decision making in sport
- ❏ How selective perception, biases in memory and pressures towards cognitive consistency influence decision making
- ❏ How a person's perceptual limitations and prior knowledge can affect judgement and decision making in sport

Assessment advice

- Judgement and decision making in sport has received much attention in recent years because of its immense practical value for athletes, coaches and officials. Students should be mindful of the areas currently under debate and be prepared to critique strengths and weaknesses of individual studies.
- A number of judgement and decision-making biases have been identified in the literature, and students should attempt to provide practical recommendations of how knowledge of such biases can aid the training of sports officials.

- Because a large number of judgement and decision-making tendencies have been observed, we are only able to offer a brief outline of each one. We have offered a number of suggested readings, and students would do well to access these papers to broaden and deepen their knowledge of each topic area.

Sample question

Could you answer this question? Below is a typical essay question that could arise on this topic.

 Sample question   *Essay*

> With reference to theory and research, outline how perceptual limitations and prior knowledge can influence athletes' and officials' decision making in sport.

Guidelines on answering this question are included at the end of this chapter, whilst guidance on tackling other exam questions can be found on the companion website at **www.pearsoned.co.uk/psychologyexpress**

How do we decide?

Coaches, athletes and officials muse over endless decisions – weighing up the advantages and disadvantages of different courses of action in the hopes of gaining the greatest return for their choices. We might assume that the more time one has to decide, the better decisions one will make. Although this supposition for critical thinking might be true, the dynamics of some sports snatch the time from players and officials to choose among alternatives. Remarkably, empirical research demonstrates that with little or no time to decide, people are capable of making exceptionally good decisions. Then again, they are also capable of making incredibly poor decisions. So what is the best route to follow when making a decision? Before we can answer this question, we need to define decision making.

Understanding decision making

The terms 'judgement' and 'decision making' are used interchangeably, yet they differ on one crucial element. Judgements refer to 'a set of evaluative and inferential processes that people have at their disposal and can draw on in the process of making decisions' (Koehler & Harvey, 2004, p. xv). This process of judgement is separated from the consequence of the decision. Decision making, on the other hand, involves choosing among alternatives and the consequences of the choice itself. It would be sensible to keep this distinction in mind when reading about judgement and decision making in sport psychology.

Systems 1 and 2

We can begin to understand judgement and decision making in sport by first considering how we think. Imagine we have two systems in the mind and we label these System 1 and System 2 (Table 8.1) (Stanovich & West, 2000). System 1 works automatically and quickly with minimal effort and no sense of voluntary control. For instance, most people could easily give an answer to 2 + 2 or state the capital of France. This system involves learned associations between ideas and learned skills. In sport settings, we are treated to mesmeric displays of superlative skills. Many of these actions are involuntary and can run on automatic pilot without a focus on the conscious control of attention. In basketball, for example, a point guard makes a pass to a shooting guard who, despite being challenged by an opponent, instantly handles the ball well, side-stepping his opponent to create his own shot.

In contrast, System 2 involves effortful mental activities such as complex computations. Imagine calculating 25 times 25 in your head. In this example, System 2 requires attention but is disrupted when attention is drawn away from the task. We recognise System 2 in sport when we watch a 100 m sprinter in the starting blocks paying attention to the sound of the starting gun or when a middle-distance runner decides to increase her speed for the final two laps of the track. However, our attention funds are limited. So if we try to allocate our attention to too many tasks, we will inevitably fail in those tasks.

It would be remiss to forget that we can do several easy and straightforward tasks at once, such as having a conversation while driving a car. However, whilst sitting in the passenger seat of a road rally car, we would recognise it as sensible to read the pace notes rather than distract the driver with irrelevant conversation. The rally car driver must focus attentively on driving to complete the course successfully. But when the rally car driver focuses intensely on the driving task, it is possible that the driver becomes blind to stimuli that would normally attract attention. This inattentional blindness (as it is known) is discussed in Chapter 5.

Table 8.1 **Properties of System 1 and System 2 (Stanovich & West, 2000)**

System 1	System 2
Associative	Rule-based
Holistic	Analytic
Automatic	Controlled
Acquisition by biology, exposure and experience	Acquisition by cultural and formal tuition
Relatively fast	Relatively slow
Relatively undemanding of cognitive capacity	Demanding of cognitive capacity

Theories of decision making

Over the past 70 years, the field of judgement and decision making has matured from a few incipient theories to several hundred that bridge the fields of psychology, economics and other disciplines (Bar-Eli, Plessner, & Raab, 2011). Suffice it to say that many of these theories are not specific to sport but some are observable in athletic populations, allowing us to describe these phenomena as they apply to athletes and officials. Before we begin, it is necessary to sketch a brief overview of judgement and decision-making theories, beginning with deterministic and static assumptions and moving to those that are more dynamic and probabilistic.

Subjective utility theory

Edwards' (1954) subjective expected utility (SEU) theory is a theory with deterministic and static assumptions. SEU theory has two chief parameters: uncertainty (i.e. the probability of success) and utility (i.e. the value of the chosen option). When the product of these parameters is calculated, the option with the uppermost outcome is selected. However, this model has received some criticism as people do not always choose the option with the highest subjective utility. Imagine that a rugby player in a game has two options, such as going for a try (high value to score directly) or passing to a teammate (low value to score directly). According to the model, we would expect the rugby player to attempt the try. However, other contextual and dynamic factors (such as competition pressure and experience) will no doubt contribute to this decision.

Prospect theory

Prospect theory emerged as a more psychologically accurate description of preferences than the SEU theory (Kahneman & Tversky, 1979). It assumes two phases: editing and evaluation. In the editing phase, the decision-maker structures the decision problem by coding potential outcomes as gains or losses relative to a reference point. This reference point could be the status quo, an expectation or an aspiration. In the evaluation stage, a value function and a weighting function are applied to prospects (Hardman, 2009). According to the predictions of prospect theory, those in a losing situation (e.g. losing money gambling at a race track) make riskier decisions than those in a winning situation (e.g., winning money gambling at a race track). Because sport requires people to make choices in a quickly changing environment, a theory with static and deterministic assumptions could not be expected to describe all the choices a person makes. For example, you might wish to pass every ball to your star player but the opposition will quickly make arrangements to reduce this option. Thus, dynamic and probabilistic models seem most appropriate for a sport setting.

Decision field theory

Busemeyer and Townsend's (1993) decision field theory (DFT) is an example of a dynamic and probabilistic model. This model extends the SEU theory by adding a temporal dimension. A key assumption within this model is that one's inclination towards options ebbs and flowsover time. If we continue with our rugby example, the rugby player recognises that passing to his teammate poses the lowest subjective expected utility (lowest value to score directly), but in an instant, the rugby player can see a defender about to tackle him so he changes his mind and decides to pass to his teammate because passing now offers the highest subjective expected utility (highest value to score). In a dynamic sport like rugby, people often need to make sequential decisions under time pressure and such decisions depend on preferences of and risks taken by athletes (Bar-Eli, Plessner, & Raab, 2011).

Simple heuristics

A radical departure from the previous theories is the simple heuristics approach developed by Gigerenzer, Todd and the ABC Research Group (1999). This approach has its genesis in Hebert Simon's 'bounded rationality' concept. This concept explains that human rationality, when measured against any 'ideal' and/ or normatively rational models, is bounded by restricted cognitive information-processing ability. Factors that restrict cognitive information-processing ability include inadequate information, temporal constraints and emotions (Bar-Eli, Plessner, & Raab, 2011). Rather than aiming for the best solution to a problem, people tend to choose the first alternative that gives an acceptable solution to the problem. This is known as *satisficing*. Rather than calculating the utility of options, it uses a 'rule of thumb' based on experience (Gigerenzer, 2004). For example, a cricketer attempting to catch a ball might use simple rules (called heuristics) to judge the flight of the ball, running speed and elements of the environment (e.g. field boundary).

Further reading Decision making	
Topic	*Key reading*
System 1 and System 2	Stanovich, K. E., & West, R. F. (2000). Individual differences in reasoning: Implications for the rationality debate. *Behavioral and Brain Sciences, 23*, 645–726.
Theories of decision making	Bar-Eli, M., Plessner, H., & Raab, M. (2011). *Judgment, decision making and success in sport*. Chichester, UK: Wiley-Blackwell.

Test your knowledge

8.1 Define 'judgement' and 'decision making'. Explain the crucial difference between them.

8.2 Outline Systems 1 and 2.

8.3 Using examples, outline the different theories of decision making.

Answers to these questions can be found on the companion website at: **www.pearsoned.col.uk/psychologyexpress**

Contextual dependence in decision making

All judgements and decisions depend on the way we see and interpret the world. For this reason, all decisions depend on context (Plous, 1993). Research on judgement and decision making illustrates this context dependence with various processes that include:

- learned associations
- biases in memory
- pressures towards cognitive consistency.

Learned associations

The human brain has evolved to be especially sensitive to patterns. Because of this, people often see patterns or connections in seemingly random data. We see faces in clouds, we create objects in the stars, and we see animals in inkblots. The tendency to identify patterns in random data can often lead to false perceptions of causality. The best-known example is the *gambler's fallacy*. This is when people expect an outcome in an independent trial (of a random process) based on previous independent trials (e.g. 'the last three coin tosses have been heads, so the next one must be a tail'). In sport settings, people have also been known to display such false causal reasoning.

For many decades, many sports fans, coaches and athletes were under the impression that athletes have 'hot streaks' – specifically, that in sports such as basketball, players had a greater chance of making a successful shot if they had been successful in their previous two or three shots. This became known as the *hot-hand phenomenon*. It was first subjected to critical scientific study in a paper by Gilovich, Vallone and Tversky (1985). They explored the shooting records from professional basketball teams but found no evidence for a positive correlation between the outcomes of successive shots. Simply, having missed a basket on a previous attempt did not decrease the chances of making a basket on the next attempt. And having scored a basket on the last attempt did not increase the chances of scoring a basket on the next attempt.

Many subsequent studies continued to explore the hot-hand phenomenon but rarely identified an effect in basketball or other sports. A recent study, however, did find evidence for a hot-hand effect in professional volleyball (Raab, Gula, & Gigerenzer, 2012). The authors contend that the simple belief in the hot-hand phenomenon could cause opponents to change their strategic play (when they identify someone with the hot hand) in a manner that results in more hits for the team. The hot-hand research is on-going but, with the exception of a few studies, it would appear a myth among sports fans, coaches and players.

Avugos, Köppen, Czienskowski, Raab, & Bar-Eli (2013): The hot hand reconsidered: A meta-analytic approach

Even though many studies have demonstrated that the hot-hand phenomenon does not exist, many people, sport psychologists included, continue to support the idea of successful and unsuccessful patterns of play. For this reason, Avugos et al. conducted a meta-analytic review of 22 studies that had explored the hot-hand effect in sport. Their analysis yielded an overall effect size of 0.02 ($p = 0.49$). They also explored whether the hot-hand effect was more observable in individual sports or team sport. For both populations no significant effect was observed. The authors concluded that a general hot-hand effect probably does not exist in sport.

Biases in memory

Memory is vital in determining how judgements and decisions are made. When we watch sporting performances, we gain an impression about the performer, the performances and the sport. From a cognitive perspective, we perceive, encode and interpret information and relate such information to prior knowledge stored in memory (Bar-Eli, Plessner, & Raab, 2011). The more acquainted we are with a particular sport (e.g. diving), the more we can appreciate various elements of performances (e.g. arm stand back double somersault tuck). Yet, we can also be influenced adversely by prior knowledge that biases our cognitive processes and judgements. This prior knowledge can be particularly problematic for sporting officials.

In gymnastics it is common for coaches to schedule their best athletes to perform last in team competitions. Plessner (1999) was interested in whether the order of gymnasts would affect their individual performance scores. Forty-eight gymnastics judges watched a video routine of a men's competition. However, the authors manipulated the videotape so that the target athlete would appear either first or fifth in the team order. The study showed that judges were awarding more favourable scores to the gymnast when he was the fifth performer rather than the first. Thus, judges were using their prior knowledge (that better performers should be last) to influence their scoring.

In another study, Plessner and Betsch (2001) were interested in whether association football referees would be more or less likely to award a penalty if they had already awarded a penalty. One hundred and fifteen participants watched 20 video clips of three potential fouls occurring in the penalty area (the first two scenes involved the same team and the third scene the opposition team) and were required to make penalty decisions for each of the three scenes. Consistent with their hypothesis, fewer penalties were awarded to the target team (in scene 2) when a penalty had already been awarded to the team (in scene 1). Also, a greater number of penalties were awarded to the opposition team (in scene 3) when a penalty had already been awarded to the target team (in scene 1 or 2). This study shows that referees use prior decisions to influence their current decisions.

In another study of referee decisions, Jones, Paull and Erskine (2002) were interested in whether a team's aggressive reputation would influence the decision to award fouls. Thirty-eight football referees were randomly assigned to either an experimental or a control group and were presented with the same 50 video clips. For each incident, the referees had to indicate what action they would take as if they were officiating the game. However, the experimental group received extra information that the 'blue team' had a reputation for foul and aggressive play. The study showed that the blue team (but not the red team) were awarded significantly more yellow and red cards by the experimental group than the control group. This suggests that officials use prior knowledge of teams when making judgements and decisions in sport competitions.

CRITICAL FOCUS

Colour in judgement and decision making

Hill and Barton (2005) explored the relationship between shirt colour and success in Olympic sport. They explored one-on-one combat events (e.g., boxing, tae kwon do) during the 2004 Olympic Games in Athens, where contestants were randomly assigned red or blue outfits or body protectors. The data showed that contestants had a greater incidence of victory when wearing red (winning on average 55 per cent of contests). The authors suggested that humans share with other primates a biologically based tendency to view red as a signal of danger (or attack readiness), providing a competitive advantage for contestants assigned red outfits.

Hagemann, Strauss and Leißing (2008) disagreed with Hill and Barton's interpretation and suggested that this phenomenon is due to a perceptual bias in the official. Simply, officials are at a disadvantage when viewing sport because athletes make rapid movements and it is difficult to make objective judgements. They performed an experiment where tae kwon do officials watched video-taped excerpts from sparring rounds of five male competitors of similar abilities. They showed the referees the original excerpts and also excerpts in which they reversed the colours worn by each competitor using digital graphics, animation and image compositing software. In other words, those who were actually wearing red protective gear in the sparring rounds were now wearing blue protective gear in the video-taped excerpt. They demonstrated that officials favoured tae kwon do competitors wearing red rather than blue protective gear.

This bias is similar to those observed in other contexts. For example, Frank and Gilovich (1988) found that American football officials were more likely to penalise a team wearing a black, rather than a white uniform. They provided a hypothesis based on the assumption that in most cultures humans recognise a strong association between the colour black and aggression.

Further reading The psychological demands of officiating

Topic	Key reading
Psychological demands of officiating	Mascarenhas, D., O'Hare, D., & Plessner, H. (2006). The psychological and performance demands of association football refereeing. *International Journal of Sport Psychology*, *37*, 99–120.
Improving decision making among officials	Plessner, H., Schweizer, G., Brand, R., & O'Hare, D. (2009). A multiple-cue learning approach as the basis for understanding and improving soccer referees' decision making. *Progress in Brain Research*, *174*, 151–158.
Motor and visual experience	Pizzera, A., & Raab, M. (2012). Perceptual judgments of sports officials are influenced by their motor and visual experience. *Journal of Applied Sport Psychology*, *24*, 59–72.

CRITICAL FOCUS

Memory alterations

As police reports of witness information testify, people's memory of critical incidents often changes over time. Loftus and Palmer (1974) illustrated the constructive nature of memory by showing participants a filmed automobile accident. After the film, the participants estimated how fast the cars were travelling when they *contacted* each other. Similar numbers of other participants were asked the same question but the word *contacted* was substituted with other words like *smashed*, *bumped* and *hit*. One week later, the participants were asked whether they had seen any broken glass in the film, even though there was no broken glass shown in the film. Those who were asked previously about cars that 'smashed' into each other were more likely to claim that they saw broken glass. It appears that the word *smashed* became attached to their memories and altered them.

Pressures towards cognitive consistency

When people commit to a course of action, their perceptions often change to remain consistent with that commitment – this is known as *cognitive dissonance*. Leon Festinger (1957) proposed the theory of cognitive dissonance to understand the relationships among cognitions or pieces of knowledge. Such knowledge might be an attitude, value, emotion or behaviour and we hold many of these at once, forming *irrelevant*, *consonant* or *dissonant* relationships with one another.

- *Cognitive irrelevance* describes two cognitions that have nothing in common.
- *Cognitive consonance* occurs when one cognition follows on from, or fits with, another cognition, reinforcing the initial piece of knowledge.
- In contrast, *cognitive dissonance* occurs when a cognition contradicts an initial thought or belief (i.e. the relationship between the two cognitions is dissonant). When this occurs, tension arises until the person reduces it by (a) devaluing the importance of dissonant beliefs, (b) adding more consonant

beliefs to outweigh the dissonant beliefs, and (c) changing dissonant beliefs so that they are not inconsistent.

The most widely used example of cognitive dissonance is the fox and the grapes. When the fox fails to reach the grapes, he decides he does not want them after all. Cognitive dissonance is one of the best-researched topics in social psychology, but has rarely been explored in athletic settings.

Further reading Contextual dependence

Topic	Key reading
The hot-hand effect in sport	Avugos, S., Köppen, J., Czienskowski, U., Raab, M., & Bar-Eli, M. (2013). The 'hot hand' reconsidered: A meta-analytic approach. *Psychology of Sport and Exercise, 14*, 21–27.
Cognitive dissonance in sport	Burke, S., Sparkes, A. C., & Allen-Collinson, J. (2008). High altitude climbers as ethnomethodologists making sense of cognitive dissonance: Ethnographic insights from an attempt to scale Mt Everest. *The Sport Psychologist, 22*, 336–355.
Colour effects in competitive contexts	Elliot, A. J., & Maier, M. A. (2012). Color-in-context theory. In P. Devine & A. Plant (Eds.), *Advances in experimental social psychology* (Vol. 45, pp. 61–125). Burlington: Academic Press.

Test your knowledge

8.4 Describe the evidence for the hot-hand phenomenon in sport.

8.5 Outline how memory biases can contribute to officials' decision making.

8.6 Using sport examples, describe the theory of cognitive dissonance.

Answers to these questions can be found on the companion website at: **www.pearsoned.col.uk/psychologyexpress**

Judging personal performances

Athletes are continually confronted with decisions: Should I spend more time in training? Should I devote more time to technical skills or weight training? Can I ask my coach for more feedback? Similar choices are countenanced in a competitive setting. As an illustration, a badminton player might decide upon a particular strategy for a game based on the impression she has of her opponent's strengths and weaknesses. She might use information from a previous victory or defeat, or if she has not met her opponent before, she might use information gained from watching her opponent warming up. Tied up within this simple outline are three prominent processes:

- person perception
- social comparison
- causal attribution.

Person perception

In regular social interactions, people search for information that helps them form an impression of other persons. In sport settings, people apply similar principles to make judgements of forthcoming opponents. But what information do athletes use when forming an impression of an opponent? This was the focus of two studies that explored how an opponent's clothing and body language might contribute to the first impressions fashioned by athletes (Greenlees, Buscombe, Thelwell, Holder, & Rimmer, 2005; Greenlees, Bradley, Holder, & Thelwell, 2005). In these studies, athletes were required to watch a video clip of a target 'opponent' warming up and to outline their impressions of that target. However, the video clips were altered so that some athletes viewed the target player in regular sportswear and others viewed the target player in sport-specific sportswear. The video clips were also altered so that the target player displayed either positive body language (good posture and eye contact) or negative body language (slumped posture and limited eye contact). The studies showed that clothes influenced observers much less than body language. In particular, athletes rated those exhibiting positive body language as more assertive, competitive, confident, experienced and fitter than those displaying negative body language, and were more confident of success against the target displaying negative body language. This suggests that body language is crucial when forming judgements of our opponents.

CRITICAL FOCUS

The primacy effect

In a classic study of judgement and decision making, Asch (1946) demonstrated how the order in which information is presented can influence how a person is perceived. Asch presented participants with a number of adjectives to describe a target person (intelligent, industrious, impulsive, critical, stubborn and envious). Participants received this information in one of two ways – favourable adjectives first (as above) or unfavourable adjectives first (the order reversed). When participants were asked to report their impressions of that person, they reported more positive impressions when they received the favourable adjectives first. This became known as the *primacy effect*.

In sport settings it is also possible that athletes' judgements and impressions are influenced by the order of information. In a study of football players and coaches, Greenlees, Dicks, Holder and Thelwell (2007) were interested in whether the order in which information about an opponent is received would influence the judgements formed of that opponent. In the study, all participants were required to watch a video of a target player warming up, but half watched a declining performance pattern (successful to unsuccessful) and half watched an ascending performance pattern (unsuccessful to successful). When asked to report their impressions, the target player was judged as having greater ability, control, attitude, speed of thought, and athleticism in the declining performance pattern. Thus, even though all participants viewed the same video footage, the target player was judged as having greater ability when the video footage showed the player's better performances at the start. Initial impressions count!

Social comparison

To make judgements about ourselves, we often search for information about others. According to social comparison theory, people appraise their abilities and attributes by comparing themselves to others (Festinger, 1954). For example, after a 10-kilometre race, we might scan the finishing times to judge our performance relative to other runners' performances. Or if you scored 70 in an exam, you might want to know how others performed to judge how well you did. You will feel much better if the average score in the exam is 60 than if it is 80.

In sport competitions, it is common for athletes to compare themselves with others. In a study of Olympic medallists, Medvec, Madey and Gilovich (1995) were interested in how finishing first, second or third would relate to the happiness experienced by athletes. They coded the facial expressions of Olympic medallists and, as people might expect, gold medallists displayed the most joy. However, it was the bronze medallists, rather than silver medallists, who exhibited the second greatest levels of joy. This seems strange because the silver medallists outperformed the bronze medallists. What seems critical here is not that silver medallists outperformed bronze medallists, but rather that silver medallists were perhaps thinking about how they didn't win gold. Bronze medallists, on the other hand, can easily recall their gratitude for having won a medal rather than being placed fourth and leaving without the accolade of being an Olympic medallist.

This process of thinking about 'what might have been' is termed counterfactual thinking. Upward counterfactual thoughts (thinking about how outcomes could have been better) have been linked to a greater occurrence of negative emotions, whereas downward counterfactual thoughts (thinking about how outcomes could have been worse) have been linked to a greater occurrence of positive emotions (or fewer negative emotions).

Causal attribution

In addition to counterfactual thoughts, sport psychologists are also interested in the explanations provided for good and poor performances. These explanations (known as attributions; see Chapter 2) can motivate individuals by contributing to emotions, expectations and decisions (Weiner, 1985).

Because the outcomes of competitions are important to athletes, we can often see biases in the attributions made for success and failure. For example, athletes are much more likely to identify 'poor officiating' or 'weather conditions' as reasons for defeat, but rarely do we see athletes attribute their victories to weather conditions that favoured them (and not their opponent), or officials being biased in their favour. The tendency to identify internal factors as a cause of success (e.g. personal ability and effort) and external factors as a cause for failure (e.g. officials and bad luck) has been termed the *self-serving bias*. Although other explanations are available, most researchers contend that the self-serving bias occurs as a mechanism for enhancing or protecting personal self-esteem (Miller & Ross, 1975). To protect our self-esteem we identify external factors as causing our failures, and to enhance our self-esteem we identify internal factors as causing our successes.

Because the self-serving bias occurs as a *self*-esteem protecting mechanism, it might seem strange that in addition to personal success and failure, people also bias the attributions made for group outcomes and the outcomes of others. In particular, we can see self-serving attributions in team sport settings and in the attributions made by coaches and sports fans (Allen, 2012). Social identity theory (Tajfel & Turner, 1986) contends that people identify themselves with various social groups (e.g., male, English, Black, Manchester United fan) and make judgements that protect the groups with which they associate themselves. In particular, the performances of the group (or groups we associate ourselves with) are considered a reflection upon the self. Therefore, coaches and sports fans bias their attributions in a similar manner to athletes to protect or enhance their personal self-esteem.

Understanding this bias is important, as the attributions made by athletes and sports coaches can influence decisions and expectations (Weiner, 1985). For example, if a coach considers that his team have lost because of biased officiating, he may be less inclined to change training patterns to work on other elements that might have contributed to team defeat.

Further reading Judging personal performance in sport

Topic	Key reading
Person perception	Greenlees, I. (2007). Person perception and sport performance. In S. Jowett & D. Lavallee (Eds.), *Social psychology in sport* (pp. 195–208). Champaign, IL: Human Kinetics.
Counterfactual thinking in sport	McGraw, A. P., Mellers, B. A., & Tetlock, P. E. (2005). Expectations and emotions of Olympic athletes. *Journal of Experimental Social Psychology, 41*, 438–446.
Self-serving bias in sport teams	Martin, L. J., & Carron, A. V. (2012). Team attributions in sport: A meta-analysis. *Journal of Applied Sport Psychology, 24*, 157–174.

Test your knowledge

8.7 Using examples, describe how our own body language might influence the judgements made by our opponents.

8.8 What are counterfactual thoughts and how do they relate to the emotions experienced by athletes?

8.9 Using examples, describe the self-serving bias of athletes, teams and coaches.

Answers to these questions can be found on the companion website at: **www.pearsoned.col.uk/psychologyexpress**

Chapter summary – pulling it all together

→ Can you tick all of the points from the revision checklist at the beginning of this chapter?

→ Attempt the sample question from the beginning of this chapter using the answer guidelines below.

→ Go to the companion website at www.pearsoned.co.uk/psychologyexpress to access more revision support online, including interactive quizzes, flashcards, You be the marker exercises as well as answer guidelines for the Test your knowledge and Sample questions from this chapter.

Further reading for Chapter 8

Bar-Eli, M., Plessner, H., & Raab, M. (2011). *Judgment, decision making and success in sport*. Chichester, UK: Wiley-Blackwell

---

Answer guidelines

 Sample question   ***Essay***

With reference to theory and research, outline how perceptual limitations and prior knowledge can influence athletes' and officials' decision making in sport.

Approaching the question

This question examines the influence of perceptual limitations and prior knowledge on athletes' and officials' decision making in sport. Therefore, when writing your answer it is important to devote equal time to each section (i.e. perceptual limitations and prior knowledge). The question also gives a directive to refer to theory and research in your answer. It would be sensible to begin with a definition of each element (e.g. perceptual limitations) before discussing the theoretical background for each element. There is also a range of research available on each topic within and outside the sport psychology literature that will offer you various research examples to include in your answer. It should be possible to describe, using examples, how theory can be applied to real-world sport settings.

Important points to include

Once the definition of each element has been presented, it would be sensible to include theoretical explanations of perceptual limitations and prior knowledge. You will notice that each element might have various accompanying theoretical explanations and it would be impossible to include all of these in your answer.

You can achieve a better grade by going into depth on two or three topic areas rather than providing a brief overview of each area. It would make sense to justify why you are choosing to explain your answer in a particular way.

Make your answer stand out

When we read articles and books about a particular topic, we come across authors attempting to convince us of the value of their authority, information or arguments. When we write answers to study questions, we are aiming to achieve a similar goal. In your answer you should look to persuade the reader in addition to outlining the area. To achieve this goal, you should aim to present a central argument supported with evidence. You can anticipate the reader's questions and prepare an answer that includes alternative explanations. In short, it is important to synthesise the available material on theoretical approaches and research. You ought to present a balanced argument that establishes a particular stance from the outset and logically summarises the content at the end.

Explore the accompanying website at www.pearsoned.co.uk/psychologyexpress
→ Prepare more effectively for exams and assignments using the answer guidelines for questions from this chapter.
→ Test your knowledge using multiple choice questions and flashcards.
→ Improve your essay skills by exploring the You be the marker exercises.

Notes

Mental toughness

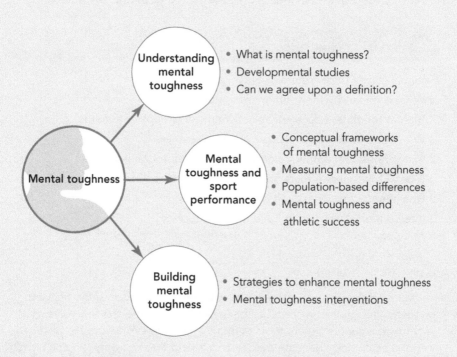

- **Understanding mental toughness**
  - What is mental toughness?
  - Developmental studies
  - Can we agree upon a definition?

- **Mental toughness and sport performance**
  - Conceptual frameworks of mental toughness
  - Measuring mental toughness
  - Population-based differences
  - Mental toughness and athletic success

- **Building mental toughness**
  - Strategies to enhance mental toughness
  - Mental toughness interventions

A printable version of this topic map is available from
www.pearsoned.co.uk/psychologyexpress

Introduction

The term 'mental toughness' pervades sporting parlance. Coaches talk about it, athletes talk about it and fans talk about it. Yet, sport psychologists are still uncertain what is meant by the neologism: *mental toughness*. This doubt suggests that the concept is vague, is difficult to define and/or has multiple meanings. In this chapter we are going to consider how sport psychologists can begin to uncover the basic components of mental toughness, and how mental toughness might contribute to athletic behaviours and sporting success. We shall provide an overview of theoretical frameworks including their strengths and weaknesses, and outline the different ways in which researchers can measure mental toughness in athletic populations. The key areas we cover are mental toughness definitions, the relative importance of mental toughness for peak performance in sport, questionnaire-based assessments, population-based differences, and whether mental toughness can be developed in athletes.

→ *Revision checklist*

Essential points to revise are:
- ❏ What is meant by the term 'mental toughness'
- ❏ Mental toughness differences between sub-groups of athletes
- ❏ Whether mental toughness is open to alteration
- ❏ The various conceptual frameworks of mental toughness
- ❏ Mental toughness effects on athletic behaviour and success
- ❏ How mental toughness can be measured
- ❏ Intervention strategies to build mental toughness

Assessment advice

- As you read through this chapter you will notice that much of the research on mental toughness in sport has been published in the last few years. It is very much a contemporary topic of inquiry. In fact, revision guides such as this one can quickly become outdated in a field that is progressing so rapidly. Therefore, it can be difficult to find up-to-date reviews that include all the important information. A useful strategy is to identify the key researchers in the field and then look up recent citations of these authors.

- Be aware that mental toughness has aroused much debate regarding its definition and main components. For this reason, there will not always be a correct right-or-wrong answer to questions regarding its components and conceptualisation. Don't be afraid to draw attention to this in your exam. In fact, this will give you much to discuss.

• Try to be critical in your evaluation of the literature. If a construct cannot be defined then it cannot be measured. Consider the problems regarding definitions and conceptualisation as you discuss the research that has explored the correlates and consequences of mental toughness.

Sample question

Could you answer this question? Below is a typical essay question that could arise on this topic.

 Sample question   *Essay*

To what extent do psychologists understand mental toughness and its contribution to sporting excellence? Critically discuss with reference to contemporary theory and empirical evidence.

Guidelines on answering this question are included at the end of this chapter, whilst guidance on tackling other exam questions can be found on the companion website at **www.pearsoned.co.uk/psychologyexpress**

Understanding mental toughness

To consider research scientific, it ought to be replicable, falsifiable, precise and parsimonious. In mental toughness research, academic researchers state hypotheses accurately to help replicate their own and others' research. Precise hypotheses emerge from operational definitions of the variables they study. And operational definitions state precisely how a variable should be measured. So, to measure a construct appropriately, operational definitions are imperative.

What is mental toughness?

Researchers have spent more than a decade trying to corral and define mental toughness. So far, there is no consensus within the sport psychology community regarding a suitable definition. This suggests that either mental toughness cannot be conceptualised or further refinements regarding the conceptual structure of mental toughness are required from inductive research efforts. This research process has already begun. Using interviews and focus groups, researchers have searched for attributes that are required to be a mentally tough performer (Bull, Shambrook, James, & Brooks, 2005; Jones, Hanton, & Connaughton, 2007). Although these studies have generated a catalogue of attributes, characteristics, behaviours, cognitions and emotions to describe and measure mental toughness, the catalogue appears unfinished and difficult to conceptualise because so many elements are included.

We shall briefly explore some of this research. Jones, Hanton and Connaughton (2002) invited ten international performers to participate in either a focus group or a one-to-one interview. An inductive content analysis of the data gathered identified 12 key attributes of mental toughness that covered self-belief, desire/motivation, dealing with pressure and anxiety, focus (related to performance and lifestyle), and factors related to pain and hardship. In another study, Bull, Shambrook, James and Brooks (2005) interviewed 12 English cricketers identified as being the mentally toughest during the previous 20 years. An inductive thematic analysis of the interview transcripts identified three global themes: personality characteristics (e.g. confidence, competitiveness), tough attitudes (e.g. willing to take risks), and tough thinking (e.g. decision making, overcoming self-doubts). A third study by Thelwell, Weston and Greenlees (2005) on 43 professional athletes identified ten key attributes of mental toughness in association football. These attributes were similar to those identified by Jones, Hanton and Connaughton (2002) but differed in terms of relative importance.

These studies raise at least two debatable issues. Firstly, if scholars aim to conceptualise mental toughness, they should also consider its antonym – mental weakness. Mental weakness, however, may not always be a weakness. Gucciardi, Gordon and Dimmock (2008) organised attributes of mental toughness and their opposites. Within their bipolar, rank-ordered, mental toughness characteristics, self-belief was anchored at the 'mentally strong' pole and self-doubt at the 'mentally weak' pole. Though it is widely believed that a positive linear relationship exists between self-confidence and performance, as you will recall from Chapter 4, research by Woodman, Akehurst, Hardy and Beattie (2010) demonstrated that some self-doubt benefited performance in a sporting task. An element of self-doubt might indicate that more effort is needed, which in turn could improve performance (Eysenck, Derakshan, Santos, & Calvo, 2007). The distinction between mental toughness and mental weakness is thorny.

Secondly, if researchers continue to hunt down the characteristics of mental toughness in different sports (e.g. cricket, Australian football), it is unlikely that any consensus will ever be reached on a definition of the construct. Understandably, the mental demands of canoe-slalom differ from golf, which differs from tennis, which differs from motor sport. But perhaps some commonality across sports can be found.

Developmental studies

Mental toughness could be thought of as a life skill that develops naturally as children and adolescents mature (Gucciardi & Jones, 2012). Indeed, mental toughness does seem to develop naturally through experience, and in youth sport samples older athletes tend to demonstrate greater levels of mental toughness than younger athletes (Gucciardi, 2009). Thus, sport participation could act as a catalyst for developing mental toughness characteristics more commonly observed in adults. This possibility can aid our conceptualisation of mental toughness – in particular, mental toughness continuity.

Psychological variables typically fall on a continuum from being trait-like to state-like (Vealey, 2002). For example, emotions fluctuate greatly within and between competitions and therefore are considered state-like (see Chapter 3), whereas components of personality can remain relatively stable over the lifespan and therefore are considered trait-like (see Chapter 1). Mental toughness falls somewhere in the middle of these two extremes. Indeed, athletes are not mentally tough one week and mentally weak the next, but mental toughness does appear open to change. Critical incidents (e.g. serious injury) or mental toughness training programmes (e.g. Gucciardi, Gordon, & Dimmock, 2009a; Parkes & Mallett, 2011) may be sufficient to observe meaningful changes in athlete mental toughness.

Psychological constructs that have more trait-like properties are more resistant to change. For example, changes in personality occur over many years (think about how your own personality has changed over the last 10 years), but changes in emotions can occur in no time at all. If mental toughness is considered a developmental life skill, it is likely that only interventions lasting many weeks or months will start to show meaningful long-term changes in athlete mental toughness.

CRITICAL FOCUS

The heritability of mental toughness

Behavioural genetic studies investigate the relative contributions of genetic and environmental influences on individual differences in a person's behaviour. A common approach to exploring heritability estimates is to compare traits in monozygotic (identical) twins (who share 100 per cent identical genes) and dizygotic (fraternal) twins (who share 50 per cent identical genes). If monozygotic twins show greater similarity in behavioural traits (than dizygotic twins) then this is considered evidence of heritability. In a study by Horsburgh, Schermer, Veselka and Vernon (2009), a mental toughness questionnaire was completed by 152 pairs of monozygotic twins and 67 pairs of dizygotic twins. Heritability estimates for the mental toughness variables ranged from 0.36 to 0.56, and unique environmental estimates ranged from 0.44 to 0.64. This study therefore provided evidence that a significant proportion of the variance in people's mental toughness is genetically inherited.

Can we agree upon a definition?

To measure something accurately we must first know what we are measuring. Like the definitions offered for motivation (see Chapter 2), definitions of mental toughness can sometimes be considered too narrow to capture adequately all elements of the construct, and sometimes so broad that they could incorporate almost the entire field of psychology. Let us consider two definitions from the research. Clough, Earle and Sewell (2002) consider mentally tough athletes to have 'a high sense of self-belief and an unshakable faith that they control their own destiny, these individuals can remain relatively unaffected by competition and adversity' (p. 38). Another definition was provided by Gucciardi, Gordon and Dimmock (2009b), who describe mental toughness as 'a collection of experientially developed and inherent sport-specific and sport-general values, attitudes, emotions, and cognitions that influence the way in which an individual approaches, responds to, and appraises both negatively and positively construed pressures, challenges, and adversities to consistently achieve his or her goals' (p. 67).

The first definition provides insight into the types of feature that characterise mentally tough athletes, and the second provides a description of the outcomes and processes of being mentally tough. There is no right or wrong definition here. Both descriptions are useful (as are several others) and can help us in our understanding of mental toughness effects on athletic success. Students should remain mindful of these definitions as we progress through this chapter.

✱ Sample question   *Essay*

Outline the conceptual difficulties with developing a standard definition of mental toughness.

Further reading Defining and understanding mental toughness in various sports

Topic	Key reading
Mental toughness in Australian football	Gucciardi, D. F., Gordon, S., & Dimmock, J. A. (2008). Towards an understanding of mental toughness in Australian football. *Journal of Applied Sport Psychology, 20*, 261–281.
Mental toughness in association football	Thelwell, R., Weston, N., & Greenlees, I. (2005). Defining and understanding mental toughness within soccer. *Journal of Applied Sport Psychology, 17*, 326–332.
Mental toughness in cricket	Bull, S. J., Shambrook, C. J., James, W., & Brooks, J. E. (2005). Towards an understanding of mental toughness in elite English cricketers. *Journal of Applied Sport Psychology, 17*, 209–227.

Mental toughness and sport performance

Conceptual frameworks of mental toughness

One of the first conceptualisations of mental toughness to emerge was based on research findings into the construct of hardiness. Hardiness was conceptualised as a combination of three factors – commitment, control and challenge (3Cs) – that relate to courage and motivation to appraise stressful situations in a positive way. Clough, Earle and Sewell (2002) recognised that the components of hardiness did not adequately capture what athletes consider mental toughness and so added a fourth factor, confidence, to propose a four-dimensional structure of mental toughness – the 4Cs (Table 9.1). The four dimensions assess the degree to which athletes are *committed* to achieving their goals (1), believe that they are capable of *controlling* negative experiences (2), view negative experiences as a *challenge* they can overcome and also as an essential mechanism for growth (3) and are *confident* in their ability to overcome negative experiences (4).

Table 9.1 Dimensions of mental toughness (based on Clough, Earle, & Sewell, 2002)

Dimension	Description
Commitment	People who score high on this dimension are extremely committed to achieving their goals.
Control	People who score high on this dimension hold a strong belief that they are able to control their environment, particularly following unsuccessful performances.
Challenge	People who score high on this dimension tend to view failure as a challenge and a mechanism for personal improvement.
Confidence	People who score high on this dimension hold a strong belief that they are capable of overcoming negative experiences.

Jones, Hanton and Connaughton (2007) proposed a framework of mental toughness based on data gathered from Olympic and World Champion athletes, coaches and sport psychologists. The qualitative study identified 30 key attributes that were essential to mental toughness, and these attributes could be grouped into 13 subcategories that, in turn, could be grouped into four general dimensions. The framework identifies one general dimension of mental toughness (attitude/mindset) and three time-dependent dimensions (training, competition and post-competition). The *attitude/mindset* dimension describes how an athlete achieves and maintains the right focus and belief. The three time-specific dimensions describe the mental skills and strategies that sport performers must possess and master in *training* (e.g. using goals for motivation), *competition* (e.g. handling pressure), and *post-competition* (handling success and failure).

A third framework of mental toughness was forwarded by Gucciardi, Gordon and Dinmmock (2009b) (Figure 9.1). Rather than providing a dimensional account of mental toughness components, Gucciardi and colleagues forwarded a process model of mental toughness that is grounded in the more general framework

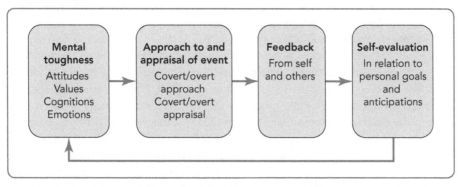

Figure 9.1 The personal construct psychology model of mental toughness (Gucciardi, Gordon, & Dimmock, 2009b)

of personal construct psychology (Kelly, 1991/1955). The model describes the processes by which mental toughness operates and the associated outcomes. In particular, the key components of mental toughness (some of which are similar across sports and some of which are sport specific) influence the way people covertly and overtly approach, appraise and respond to pressure situations. Sources of feedback (from self and others) are then used to self-evaluate in relation to one's personal goals. This self-evaluation can influence back upon mental toughness.

CRITICAL FOCUS

Physiological toughness

If athletes can vary in their levels of mental toughness then can they also vary in their levels of physiological toughness? Building on proposals outlined by Dienstbier (1989), Crust (2008) proposed that mental toughness might be related to physiological processes. Indeed, the tendency to interpret potential stressors as a challenge (rather than a threat) is often considered a characteristic of mental toughness (e.g. Clough, Earle, & Sewell, 2002) and challenge responses are associated with different physiological changes from threat responses (Jones, Meijen, McCarthy, & Sheffield, 2009). In particular, Crust (2008) proposed that mental toughness should be linked to greater epinephrine reactivity and lower cortisol reactivity. To date, the physiological correlates of mental toughness have not been explored. But mental toughness has been associated with a greater pain tolerance (Crust, 2008).

Measuring mental toughness

Qualitative (interview) methods have generally been used in studies focusing on the conceptualisation of mental toughness, and quantitative (questionnaire) methods have generally been used to assess the correlates and consequences of mental toughness. Surprisingly, no studies have used observational (video viewing) methods to examine mental toughness at the elite level.

Both general and sport-specific questionnaires have been developed to aid the research process. The most widely used measure of mental toughness in sport is the Mental Toughness Questionnaire 48 (MTQ-48; Clough, Earle, & Sewell, 2002). This self-report measure assesses four components of mental toughness as described in the 4Cs model. Initial validation efforts generally supported the construct validity of the scale (Clough, Earle, & Sewell, 2002), although there has been some criticism of the measure following an unsuccessful validation attempt by Gucciardi, Hanton and Mallett (2012). Clough, Earle, Perry and Crust (2012) responded to these concerns by highlighting the limitations of statistical techniques used to validate scales and potential limitations in the way the data were collected in the Gucciardi, Hanton and Mallett (2012) study. They contend that psychometric analysis is an on-going process and that in many samples the MTQ-48 is an appropriate measure of a person's mental toughness.

The Sports Mental Toughness Questionnaire (SMTQ; Sheard, Golby, & van Wersch, 2009) is another general measure of mental toughness that was developed based on themes emerging from qualitative studies. It assesses three components of mental toughness – confidence, constancy and control. Initial validation efforts supported the use of the SMTQ in athletic samples (Sheard, Golby, & van Wersch, 2009) and the scale has shown evidence of concurrent validity with the MTQ-48 (Crust & Swann, 2011). Two sport-specific measures have also been developed: the Australian Football Mental Toughness Inventory (AFMTI; Gucciardi, Gordon, & Dimmock, 2009c) and the Cricket Mental Toughness Inventory (CMTI; Gucciardi & Gordon, 2009). The AFMTI is domain specific and assesses four components of mental toughness in Australian football: thrive through challenge, sport awareness, tough attitude and desire success. The CMTI is also domain specific and assesses five components of mental toughness in cricket: affective intelligence, attentional control, resilience, self-belief and desire to achieve. Domain-specific measures may be more suitable for understanding mental toughness in a particular sport but are unsuitable for population comparison studies across different sports.

Population-based differences

A number of studies assessing mental toughness in athletes have identified population-based differences. In addition to the research by Gucciardi (2009), which showed older youth sport athletes to have greater levels of mental toughness than younger youth sport athletes, research has also shown differences in mental toughness between male and female athletes and between athletes with different levels of experience (Nicholls, Polman, Levy, & Backhouse, 2009). In particular, men show higher levels of mental toughness than women, and athletes with greater experience show greater levels of mental toughness. Mental toughness develops naturally as people become more familiar with the general requirements of an activity and it is not surprising that older athletes, and athletes with greater experience, should show greater mental toughness. The observation of gender differences is less easy to explain but could reflect differences in the relative expression of mental toughness attributes between men's sports and women's sports. Alternatively, gender differences could reflect a straightforward social desirability effect (men are simply less willing to report that they are not mentally tough).

Mental toughness and athletic success

Assessments of mental toughness have often been used to try to predict behaviour and success in sport. It has been observed that athletes with greater levels of mental toughness report a lower incidence of athletic burnout (Gucciardi & Gordon, 2009), have greater levels of optimism and use more approach-based coping strategies (Nicholls, Polman, Levy, & Backhouse, 2008), and show an increased occurrence of risk-taking behaviour (Crust & Keegan, 2010). It has also been shown that mental toughness is not strongly related to emotional responses

(Crust, 2009; Gucciardi & Jones, 2012) but can predict athletes' use of self-talk, emotional control strategies and relaxation strategies (Crust & Azadi, 2010).

There is less evidence that assessments of mental toughness can predict athletic success. Research by Shin and Lee (1994) observed that elite-level athletes had greater mental toughness than recreational-level athletes, but research by Nicholls, Polman, Levy and Backhouse (2009) observed no differences in mental toughness between athletes competing at the elite and recreational levels. In other research, more successful international rugby league athletes (Golby, Sheard, & Lavallee, 2003) and university-level rugby league athletes (Sheard, 2009) have been shown to have greater levels of mental toughness and/or hardiness. Importantly, these studies were cross-sectional in nature and therefore did not address cause and effect. To understand better the contribution of mental toughness to athletic success, it can be useful to consider studies that have attempted to develop mental toughness in athletic samples.

Test your knowledge

9.1 Outline the different conceptual frameworks of mental toughness in sport.

9.2 Describe the different assessments methods of mental toughness in athletic samples.

9.3 Has mental toughness been shown to predict athletic behaviour or success in sport?

Answers to these questions can be found on the companion website at: **www.pearsoned.col.uk/psychologyexpress**

Further reading Mental toughness and sport

Topic	Key reading
Conceptual models of mental toughness	Gucciardi, D. F., & Gordon, S. (2011). *Mental toughness in sport: Developments in research and theory.* Abingdon, UK: Routledge.
Measuring mental toughness	Clough, P., Earle, K., Perry, J. L., & Crust, L. (2012). Comment on 'Progressing measurement in mental toughness: A case example of the Mental Toughness Questionnaire 48' by Gucciardi, Hanton, & Mallett (2012). *Sport, Exercise, and Performance Psychology, 1,* 283–287.
Population-based differences	Nicholls, A. R., Polman, R. C. J., Levy, A. R., & Backhouse, S. H. (2009). Mental toughness in sport: Achievement level, gender, age, experience, and sport type differences. *Personality and Individual Differences, 47,* 73–75.
Mental toughness and sport performance	Gucciardi, D. F., Gordon, S., & Dimmock, J. A. (2009a). Evaluation of a mental toughness training programme for youth-aged Australian footballers: I. A quantitative analysis. *Journal of Applied Sport Psychology, 21,* 307–323.

Building mental toughness

Strategies to enhance mental toughness

Several factors are known to enhance or hinder the development of mental toughness characteristics. Four factors – the *sport process* (e.g. training, experience), *sporting personnel* (e.g. coach, teammates), *non-sporting personnel* (e.g. parents, friends) and *environmental influences* (e.g. training environment) – were all identified by elite female gymnasts as contributing to the development of mental toughness (Thelwell, Such, Weston, Such, & Greenlees, 2010). Also, elite coaches identified five factors that contribute to the development of mental toughness characteristics in Australian football: the *coach–athlete relationship, coaching philosophy*, the *training environment* and *specific strategies* (e.g. use of training diaries) were deemed helpful for mental toughness development, but *negative experiences* (e.g. coaches focusing on player's weaknesses) were deemed unhelpful (Gucciardi, Gordon, Dimmock, & Mallett, 2009). Building on these research findings, Crust and Clough (2011) outlined several ways in which mental toughness could be developed in youth sport. They point towards the development of independent problem solving and personal responsibility through a challenging yet supportive learning environment, a greater involvement in decision making regarding their development as they mature, and coach encouragement and support following athlete set backs and failure.

Mental toughness interventions

A number of studies have attempted to develop mental toughness characteristics in athletes. For example, Gucciardi, Gordon and Dimmock (2009a) compared the efficacy of two training programmes for developing mental toughness in youth athletes: a standard psychological skills training programme (PST) that incorporated arousal regulation, mental rehearsal, attentional control and self-efficacy, and a targeted mental toughness training programme (MTT) that incorporated factors such as tough attitude, resilience, emotional intelligence and physical toughness. They found that after seven sessions both groups reported positive changes in reported mental toughness. In another study, Parkes and Mallett (2011) implemented an intervention they termed *the optimistic footballer*. Through a series of practical sessions, targeting factors such as automatic thoughts, pervasiveness and personalisation, male rugby players showed positive changes in reported resilience, confidence and optimism. These findings show that mental toughness characteristics can be developed in sport performers (at least to some extent), but the effectiveness of such mental toughness training interventions for real-world outcomes (success and failure) remains unknown.

Andersen (2011): Who's mental, who's tough, and who's both? Mutton constructs dressed up as lamb

The chapter by Andersen (2011) addressed a number of important points that students should consider in their learning of mental toughness and mental toughness interventions. This review stands out because it sheds light on many of the problems and issues in the mental toughness literature. In addition to outlining problems concerning the definition of mental toughness and measures of mental toughness, Andersen (2011) comments on the potential problems with targeting mental toughness in applied practice. In particular, Andersen considers whether mental toughness training sessions are genuinely effective or whether the positive changes observed are simply an artefact of the relationships developed between practitioners and clients. He also comments on the problems with categorising people as mentally weak and self-fulfilling prophecies (if people score low on mental toughness questionnaires, this might affect their behaviour in a negative way), and that mental toughness might not necessarily be beneficial for all sport performers, and therefore to develop mental toughness in these populations could cause problems. For example, research has shown that some level of self-doubt might benefit sport performance under certain circumstances (Woodman, Akehurst, Hardy, & Beattie, 2010).

Test your knowledge

9.4 Outline the factors, as identified in research on athletes and coaches, that contribute to the development of athlete mental toughness.

9.5 What strategies can coaches use to develop mental toughness in athletes?

9.6 Outline the relative success of interventions that have attempted to build mental toughness in athletes.

Answers to these questions can be found on the companion website at:
www.pearsoned.col.uk/psychologyexpress

Chapter summary – pulling it all together

→ Can you tick all of the points from the revision checklist at the beginning of this chapter?

→ Attempt the sample question from the beginning of this chapter using the answer guidelines below.

→ Go to the companion website at www.pearsoned.co.uk/psychologyexpress to access more revision support online, including interactive quizzes, flashcards, You be the marker exercises as well as answer guidelines for the Test your knowledge and Sample questions from this chapter.

Further reading for Chapter 9

Gucciardi, D. F., & Gordon, S. (2011). Mental toughness in sport: Developments in research and theory. Abingdon, UK: Routledge.

Answer guidelines

 Sample question   *Essay*

To what extent do psychologists understand mental toughness and its contribution to sporting excellence? Critically discuss with reference to contemporary theory and empirical evidence.

Approaching the question

Whenever you approach an essay question, it is always useful to think about structure. You could begin your answer by discussing the issues surrounding adequate definitions of mental toughness and what the term means to athletes. Even though mental toughness has been difficult to define, it can be useful to include one or two direct quotations to illustrate how researchers define the term in their assessments. You could then go on to discuss the various conceptual models of mental toughness and the questionnaire-based measures that have been developed to test these models. The relationship between mental toughness and athletic behaviours could then be discussed with reference to particular studies, and in particular, interventions that have attempted to build mental toughness in athletic populations. You could end your essay by describing various strategies that coaches could use to build mental toughness in athletes.

Important points to include

When you formulate your answer, be sure to include a discussion of the difficulties in trying to formulate an accurate definition of mental toughness. Better answers will provide example definitions from the literature and consider the characteristics of mental toughness across different sports, mental toughness continuity, and mental toughness processes. Students should outline the differences between conceptual models of mental toughness. Although many similarities can be found in qualitative studies that identify mental toughness characteristics, how researchers classify such characteristics can be quite different (Clough, Earle, & Sewell, 2002; versus Jones, Hanton & Connaughton, 2007). Be sure to include an outline of how mental toughness can be developed in athletes. Good answers will provide an outline of important studies that have attempted to develop mental toughness in athletic populations (e.g. Gucciardi, Gordon, & Dimmock, 2009a) and better answers will consider both the potential benefits and costs of developing mentally tough athletes (Andersen, 2011).

Make your answer stand out

A useful way to show your examiner that you have developed a critical understanding of the literature is to provide a brief outline of key studies to illustrate important points. For example, when outlining the predictive utility of mental toughness measures, you could describe the methods and main findings of one or two studies that have used the inventory to predict components of athletic behaviour. An examiner will also be impressed that you are familiar with research on the heritability of mental toughness (Horsburgh, Schermer, Veselka, & Vernon, 2009) and research on physiological toughness (Crust, 2008). But the best way to impress your examiner is to be critical. For example, even though mental toughness interventions seem to be effective in developing mental toughness characteristics, the long-term costs and benefits of such interventions are unknown. Students should draw attention to the strengths and weaknesses of mental toughness research in their essay conclusion.

Explore the accompanying website at www.pearsoned.co.uk/psychologyexpress

→ Prepare more effectively for exams and assignments using the answer guidelines for questions from this chapter.
→ Test your knowledge using multiple choice questions and flashcards.
→ Improve your essay skills by exploring the You be the marker exercises.

Notes

Notes

Notes

Sport psychology in practice

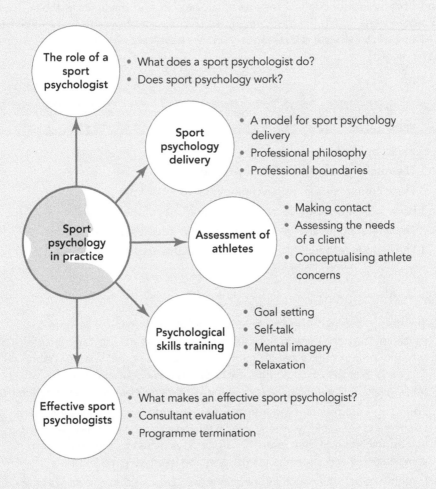

- **The role of a sport psychologist**
  - What does a sport psychologist do?
  - Does sport psychology work?

- **Sport psychology in practice**

- **Sport psychology delivery**
  - A model for sport psychology delivery
  - Professional philosophy
  - Professional boundaries

- **Assessment of athletes**
  - Making contact
  - Assessing the needs of a client
  - Conceptualising athlete concerns

- **Psychological skills training**
  - Goal setting
  - Self-talk
  - Mental imagery
  - Relaxation

- **Effective sport psychologists**
  - What makes an effective sport psychologist?
  - Consultant evaluation
  - Programme termination

A printable version of this topic map is available from
www.pearsoned.co.uk/psychologyexpress

Introduction

So what do sport psychologists do? The answer to this question might seem obvious at first but it also embraces an explanation of how sport psychologists do what they do and what they are allowed to do – and these issues are multifaceted. It is possible broadly to define what sport psychologists do as 'helping athletes improve sport performance and psychological well-being'. These goals are juxtaposed when sport psychologists begin consulting with an athlete (or coach), but the extent to which either goal takes primacy often depends upon various independent factors (e.g. consulting philosophy, client needs, organisational demands). In this chapter, we begin by exploring what sport psychologists do, how they do what they do, and the limits of their competencies. Within this assessment, we shall explore how sport psychologists deliver their services and the stages of delivery typical of most sport psychologists.

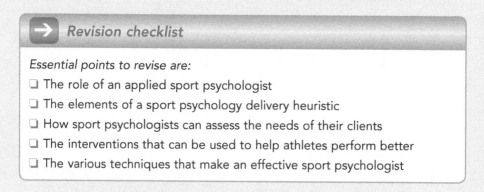

Revision checklist

Essential points to revise are:
- ❏ The role of an applied sport psychologist
- ❏ The elements of a sport psychology delivery heuristic
- ❏ How sport psychologists can assess the needs of their clients
- ❏ The interventions that can be used to help athletes perform better
- ❏ The various techniques that make an effective sport psychologist

Assessment advice

- The field of applied sport psychology broadens and deepens as more sport psychologists participate in publishing academic research, recount their tales of the field in books and scholarly journals, and supervise the next generation of sport and exercise psychologists. Therefore, issues about effectiveness, ethics, training and accountability have become important debates in the literature.

- Sport psychologists emerge from departments of physical education, sport science and psychology among others (e.g. psychiatry) with diverse training and appreciation of their role. These pathways influence the philosophy, competencies and expectations of sport and exercise psychologists.

- Cognitive and behavioural interventions (e.g. goal setting and self-talk) are one element of sport psychology practice. However, they appear to be used extensively by sport psychologists. It would be sensible to review the value of these interventions to help athletes perform better or enhance psychological well-being.

Sample question

Could you answer this question? Below is a typical essay question that could arise on this topic.

 Sample question   *Essay*

What are the characteristics and practices of effective sport psychologists? Discuss with reference to the literature.

Guidelines on answering this question are included at the end of this chapter, whilst guidance on tackling other exam questions can be found on the companion website at **www.pearsoned.co.uk/psychologyexpress**

The role of a sport psychologist

What does a sport psychologist do?

Sport psychologists work with amateur and professional athletes to improve performance and/or psychological well-being. When an athlete's performance improves, one might expect a corresponding improvement in psychological well-being, or perhaps an improvement in psychological well-being increases the chances that an athlete performs better. Whatever may be the case, a common denominator emerges among most sport psychologists: to meet the needs of the athlete. To meet the athlete's needs, however, a sport psychologist requires at least education, supervised training and critical reflection because the art of helping athletes is founded upon sound principles from counselling psychology, sport psychology and several other fields that contribute to good practice in sport psychology delivery. Specialised training programmes exist in different countries to support those wishing to become qualified sport and exercise psychologists: for example, the postgraduate training programme for chartered status within the British Psychological Society (BPS), and certified consultancy registration within the Association for Applied Sport Psychology (AASP).

Few sport psychologists work exclusively as practitioners. Most will work in a university setting where they contribute to *teaching* (the next generation of sport psychologists – such as yourself), *research* (conducting empirical studies to develop knowledge of sport psychology) and *consultancy* (working directly with sport performers). Most sport psychologist split their time relatively evenly between these three activities.

Does sport psychology work?

The short answer is yes. But, then again, you might expect a book on the topic of sport psychology to reach this conclusion! Perhaps the best approach to identifying the relative success of sport psychology consultancy is to ask those who have used, or are currently using, a sport psychologist. Most athletes who have employed a sport psychologist report that psychological skills training (PST) is helpful and many incorporate such skills into their competition day routines. There are relatively few instances of athletes reporting that interventions were not effective, and even fewer cases of athletes reporting that interventions were positively unhelpful (see Hemmings & Holder, 2009, for case examples). Nevertheless, the gains that athletes take away from working with a sport psychologist often depend on the quality of the delivery. Thus, sport psychology consultancy can be effective provided it is delivered in an appropriate manner.

Sport psychology delivery

A model for sport psychology delivery

Sport psychology delivery rarely follows a smooth outline from an initial assessment through various logical steps to a formal adjournment when the athlete's needs are met. However, several key elements are typical in most consultations. Poczwardowski and Sherman (2011) presented a practical model of sport psychology delivery. This model is a revision of their original *sport psychology service delivery* (SPSD) heuristic (Poczwardowski, Sherman, & Henschen, 1998), which reflects experienced consultants' views about the stages of delivery. The original model contained 11 elements of effective sport psychology practice (viz., professional boundaries; professional philosophy; making contact; assessment; conceptualising athletes' concerns and potential interventions; ranges, types and organisation of service; programme implementation; managing the self as an intervention instrument; programme and consultant evaluation; conclusions and implications; and leaving the setting). The new elements included: the consultant–client relationship; consultant variables; client variables; and immersion and goodness of fit. For coherence, we shall combine various elements of this framework within this chapter to illustrate how sport psychologists deliver sport psychology services.

Professional philosophy

The foundation of service delivery in sport psychology requires education, training and professional experience founded upon appropriate professional ethics and a congruent philosophy for professional practice. Many sport psychologists receive a formal education in physical education, sport science or psychology before they gather professional experience with coaches, athletes and performers. Professional ethics are essential for the betterment of the profession because if issues of confidentiality, welfare and boundaries in relationships with clients have no regulation, the trust and professionalism expected of a helping profession such as sport psychology is undermined and devalued. These elements mould together with one's professional philosophy to represent what the consultant does and why the consultant works that way.

Various psychological approaches (e.g. person-centred, psychoanalytic, existential, Gestalt, rational-emotive and behavioural) are adopted by sport psychologists for service delivery. The service delivery emerging from these approaches means that sport psychologists attempt to support a client through their specific approach.

- The *person-centred* approach is a form of talk psychotherapy that attempts to provide the client with greater self-awareness about how their thoughts, feelings and behaviour may be negatively affected. The practitioner typically creates a non-judgemental environment by displaying congruence, empathy and positive reinforcement.

- The *psychoanalytic* approach views human behaviour as deterministic. It considers a person's current behaviour as determined from past experiences. The practitioner typically looks to identify and make sense of these past (often unconscious) experiences.

- The *existential* approach is generally not concerned with the client's past. The emphasis is on choices and the future. The practitioner attempts to increase awareness of the present and focus on the future.

- The *Gestalt* approach to service delivery is similar to the existential approach, but focuses on personal responsibility.

- The *rational-emotive* approach focuses on resolving emotional and behavioural issues in the interests of increasing the client's happiness and well-being. The practitioner will target the client's problems by focusing on values and goals.

- The *behavioural* approach is concerned with some sort of behaviour change. The practitioner often focuses on unlearning negative behaviours using positive reinforcement.

The approach to service delivery depends very much on the beliefs of the sport psychologist. There is no right or wrong approach to adopt, but practitioners need to remain mindful that some clients will respond better to some approaches than others.

Professional boundaries

Sport psychologists have professional boundaries based on their education and training. For instance, a sport psychologist in her first year of training will differ from an experienced sport psychologist in the amount of supervised work undertaken, the intervention models and techniques used, as well as the types of issue addressed (Poczwardowski, Sherman, & Henschen, 1998). The British Psychological Society has set ethical practice guidelines for trainee and qualified sport and exercise psychologists. Similar guidelines for ethical practice are recommended by the American Psychological Association (APA) and the Association for Applied Sport Psychology (AASP). When sport psychologists assess their ability to support a client, they might need to ask whether they are (1) prepared to deliver the services requested by the client, (2) trained and supervised to offer effective consultations, and (3) supported by a network of trained colleagues (e.g. peer consulting). The success of the work that sport psychologists' do often depends upon their counselling competencies. These include an awareness of one's expertise and competency limits, confidentiality, client welfare, professional relationships, assessment techniques, and moral and legal standards (Ward, Sandstedt, Cox, & Beck, 2005).

CRITICAL FOCUS

Crossing professional boundaries

In December 2008 the *International Journal of Sport and Exercise Psychology* published a special issue on sexual harassment and abuse in sport. The collection of articles provided some worrying information about the conduct of persons in positions of authority in adult and youth sport contexts. For example, a study by Volkwein, Schnell, Sherwood and Livezy (1997) showed that 18.7 per cent of athletes in their study had experienced derogatory remarks or sexist jokes from their coaches. In a national survey of 1,200 recently retired Olympic athletes, Kirby and Greaves (1996; cited in Vanden Auweele et al., 2008) found that 22 per cent of the 266 respondents reported that they had had sexual intercourse with persons in positions of authority in sport, and that 9 per cent reported that they had experienced forced sexual intercourse with such persons. In other research it has been reported that between 4 and 10 per cent of male, and 2 and 3 per cent of female, psychologists have had sexual relationships with clients (Andersen, 2005), and in a survey of AASP members, 4 per cent of male members reported that they had at one point been sexually involved with an athlete client (Petrie & Buntrock, 1995).

Sexual interaction between clients and practitioners is strictly prohibited by governing bodies (e.g. AASP, BPS). The potential harm resulting from client–practitioner sexual intimacy is great, and the literature shows the damage that can occur – including feelings of depression, betrayal, exploitation and abuse (Andersen, 2005). However, sexual attraction between athletes and service providers (e.g. a sport psychologist) are common (Andersen, 2005). The critical consideration is how such erotic transference and counter transference is resolved. Denial, suppression and/or repression are natural but unhelpful responses (Stevens & Andersen, 2007). Although there are no clear guidelines on correct actions in deeply personal and emotional situations (as every situation is different), open and honest discussions are useful practice to determine how to move forward with clients.

 Sample question   *Essay*

How would you deal with a client expressing feelings of sexual attraction towards you in a professional setting?

Further reading Professional boundaries

Topic	Key reading
BPS code of ethics and conduct	http://www.bps.org.uk/what-we-do/ethics-standards/ethics-standards
Practitioner–client sexual attraction	Andersen, M. B. (2005). Touching taboos: Sex and the sport psychologist. In M. B. Andersen (Ed.), *Sport psychology in practice* (pp. 171–191). Champaign, IL: Human Kinetics.
Unwanted sexual experiences in sport	Vanden Auweele, Y., Opdenacker, J., Vertommen, T., Boen, F., Van Niekerk, L., De Martelaer, K., & De Cuyper, B. (2008). Unwanted sexual experiences in sport: Perceptions and reported prevalence among Flemish female student-athletes. *International Journal of Sport and Exercise Psychology, 6*(4), 354–365.

Assessment of athletes

Making contact

Making contact, or gaining entry, to work with athletes and coaches represents a delicate step for most consultants because some clients remain sceptical about sport psychologists and the services they offer. The challenge for sport psychologists, therefore, is to help tangibly in the first encounter, by exciting the athlete about the process of change through concrete, jargon-free language within an empathetic relationship. Rather than imposing one's ideas and promising more than one can deliver, it seems sensible to be patient, honest and helpful. The sport psychologist can gain trust, respect and credibility by demonstrating the limits of his or her knowledge and experience in the sport, establishing the lines of confidentiality, clarifying his or herrole and services, and adhering to agreed timelines and goals.

Assessing the needs of a client

Once the consultant gains entry, the process of assessment begins. Assessment is complex and evolves throughout the consultation process. Sport psychologists will explore several components, such as the athlete's needs, values, emotions, goals, history and childhood, family issues and team issues. Consultants often triangulate their assessment techniques. For instance, a consultant might interview the athlete, ask him or her to complete psychometric assessments, and also speak with his or her coach. Structured interviews (i.e. a set of prepared questions) and semi-structured interviews (i.e. a list of general discussion topics) form one element of assessment in sport psychology.

The sport psychologist listens to the needs of the athlete, and these might include performance fears and insecurities, and sometimes non-performance issues and even issues outside of sport. Psychometric testing is used by some consultants. These tests are used when the test is considered valid and reliable and the consultant is trained to administer and evaluate the test. The consultant can also provide the client with a relevant interpretation of the test and triangulate the results with other assessments (e.g. observation, interview). Once the client's problems and concerns are conceptualised, the intervention can be designed, refined and evaluated.

Two common inventories for gathering information with a new client are the Test of Performance Strategies-2 (TOPS-2; Hardy, Roberts, Thomas, & Murphy, 2010) and the *performance profile* (Butler & Hardy, 1992). The TOPS-2 requires athletes to answer a number of questions regarding their current use of psychological skills (e.g. self-talk, goal setting) in training and competition. Although the questionnaire does not provide an indication of the quality of such psychological skill usage, it does provide useful information about the familiarity that athletes have with these psychological skills and the situations under which they are typically implemented by athletes.

The performance profile is another inventory commonly used by sport psychologists. It requires athletes to identify the most important characteristics of successful performance in their sport (including physical abilities, tactical strategies and psychological characteristics) and then to rate their own personal competence in each of the areas on a scale from 1 (lowest ability) to 10 (ideal level of performance). The performance profile is useful not only for gathering important information about clients, but for athletes as it can help facilitate self-awareness and intrinsic motivation (see Chapter 2), and can serve as a basis for goal setting, monitoring progress and evaluating performance (Weston, Greenlees, & Thelwell, 2013).

CRITICAL FOCUS

Should sport psychologists use psychometric tests?

Some sport psychologists rarely, if ever, use psychometric tests with clients. They argue that such tests offer little practical value in the consultation process and undermine the relationship they are forging with the new client. This view, however, is inconsistent with the data and unacceptable to evidence-based practice in sport psychology (Gardner & Moore, 2007). Psychometric tests might form part of the assessment strategy to explore specific non-clinical issues and overcome biases in personal style, beliefs and philoso-phies. Taylor and Schneider (1992) presented the Sport-Clinical Intake Protocol (SCIP) for sport psychology that follows a structured interview style with sport and non-sport issues. The SCIP helps the sport psychologist to collect consistent and comprehensive data without creating an artificial atmosphere.

Conceptualising athlete concerns

Understanding the athlete's concerns to organise and generate potential interventions requires a suitable assessment process. Although an initial interview might highlight possible performance problems, it would be prudent to search for other sources of information about this performance problem. For example, the sport psychologist might conduct more interviews with the athlete, include psychometric testing, observe the athlete at practice and in competition and, with the athlete's permission, speak to the coach or significant others (e.g. coach, parent, partner, physiotherapist). Sometimes, the issue presented by the athlete initially might not reflect the 'real' issue that athletes wished to discuss. Arnold Lazarus (1981) offered a multimodal assessment to assist in this process with the acronym BASIC ID. This acronym represents Behaviour, Affect, Sensation, Imagery, Cognition, Interpersonal and Drugs/Biology (see Table 10.1).

Table 10.1 Examples of questions used by sport psychology consultants

	Questions a sport psychologist might ask in an assessment
Behaviour	What would you like to stop doing? What would you like to start doing?
Affect	Which emotions do you feel most often? What do you do when you feel anxious?
Sensation	What sensations do you feel before you compete? Do any of these sensations cause you to behave in or feel a particular way?
Imagery	What images of the past, present or future are bothering you? Do these images affect how you behave or feel?
Cognition	What negative things do you say about yourself? How do these things affect how you behave or feel?
Interpersonal	Which problems with other people (e.g. coach, partner) bother you? How do these problems affect the way you behave or feel?
Drugs/Biology	What illnesses or medical concerns do you have?

Keeping records for each professional encounter is a worthy practice for a sport psychologist. Such records protect the sport psychologist, assist the client's welfare and meet professional ethics codes. They also help communication between psychologist and clients, form creditable assessment and treatment plans, help write reports and assure contractual commitments with third-party payers (Luepker, 2010). Such progress notes would show the content of each session, the interventions chosen and specific references about who said what in the sessions. Luepker (2010) suggested that adequate records should be legible, relevant, reliable, logical, chronological and concise.

Test your knowledge

10.1 Outline the various psychological approaches/professional philosophies of sport psychology consultants.

10.2 Why do you think some sport psychologists are reluctant to use psychometric tests?

10.3 What questions might a sport psychologist ask a client during a multimodal assessment?

Answers to these questions can be found on the companion website at: www.pearsoned.col.uk/psychologyexpress

Psychological skills training

The service offered by a sport psychologist often depends upon contextual factors (e.g. time available for psychological preparation; specific needs of the client or organisation). Sometimes a strategy for delivering one's services is organised alongside a coach and/or performance director. Together, they might decide that an initial psychoeducation programme is necessary and then organise what, when, how and where the programme will be delivered. This planning phase leans upon the experience of the consultant to suggest the best plan for the organisation and clients whom he or she will work alongside.

Basic psychological skills (i.e. goal setting, self-talk, mental imagery and relaxation) and psychological skills training (PST) more generally often form part of a psychoeducation programme with athletes and coaches (Hardy, Jones, & Gould, 1996). Evidence suggests that PST can improve sport performance (Greenspan & Feltz, 1989). However, it would be foolish to overstate this finding (Gilbourne & Richardson, 2006), especially because since the mid-1990s, no quantitative reviews of the efficacy of PST in sport psychology have been published. We shall briefly discuss four basic psychological skills that are commonly recommended by sport practitioners: goal setting, self-talk, mental imagery and relaxation. Because these have already been discussed in previous chapters, we only provide a brief outline of each skill and how it relates to sport performance.

Goal setting

Goal setting is a popular technique to improve sport performance. It is suggested to enhance motivation by focusing attention on a task/outcome, increasing effort and intensity, encouraging persistence and seeking new strategies (Burton & Weiss, 2008). Goal setting benefits sport performance but only small to moderate effects have been shown (Kyllo & Landers, 1995). Although more beneficial effects have been shown in business (Locke, Shaw, Saari, & Latham, 1981), methodological and conceptual problems arise in sport settings. There is also a difference between setting goals and attaining goals: one might set goals but if that person cannot solve problems related to starting and persisting until the goal is attained, then it is unlikely that goal setting will be effective.

Specific, difficult goals elicit better performances than do-your-best instructions or no goals (Burton & Weiss, 2008). Three types of goal feature within the goal-setting literature: process, performance and outcome goals. *Process goals* emphasise improving performance by focusing upon form, technique and strategy. *Performance goals* emphasise improving general performance, whereas *outcome goals* denote achieving objective outcomes (e.g. winning). The setting of short-term process and performance goals in conjunction with long-term outcome goals may be the most effective combination of goal strategies.

Self-talk

People often talk to themselves. When sport psychologists use the term 'self-talk' they are referring to the voice or internal dialogue that sounds in one's mind (Cornelius, 2002). Athletes have been found to use positive self-statement for a number of reasons. These include learning new skills, correcting bad habits, focusing attention and building self-confidence (Hardy, 2006). Self-talk can differ in terms of *direction* (positive or negative), *content* (instructional or motivational) and *overtness* (silent or out-loud self-statements). These characteristics can influence how self-talk affects the thoughts, feelings and behaviours of sport performers. Research has shown that the use of self-talk strategies differentiates successful from less successful athletes. In particular, successful athletes report fewer negative thoughts, greater focus and task-related thoughts, and positive expectancies (Orlick & Partington, 1988; Hardy, Hall, & Hardy, 2004).

KEY STUDY

Hatzigeorgiadis, Zourbanos, Galanis, & Theodorakis (2011): Self-talk and sports performance: A meta-analysis

Hatzigeorgiadis and colleagues performed a meta-analysis of self-talk interventions and sport performance. The meta-analysis included data obtained from 32 previously published empirical studies. The meta-analyses established positive self-talk as an effective strategy for improving sport performance. Several factors were also identified that moderated the effectiveness of self-talk interventions. Self-talk was found to be more effective when learning new skills compared with refining well-learned tasks. Self-talk was also more effective for improving performance in tasks involving fine, compared with gross, motor demands. Moreover, for fine tasks, instructional self-talk was more effective for performance enhancement than was motivational self-talk. Overall, the meta-analysis demonstrated the effectiveness of self-talk as a strategy to facilitate learning and enhance performance in sport.

Mental imagery

Mental imagery is the ability to create or recreate experiences in the mind (Murphy, Nordin, & Cumming, 2008). It is, for instance, purported to enhance motor control (e.g. more consistent routines), regulate emotions (e.g. increase enjoyment) and fuel motivation (e.g. improve decision making). There are two main imagery perspectives: internal and external.

- *Internal imagery* involves seeing what is happening from within ourselves, as if we were actually doing the activity (e.g. looking down at the tennis ball before we serve).
- *External imagery* involves seeing ourselves as though we were looking at an actor in a movie (e.g. watching ourselves like a spectator).

Martin, Moritz and Hall (1999) developed a conceptual model of mental simulations that outlined five distinct types of imagery (Table 10.2). Each type is proposed to have different functions and can be more or less effective depending on the target of that intervention. For example, Jones, Mace, Bray, MacRae and Stockbridge (2002) found that motivational–general mastery imagery was effective in regulating anxiety levels and facilitating performance in a climbing task.

Table 10.2 **Imagery types and their functions (Martin, Moritz, & Hall, 1999)**

Imagery type	Imagery function
Cognitive–general imagery	Imagining game plans, successful strategies, routines
Cognitive–specific imagery	Imagining specific sport skills
Motivational–specific imagery	Imagining individual goals (e.g. winning a medal)
Motivational–general arousal imagery	Imagining feelings associated with arousal and stress
Motivational–general mastery imagery	Imagining being confident and mastering challenging situations

One discussion within the sport literature on mental imagery is whether athletes should use internal or external imagery (Hardy, 1997; 2012). Traditionally, practitioners had encouraged athletes to use internal imagery because it was thought that such images would be easier to generate (particularly from a kinaesthetic standpoint). However, subsequent research has shown that external imagery is just as effective in facilitating performance as internal imagery. When engaging in mental imagery, athletes should be encouraged to make the images as vivid as possible. This involves not only 'seeing' the action but also focusing on sounds (e.g. the noise of the crowd), smells (e.g. the grass) and touch (e.g. the feel of the racket).

Relaxation

Relaxation is an approach to reduce arousal for sport performers. Relaxation can be mental (e.g. reducing worry) or physical (e.g. reducing physiological arousal manifested in heart rate, blood pressure, respiration rate and muscle tension). To reduce worry or tension, a performer might use cognitive techniques and relaxation exercises. For instance, a cognitive technique might involve cognitive restructuring, where an athlete changes the content of a destructive thought (e.g. it's raining today and I always play poorly in the rain) to a more facilitative thought (e.g. it's raining today but there is no reason why I cannot play well by focusing on the task at hand). Techniques to reduce physiological arousal might involve breathing exercises, progressive relaxation, autogenic training or meditation (Williams, 2010).

Is applied sport psychology all about basic psychological skills?

A perusal of popular books on applied sport psychology might present the false impression that sport psychologists rely mostly on basic psychological skills such as goal setting and self-talk to improve athletic performance. Although these skills are useful and appropriate at times, they only form part of the armoury of a sport psychologist. A critical element in the success of a sport psychologist is the quality of the relationship with the client.

Test your knowledge

10.4 Outline the different types of mental imagery and their functions.

10.5 Describe the benefits of goal setting in sport.

10.6 Has self-talk been identified as an effective technique for improving sport performance?

Answers to these questions can be found on the companion website at: **www.pearsoned.col.uk/psychologyexpress**

Effective sport psychologists

Implementing a programme requires taking time to prepare as well as planning for possible set backs along the way. Once prepared, its success often depends upon the skills of the sport psychologist delivering it. An eclectic approach to sport psychology delivery might best serve the needs of most clients, owing to the diversity of the sports from which they come. In this way, the sport psychologist might employ one or more theoretical frameworks with one organising psychological theory, borrowing methods and techniques from other schools of thought (Poczwardowski, Sherman, & Henschen, 1998).

What makes an effective sport psychologist?

The most significant influence on successful therapeutic processes is the quality of the counselling relationship (Sexton & Whiston, 1994). To prevent non-compliance with a proposed intervention, or clients leaving the therapeutic process early, the therapist and the client aim to establish an open, trusting and collaborative relationship. The sport psychologist requires training and supervision to prepare suitably for this role. Reading to gain professional knowledge, peer discussions and personal therapy are all suggested to prepare the sport psychologist for professional practice.

Orlick and Partington (1988) suggested that effective consultants have a useful sport-specific knowledge about mental training, individualise the mental training programme, adopt a positive constructive attitude, are trustworthy and easy to relate to, fit in with the team, draw upon the athlete's strengths and help the athlete to overcome problems whilst providing clear and practical strategies. Other studies have confirmed the necessity of such characteristics for effective practice in applied sport psychology. Sport psychologists, like the clients they serve, also have opinions, attitudes, values, beliefs, biases and prejudices that affect their consultancy. Without an awareness of how such issues affect one's consultancy, it is unlikely that the sport psychologist can work effectively in this setting. Self-awareness is a vital step in the process of sport psychology service delivery.

Consultant evaluation

Sport psychologists are accountable for the services they offer clients. Some trial and error is inevitable when working with clients. However, not learning from mistakes is senseless and unprofessional. Some mistakes can be avoided through appropriate training, evaluation and reflection whilst heeding the advice from other more established consultants. Each consulting experience provides conclusions and implications for future consulting experience. The consultant can realise greater personal and professional benefits through *reflective practice* processes because the consultant can consider issues that can be changed and improved.

Programme termination

This stage of the consulting process is recognised in the counselling literature as *closure*. Closure represents a delicate stage because termination issues such as resistance, rejection, abandonment, sense of accomplishment and relief might emerge in this stage. Although many sport psychologists and their clients work towards client independence so that the sport psychologist becomes unnecessary to the client, each consultation has its own life cycle so endings vary in time and context. For example, a sport psychologist might end his or her consultancy with a client after three months but her professional relationship might continue in her capacity as team psychologist. In some instances, the sport psychologist needs to refer the client to a more suitably trained professional because the client's presenting issue lies outside the competency of the sport psychologist. For example, the client may present a clinical issue (e.g. an eating disorder) that requires the professional support of a clinical psychologist.

Test your knowledge

10.7 Outline how you would evaluate the relative success of your consultancy work.

10.8 Under what circumstances would you terminate work with a client?

10.9 Outline five factors that make an effective sport psychologist.

Chapter summary – pulling it all together

→ Can you tick all of the points from the revision checklist at the beginning of this chapter?

→ Attempt the sample question from the beginning of this chapter using the answer guidelines below.

→ Go to the companion website at www.pearsoned.co.uk/psychologyexpress to access more revision support online, including interactive quizzes, flashcards, You be the marker exercises as well as answer guidelines for the Test your knowledge and Sample questions from this chapter.

Further reading for Chapter 10

Andersen, M. (2005). *Sport psychology in practice*. Champaign, IL: Human Kinetics.

Williams, J. M. (2010). *Applied sport psychology: Personal growth to peak performance*. New York: McGraw-Hill.

Answer guidelines

 Sample question   *Essay*

What are the characteristics and practices of effective sport psychologists? Discuss with reference to the literature.

Approaching the question

At first this question might appear overly broad and rather vague. But when we unpack the key elements of the question, we see that two elements require discussion. First, what are the characteristics of effective sport psychologists? And second, what do effective sport psychologists do? To answer these questions it can be useful to structure your response in a manner that reflects the beginning, middle and end of the cycle of working with an athlete. You could start by describing the challenges that practitioners face when starting work with a new athlete, team or coach, and the initial assessments that practitioners might consider using. You could then describe the types of psychological skill that practitioners often incorporate into athletes' practice and competition day routines (e.g. mental imagery), including the theoretical underpinnings of such approaches. You could then end your essay by describing how practitioners evaluate their own performances and the relative successes of interventions, including the termination process. Throughout the essay you should draw attention to how characteristics of sport psychologists make these processes more or less effective.

Important points to include

When answering this question it can be useful to describe the various professional philosophies that are adopted by consultants. Even though there is no one correct approach (as every situation is different), you will have demonstrated to an examiner that you understand the various methods of consulting with athletes. You should also describe the various training that neophyte practitioners go through before becoming an accredited sport psychologist, including ethical practices. You should describe how consultants gather information in the early stages of working with a new client and provide some examples of questions that a sport psychologist might ask. When describing the various psychological skills recommended by practitioners, try to outline specific research examples that have assessed the efficacy of each of these techniques. This will show an examiner that you have read critically into the literature.

Make your answer stand out

One of the most effective methods of making your answer stand out is to provide detailed research examples for important points. For example, when describing psychological skills you could outline an important study that has demonstrated the efficacy of the applied technique, including how the study was conducted, the procedure and main findings. This shows an examiner that you have read critically into the literature. You could also provide detailed definitions of the various psychological skills and outline the strengths and weaknesses (validity and reliability) of psychological assessments such as the TOPS-2 and performance profile. Consideration of professional boundaries (professional misconduct) and ethics will also impress an examiner (especially if you can quote from established guidelines).

Explore the accompanying website at www.pearsoned.co.uk/psychologyexpress

→ Prepare more effectively for exams and assignments using the answer guidelines for questions from this chapter.

→ Test your knowledge using multiple choice questions and flashcards.

→ Improve your essay skills by exploring the You be the marker exercises.

Notes

Notes

And finally, before the exam . . .

How to approach revision from here

You should now be at a reasonable stage in your revision process – you should have developed your skills and knowledge base over your course and used this text judiciously during that period. Now, however, you have used the book to reflect on, remind yourself of and reinforce the material you have researched over the year/seminar. You will, of course, need to do additional reading and research to that included here (and appropriate directions are provided) but you will be well on your way with the material presented in this book.

It is important that in answering any question in psychology you take a research- and evidence-based approach to your response. For example, do not make generalised or sweeping statements that cannot be substantiated or supported by evidence from the literature. Remember as well that the evidence should not be anecdotal – it is of no use citing your mum, dad, best friend or the latest news from a celebrity website. After all, you are not writing an opinion piece – you are crafting an argument that is based on current scientific knowledge and understanding. You need to be careful about the evidence you present: do review the material and from where it was sourced.

Furthermore, whatever type of assessment you have to undertake, it is important to take an evaluative approach to the evidence. Whether you are writing an essay, sitting an exam or designing a webpage, the key advice is to avoid simply presenting a descriptive answer. Rather, it is necessary to think about the strength of the evidence in each area. One of the key skills for psychology students is critical thinking and for this reason the tasks featured in this series focus upon developing this way of thinking. Thus you are not expected to simply learn a set of facts and figures, but to think about the implications of what we know and how this might be applied in everyday life. The best assessment answers are the ones that take this critical approach.

It is also important to note that psychology is a theoretical subject: when answering any question about psychology, not only refer to the prevailing theories of the field, but outline the development of them as well. It is also important to evaluate these theories and models either through comparison with other models and theories or through the use of studies that have assessed them and highlighted their strengths and weaknesses. It is essential to read widely – within each section of this book there are directions to interesting and pertinent papers relating to the specific topic area. Find these papers, read these papers and make notes from these papers. But don't stop there. Let them lead you to other sources that may be important to the field. One thing that an examiner hates to see is the same old sources being cited all of the time: be innovative and, as well as reading the seminal works, find the more obscure and interesting sources as well – just make sure they're relevant to your answer!

How not to revise

- **Don't avoid revision.** This is the best tip ever. There is something on the TV, the pub is having a two-for-one offer, the fridge needs cleaning, your budgie looks lonely . . . You have all of these activities to do and they need doing now! Really . . . ? Do some revision!

- **Don't spend too long at each revision session.** Working all day and night is not the answer to revision. You do need to take breaks, so schedule your revision so you are not working from dawn until dusk. A break gives time for the information you have been revising to consolidate.

- **Don't worry.** Worrying will cause you to lose sleep, lose concentration and lose revision time by leaving it late and then later. When the exam comes, you will have no revision completed and will be tired and confused.

- **Don't cram.** This is the worst revision technique in the universe! You will not remember the majority of the information that you try to stuff into your skull, so why bother?

- **Don't read over old notes with no plan.** Your brain will take nothing in. If you wrote your lecture notes in September and the exam is in May, is there any point in trying to decipher your scrawly handwriting now?

- **Don't write model answers and learn by rote.** When it comes to the exam you will simply regurgitate the model answer irrespective of the question – not a brilliant way to impress the examiner!

Tips for exam success

What you should do when it comes to revision

Exams are one form of assessment that students often worry about the most. The key to exam success, as with many other types of assessment, lies in good preparation and self-organisation. One of the most important things is knowing what to expect – this does not necessarily mean knowing what the questions will be on the exam paper, but rather what the structure of the paper is, how many questions you are expected to answer, how long the exam will last and so on.

To pass an exam you need a good grasp of the course material and, obvious as it may seem, to turn up for the exam itself. It is important to remember that you aren't expected to know or remember everything in the course, but you should be able to show your understanding of what you have studied. Remember as well that examiners are interested in what you know, not what you don't know. They try to write exam questions that give you a good chance of passing – not ones to catch you out or trick you in any way. You may want to consider some of these top exam tips.

- Start your revision in plenty of time.
- Make a revision timetable and stick to it.
- Practise jotting down answers and making essay plans.
- Practise writing against the clock using past exam papers.
- Check that you have really answered the question and have not strayed off the point.
- Review a recent past paper and check the marking structure.
- Carefully select the topics you are going to revise.
- Use your lecture/study notes and refine them further, if possible, into lists or diagrams and transfer them on to index cards/Post-it notes. Mind maps are a good way of making links between topics and ideas.
- Practise your handwriting – make sure it's neat and legible.

One to two days before the exam
- Recheck times, dates and venue.
- Actively review your notes and key facts.
- Exercise, eat sensibly and get a few good nights' sleep.

On the day
- Get a good night's sleep.
- Have a good meal, two to three hours before the start time.
- Arrive in good time.
- Spend a few minutes calming and focusing.

In the exam room
- Keep calm.
- Take a few minutes to read each question carefully. Don't jump to conclusions – think calmly about what each question means and the area it is focused on.
- Start with the question you feel most confident about. This helps your morale.
- By the same token, don't expend all your efforts on that one question – if you are expected to answer three questions then don't just answer two.
- Keep to time and spread your effort evenly on all opportunities to score marks.
- Once you have chosen a question, jot down any salient facts or key points. Then take five minutes to plan your answer – a spider diagram or a few notes may be enough to focus your ideas. Try to think in terms of 'why and how' not just 'facts'.

- You might find it useful to create a visual plan or map before writing your answer to help you remember to cover everything you need to address.
- Keep reminding yourself of the question and try not to wander off the point.
- Remember that quality of argument is more important than quantity of facts.
- Take 30–60-second breaks whenever you find your focus slipping (typically every 20 minutes).
- Make sure you reference properly – according to your university requirements.
- Watch your spelling and grammar – you could lose marks if you make too many errors.

→ *Final revision checklist*

❏ Have you revised the topics highlighted in the revision checklists?

❏ Have you attended revision classes and taken note of and/or followed up on your lecturers' advice about the exams or assessment process at your university?

❏ Can you answer the questions posed in this text satisfactorily? Don't forget to check sample answers on the website too.

❏ Have you read the additional material to make your answer stand out?

❏ Remember to criticise appropriately – based on evidence.

Test your knowledge by using the material presented in this text or on the website: **www.pearsoned.co.uk/psychologyexpress**

Glossary

acquiescence A tendency to agree or disagree with questionnaire statements regardless of their content.

aggression Any behaviour, physical or verbal, directed towards the goal of harming or injuring another living being.

anxiety An emotional label for a specific type of arousal experience. It is an emotional state characterised by worry, feelings of apprehension and bodily tension.

applied research Scientific research into the effectiveness of psychological interventions used by practitioners.

arousal A measure of bodily energy, ranging from deep sleep to high alertness.

attribution retraining Changing attributions by verbally convincing a person that a particular cause was responsible for an outcome.

autogenic training A self-relaxation technique that involves mental images and self-statements of relaxation.

autonomous behaviour A state of functioning independently without external controlling influences.

bounded rationality The idea that rational decisions are limited by the external information available, cognitive limitations and decision-making time.

causality The relationship between two events where the second is understood to be the consequence of the first (a cause and an effect).

closed skills Skills that take place in a stable and predictable environment where movements follow a set pattern (e.g. free throw in basketball).

co-active sports Team sports where group member skills are performed at the same time but without direct interaction (e.g. rowing, swimming relay).

coaching efficacy A coach's belief in his or her ability to coach effectively to produce desired outcomes.

cocktail party effect The phenomenon of being able to focus attention on a single stimulus while filtering out other non-relevant information.

cognitive confirmation A tendency for people to favour information that confirms their beliefs or hypotheses.

cognitive consonace Occurs when one cognition follows on from, or fits with, another cognition, reinforcing the initial piece of knowledge.

cognitive dissonance Occurs when a cognition contradicts an initial thought or belief (i.e. the relationship between the two cognitions is dissonant).

cognitive irrelevance Describes two cognitions that have nothing in common.

cognitive reappraisal A coping strategy in which participants monitor negative thoughts and actively replace them with more positive thoughts.

collective efficacy A group's shared belief in its ability to perform group tasks effectively to produce desired group outcomes.

control group The group that receives no treatment, or the standard treatment, in comparison to the new treatment (experimental) group.

coping effectiveness The degree to which a particular coping strategy is effective in alleviating negative emotions caused by stress.

counterfactual thoughts Mental representations of alternatives to past events, actions or states.

correlation coefficient A measure of the strength and direction of linear relationships between two variables.

cross-sectional research Research in which independent variables have not been manipulated and data have been collected at a single time-point.

curvilinear relationship Where an increase in variable 1 is associated with an increase in variable 2 up to a certain point, after which further increases in variable 1 are associated with a decrease in variable 2.

electroencephalography (EEG) A method of recording of the brain's electrical activity over a short period of time.

emotion regulation Various psychological skills that help a person to monitor and manage their emotional states.

factor analysis A statistical method used to group a number of lower-order variables into higher-order factors.

functional magnetic reasoning image (fMRI) A procedure that measures brain activity by detecting changes in blood flow.

fundamental attribution error The tendency to over-estimate dispositional factors for observed behaviour and under-estimate situational factors.

group norms Group-held beliefs about how members should behave in a given context.

groupthink When group members try to minimise conflict and reach a consensus decision without critical evaluation of alternative ideas.

heritability estimate The proportion of variation between individuals that is influenced by genetic factors.

imagery The formation of mental images in the mind. It can be *internal* (seeing what is happening from within ourselves as if we were doing the activity) or *external* (seeing ourselves as if looking at an actor in a movie).

inattentional blindness When a person focuses intensely on a particular task and they become blind to stimuli that would normally attract their attention.

individual differences Factors that separate how individuals differ in their behaviour (e.g. personality).

ingroup deviance When a group member deviates from accepted group norms.

interdependent sports Team sports where performers are continually interacting with one another (e.g. rugby, netball).

intergroup processes Processes that take place between groups.

intragroup processes Processes that take place within groups.

kinaesthetic imagery Mental images that involve thoughts about touch, temperature, movement and feelings.

kinematics The motion of persons, points, objects or systems of objects.

linear relationship An increase or decrease in one variable coincides with an increase or decrease in another variable.

mediating relationship When one variable influences another variable via a third variable.

meta-analysis A statistical method that involves combining data from several sources to better understand patterns among study results.

moderator variables A variable that affects the strength and/or direction of a relationship between two other variables.

motivational climate The environmental influence on achievement goals. It can be a *mastery climate* (task-involving focused on effort, personal improvement and skill development) or a *performance climate* (ego-involving where the emphasis is on normative comparison and public evaluation).

negative emotions Emotions that are generally considered unpleasant (e.g. anger, anxiety).

open skills Skills that have to be continually adapted to suit a constantly changing environment (e.g. passing and moving in football).

outcome goals Denote achieving objective outcomes (e.g. winning).

overconfidence When confidence levels are above those required for optimal performance.

performance goals Emphasise improving general performance.

positive emotions Emotions that are generally considered pleasant (e.g. excitement, happiness).

positron emission tomography An imaging technique that uses a camera and tracer to produce three-dimensional images of organs in the body.

pre-performance routines A set routine that helps athletes create a stable and predictable environment during the lead-up to competition.

process goals Emphasise improving performance by focusing upon form, technique and strategy.

process losses Any aspect of intragroup interactions that inhibits effective group functioning.

proxy efficacy One's confidence in the skills and abilities of a third party to function effectively on one's behalf.

psychological need thwarting When basic psychological needs (competence, autonomy and relatedness) are inhibited.

psychological skills training The practice of psychological skills such as imagery and self-talk during training in preparation for competition.

qualitative research A method of psychological research that aims to gather an in-depth understanding of behaviour using non-numerical data collection.

quantitative research A method of psychological research that investigates behaviour using statistical, mathematical or computational analyses of numerical data.

reflective practice Reflecting on actions and behaviours to aid the process of continuous learning.

reliability Whether an assessment measure produces consistent results.

response distortion A tendency to manipulate scores by answering in a certain way.

Ringelmann effect A reduction in individual productivity that coincides with increases in group size.

role ambiguity When a person is unclear about their role responsibilities.

self-awareness When individuals become more conscious of their personality, thought processes and behaviours.

self-control The ability to control emotions, behaviours and desires in an attempt to achieve a reward or to avoid punishment.

self-efficacy Beliefs in one's ability to execute the courses of action required to produce given attainments.

self-esteem A person's judgement of his or her own worth.

self-fulfilling prophecy A false prediction of a situation which evokes new behaviours that inadvertently cause the original false prediction to become true.

self-modelling A psychological technique that involves watching selectively edited video footage of prior performances.

self-report measures Questionnaires that involve answering questions about oneself.

self-serving bias The tendency to attribute positive outcomes to the self and negative outcomes to external factors.

self-talk The voice or internal dialogue that sounds in one's mind.

simulation training Replicating the demands of competition in a training environment to practise coping with mental and physical stressors.

social desirability The tendency to answer questions in a manner that would be perceived as favourable by others.

social facilitation Increases in performance due to the presence of an audience.

social identity Self-esteem derived from membership of a relevant social group.

social loafing The tendency for people to exert less effort when working in a group than they would have when working alone.

social psychology The scientific study of psychological processes in social situations.

states Temporary thoughts, feelings or behaviours that vary relative to the situation.

stress An on-going process that involves making appraisals of situational demands and personal resources to cope with those demands.

subjective performance Performance as measured by personal judgement rather than objective scores.

systematic review A research synthesis that uses a set of specified inclusion and exclusion criteria in an attempt to answer a specific research question.

traits Thoughts, feelings and behaviours that remain relatively consistent across situations.

triangulation Using two or more methods to double-check research findings.

validity Whether an assessment device measures what it purports to measure.

working memory The system that holds information in the mind for a short period of time.

References

Abel, E. L., & Kruger, M. L. (2010). Smile intensity in photographs predicts longevity. *Psychological Science, 21*, 542–544.

Aidman, E. V. (2007). Attribute-based selection for success: The role of personality attributes in long-term predictions of achievement in sport. *Journal of the American Board of Sport Psychology, 3*, 1–18.

Allen, M. S. (2012). A systematic review of content themes in sport attribution research: 1954–2011. *International Journal of Sport and Exercise Psychology, 10*, 1–8.

Allen, M. S., Frings, D., & Hunter, S. (2012). Personality, coping, and challenge and threat states in athletes. *International Journal of Sport and Exercise Psychology, 10*, 264–275.

Allen, M. S., Greenlees, I., & Jones, M. V. (2011). An investigation of the five-factor model of personality and coping behaviour in sport. *Journal of Sports Sciences, 29*, 841–850.

Allen, M. S., Greenlees, I., & Jones, M. V. (2013). Personality in sport: A comprehensive review. *International Review of Sport and Exercise Psychology, 6*, 184–208.

Allport, G. W. (1937). Personality: A psychological interpretation. New York: Holt.

Allport, G. W., & Odbert, H. S. (1936). Trait names: A psycho-lexical study. *Psychological Monographs, 47* (1, Whole No. 211).

Ames, C. (1984). Competitive, cooperative, and individualistic goal structures: A cognitive-motivational analysis. In C. Ames & R. Ames (Eds.), *Research on motivation in education* (Vol. 1, pp. 177–207). New York: Academic Press.

Ames, C. (1992). Classrooms: Goals, structures, and student motivation. *Journal of Educational Psychology, 84*, 261–271.

Andersen, M. B. (2005). Touching taboos: Sex and the sport psychologist. In M. B. Andersen (Ed.), *Sport psychology in practice* (pp. 171–191). Champaign, IL: Human Kinetics.

Andersen, M. B. (2011). Who's mental, who's tough, and who's both? Mutton constructs dressed up as lamb. In D. F. Gucciardi & S. Gordon (Eds.), *Mental toughness in sport: Developments in research and theory* (pp. 69–88). Abingdon, UK: Routledge.

Anshel, M. H., & Kaissidis, A. N. (1997). Coping style and situational appraisals as predictors of coping strategies following stressful events in sport as a function of gender and skill level. *British Journal of Psychology, 88*, 263–276.

Asch, S. E. (1946). Forming impressions of personality. *Journal of Abnormal and Social Psychology, 41*, 258–290.

Avugos, S., Köppen, J., Czienskowski, U., Raab, M., & Bar-Eli, M. (2013). The 'hot hand' reconsidered: A meta-analytic approach. *Psychology of Sport and Exercise, 14*, 21–27.

Bandura, A. (1977). Self-efficacy: Towards a unifying theory of behavioral change. *Psychological Review, 84*, 191–215.

Bandura, A. (1986). *Social foundations of thought and action.* Englewood Cliffs, NJ: Prentice Hall.

Bandura, A. (1997). *Self-efficacy: The exercise of control.* New York: Freeman.

Bandura, A. (2006). Guide for constructing self-efficacy scales. In F. Pajares & T. Urdan (Eds.), *Self-efficacy beliefs of adolescents* (Vol. 5., pp. 307–337). Greenwich, CT: Information Age Publishing.

Bandura, A. (2012). Social cognitive theory. In P. A. M. Van Lange, A. W. Kruglanski & E. T. Higgins (Eds.), *Handbook of theories of social psychology* (Vol. 1, pp. 349–373). London: Sage.

Bar-Eli, M., Plessner, H., & Raab, M. (2011). *Judgment, decision making and success in sport.* Chichester, UK: Wiley-Blackwell.

References

Barenbaum, N. B., & Winter, D. G. (2008). History of modern personality theory and research. In O. P. John, R. W. Robins & L. A. Pervin (Eds.), *Handbook of personality: Theory and research* (3rd ed., pp. 3–26). New York: Guilford Press.

Bartholomew, K. J., Ntoumanis, N., Ryan, R. M., & Thøgersen-Ntoumani, C. (2011). Psychological need thwarting in the sport context: Assessing the darker side of athletic experience. *Journal of Sport and Exercise Psychology, 33,* 75–102.

Baumeister, R. F. (1984). Choking under pressure: Self-consciousness and paradoxical effects of incentives on skilful performance. *Journal of Personality and Social Psychology, 46,* 610–620.

Baumeister, R. F., & Leary, M. R. (1995). The need to belong: Desire for interpersonal attachments as a fundamental human motivation. *Psychological Bulletin, 117,* 497–529.

Baumeister, R. F., & Showers, C. J. (1986). A review of paradoxical performance effects: Choking under pressure in sports and mental tests. *European Journal of Social Psychology, 16,* 361–383.

Baumeister, R. F., & Steinhilber, D. (1984). Paradoxical effects of supportive audiences on performance under pressure: The home field disadvantage in sports championships. *Journal of Personality and Social Psychology, 47,* 85–93.

Beattie, S., Lief, D., Adamoulas, M., & Oliver, E. (2011). Investigating the possible negative effects of self-efficacy upon golf putting performance. *Psychology of Sport and Exercise, 12,* 434–441.

Beauchamp, M. R., Bray, S. R., Eys, M. A., & Carron, A. V. (2002). Role ambiguity, role efficacy, and role performance: Multidimensional and mediational relationships within interdependent sport teams. *Group Dynamics: Theory, Research, and Practice, 6,* 229–242.

Beauchamp, M. R., Jackson, B., & Lavallee, D. (2007). Personality processes and intra-group dynamics in sport teams. In M. R. Beauchamp & M. A. Eys (Eds.), *Group dynamics in exercise and sport psychology: Contemporary themes* (pp. 25–41). Abingdon, UK: Routledge.

Beedie, C. J., Terry, P. C., & Lane, A. M. (2000). The profile of mood states and athletic performance: Two meta-analyses. *Journal of Applied Sport Psychology, 12,* 49–68.

Beilock, S. L., & Carr, T. H. (2001). On the fragility of skilled performance: What governs choking under pressure? *Journal of Experimental Psychology: General, 130,* 701–725.

Bell, J. J., & Hardy, J. (2009). Effects of attentional focus on skilled performance in golf. *Journal of Applied Sport Psychology, 21,* 163–177.

Bell, S. T. (2007). Deep-level composition variables as predictors of team performance: A meta-analysis. *Journal of Applied Psychology, 92,* 595–615.

Biddle, S. J. H., Hanrahan, S. J., & Sellars, C. N. (2001). Attributions: Past, present, and future. In R. N. Singer, H. A. Hausenblas, & C. M. Janelle (Eds.), *Handbook of sport psychology* (2nd ed., pp. 444–471). New York: Wiley.

Boutcher, S. H. (2008). Attentional processes and sport performance. In T. S. Horn (Ed.), *Advances in sport psychology* (3rd ed., pp. 325–338). Champaign, IL: Human Kinetics.

Boyce, B. A., & Bingham, S. M. (1997). The effects of self-efficacy and goal-setting on bowling performance. *Journal of Teaching in Physical Education, 16,* 312–323.

Bray, S. R., Gyurcsik, N. C., Culos-Reed, S. N., Dawson, K. A., & Martin, K. A. (2001). An exploratory investigation of the relationship between proxy efficacy, self-efficacy and exercise attendance. *Journal of Health Psychology, 6,* 425–434.

Bray, S. R., & Shields, C. A. (2007). Proxy agency in physical activity. In M. R. Beauchamp & M. A. Eys (Eds.), *Group dynamics in exercise and sport psychology* (pp. 79–95). Abingdon, UK: Routledge.

Broadbent, D. E. (1958). *Perception and communication.* New York: Oxford University Press.

Brown, R. (1988). Group processes: Dynamics within and between groups. Oxford: Blackwell.

Bull, S. J., Shambrook, C. J., James, W., & Brooks, J. E. (2005). Towards an understanding of mental toughness in elite English cricketers. *Journal of Applied Sport Psychology, 17,* 209–227.

Burke, S., Sparkes, A. C., & Allen-Collinson, J. (2008). High altitude climbers as ethnomethodologists making sense of cognitive dissonance: Ethnographic insights from an attempt to scale Mt Everest. *The Sport Psychologist, 22,* 336–355.

Burton, D., & Weiss, C. (2008). The fundamental goal concept: The path to process and performance success. In T. S. Horn (Ed.), *Advances in sport psychology* (3rd ed., pp. 339–375). Champaign, IL: Human Kinetics.

Busemeyer, J. R., & Townsend, J. T. (1993). Decision field theory: A dynamic-cognitive approach of decision making in an uncertain environment. *Psychological Review, 100*, 432–459.

Butler, R. J., & Hardy, L. (1992). The performance profile: Theory and application. *The Sport Psychologist, 6*, 253–264.

Callow, N., & Waters, A. (2005). The effect of kinaesthetic imagery on the sport confidence of flat-race horse jockeys. *Psychology of Sport and Exercise, 6*, 443–459.

Cameron, J. E., Cameron, J. M., Dithurbide, L., & Lalonde, R. N. (2012). Personality traits and stereotypes associated with ice hockey positions. *Journal of Sport Behavior, 35*, 109–124.

Carron, A. V., Brawley, L. R., & Widmeyer, W. N. (1998). The measurement of cohesiveness in sport groups. In J. L. Duda (Ed.), *Advances in sport and exercise psychology measurement* (pp. 213–226). Morgantown, WV: Fitness Information Technology.

Carron, A. V., Colman, M. M., Wheeler, J., & Stevens, D. (2002). Cohesion and performance in sport: A meta-analysis. *Journal of Sport and Exercise Psychology, 24*, 168–188.

Carron, A. V., & Eys, M. A. (2012). *Group dynamics in sport* (4th ed.). Morgantown, WV: Fitness Information Technology.

Carron, A. V., Loughead, T. M., & Bray, S. R. (2005). The home advantage in sport competitions: Courneya and Carron's (1992) conceptual framework a decade later. *Journal of Sports Sciences, 23*, 395–407.

Carron, A. V., Widmeyer, W. N., & Brawley, L. R. (1985). The development of an instrument to assess cohesion in sport teams: The group environment questionnaire. *Journal of Sport Psychology, 7*, 244–266.

Carron, A. V., Widmeyer, W. N., & Brawley, L. R. (1989). Perceptions of ideal group size in sport teams. *Perceptual and Motor Skills, 69*, 1368–1379.

Castanier, C., Le Scanff, C., & Woodman, T. (2010). Who takes risks in high-risk sports? A typological personality approach. *Research Quarterly for Exercise and Sport, 81*, 478–485.

Cattell, R. B. (1943). The description of personality: Basic traits resolved into clusters. *Journal of Abnormal and Social Psychology, 38*, 476–506.

Cherry, E. C. (1953). Some experiments on the recognition of speech, with one and with two ears. *Journal of the Acoustical Society of America, 25*, 975–979.

Clough, P., Earle, K., Perry, J. L., & Crust, L. (2012). Comment on 'Progressing measurement in mental toughness: A case example of the Mental Toughness Questionnaire 48' by Gucciardi, Hanton, and Mallett (2012). *Sport, Exercise, and Performance Psychology, 1*, 283–287.

Clough, P., Earle, K., & Sewell, D. (2002). Mental toughness: The concept and its measurement. In I. Cockerill (Ed.), *Solutions in sport psychology* (pp. 32–45). London: Thomson.

Coffee, P., & Rees, T. (2008). The CSGU: A measure of controllability, stability, globality, and universality attributions. *Journal of Sport and Exercise Psychology, 30*, 611–641.

Coffee, P., & Rees, T. (2011). When the chips are down: Effects of attributional feedback on self-efficacy and task performance following initial and repeated failure. *Journal of Sports Sciences, 29*, 235–245.

Cohen, S., Underwood, L. G., & Gottlieb, B. H. (2000). *Social support measurement and intervention: A guide for health and social scientists.* New York: Oxford University Press.

Cohen, S., & Wills, T. A. (1985). Stress, social support and the buffering hypothesis. *Psychological Bulletin, 98*, 310–357.

Conroy, D. E., Elliot, A. J., & Hofer, S. M. (2003). A 2 × 2 achievement goals questionnaire for sport. *Journal of Sport and Exercise Psychology, 25*, 456–476.

Conroy, D. E., & Hyde, A. L. (2012). Achievement motivation processes. In G. Tenenbaum, R. C. Eklund & A. Kamata (Eds.), *Measurement in sport and exercise psychology* (pp. 303–317). Champaign, IL: Human Kinetics.

Cornelius, A. (2002). Intervention techniques in sport psychology. In J. M. Silva III & D. E. Stevens (Eds.), *Psychological foundations of sport* (pp. 177–196). Boston, MA: Allyn & Bacon.

References

Costa, P. T., & McCrae, R. R. (1992). *Revised NEO personality inventory and NEO five-factor inventory: Professional manual*. Odessa, FL: Psychological Assessment Resources.

Cotterill, S. T. (2010). Pre-performance routines in sport: Current understanding and future directions. *International Review of Sport and Exercise Psychology, 3*, 132–153.

Cottrell, N. B. (1972). Social facilitation. In C. G. McClintock (Ed.), *Experimental Social Psychology* (pp. 185–236). New York: Holt, Rinehart & Winston.

Courneya, K. S., & Carron, A. V. (1992). The home advantage in sport competitions: A literature review. *Journal of Sport and Exercise Psychology, 14*,13–27.

Cox, R. H., Martens, M. P., & Russell, W. D. (2003). Measuring anxiety in athletics: The *Revised Competitive State Anxiety Inventory–2*. *Journal of Sport and Exercise Psychology, 25*, 519–533.

Craft, L. L., Magyar, T. M., Becker, B. J., & Feltz, D. L. (2003). The relationship between the Competitive State Anxiety Inventory–2 and sport performance: A meta-analysis. *Journal of Sport and Exercise Psychology, 25*, 44–65.

Crocker, P. R. E., & Graham, T. R. (1995). Coping by competitive athletes with performance stress: Gender differences and relationships with affect. *The Sport Psychologist, 9*, 325–338.

Crust, L. (2008). A review and conceptual re-examination of mental toughness: Implications for future researchers. *Personality and Individual Differences, 45*, 576–583.

Crust, L. (2009). The relationship between mental toughness and affect intensity. *Personality and Individual Differences, 47*, 959–963.

Crust, L., & Azadi, K. (2010). Mental toughness and athletes' use of psychological strategies. *European Journal of Sport Science, 10*, 43–51.

Crust, L., & Clough, P. J. (2011). Developing mental toughness: From research to practice. *Journal of Sport Psychology in Action, 2*, 21–32.

Crust, L., & Keegan, R. (2010). Mental toughness and attitudes to risk-taking. *Personality and Individual Differences, 49*, 164–168.

Crust, L., & Swann, C. (2011). Comparing two measures of mental toughness. *Personality and Individual Differences, 50*, 217–221.

Davis, IV, H., Liotti, M., Ngan, E. T., Woodward, T. S., Van Snellenberg, J. X., van Anders, S. M., Smith, A., & Mayberg, H. S. (2008). fMRI BOLD signal changes in elite swimmers while viewing videos of personal failure. *Brain Imaging and Behavior, 2*, 84–93.

DeCaro, M. S., Thomas, R. D., Albert, N. B., & Beilock, S. L. (2011). Choking under pressure: Multiple routes to skill failure. *Journal of Experimental Psychology: General, 140*, 390–406.

Deci, E. (1980). *The psychology of self-determination*. Lexington, MA: DD Heath.

Deci, E. L., & Ryan, R. M. (1985). *Intrinsic motivation and self-determination in human behavior*. New York: Academic Press.

Deci, E. L., & Ryan, R. M. (2012). Self-determination theory. In P. A. M. Van Lange, A. W. Kruglanski, & E. T. Higgins (Eds.), *Handbook of theories of social psychology* (Vol. 1; pp. 416–437). London: Sage.

Dienstbier, R. A. (1989). Arousal and physiological toughness: Implications for mental and physical health. *Psychological Review, 96*, 84–100.

Duda, J. L., & Nicholls, J. G. (1992). Dimensions of achievement motivation in schoolwork and sport. *Journal of Educational Psychology, 84*, 290–299.

Edwards, W. (1954). The theory of decision making. *Psychological Bulletin, 51*, 380–417.

Eidelman, S., Silvia, P. J., & Biernat, M. (2006). Responding to deviance: Target exclusion and differential devaluation. *Personality and Social Psychology Bulletin, 32*, 1153–1164.

Ekman, P. (1992). An argument for basic emotions. *Cognition and Emotion, 6*, 169–200.

Elliot, A. J. (1999). Approach and avoidance motivation and achievement goals. *Educational Psychologist, 34*,169–189.

Elliot, A. J. (2006). The hierarchical model of approach-avoidance motivation. *Motivation and Emotion, 30*, 111–116.

Elliot, A. J., & Maier, M. A. (2012). Color-in-context theory. In P. Devine & A. Plant (Eds.), *Advances in experimental social psychology* (Vol. 45, pp. 61–125). Burlington: Academic Press.

Elliot, A. J., Murayama, K., & Pekrun, R. (2011). A 3 x 2 achievement goal model. *Journal of Educational Psychology, 103,* 632–648.

Epstein, J. L. (1989). Family structures and student motivation: A developmental perspective. In C. Ames & R. Ames (Eds.), *Research on motivation in education* (Vol. 3, pp. 259–295). San Diego, CA: Academic Press.

Evans, V., & Quarterman, J. (1983). Personality characteristics of successful and unsuccessful black female basketball players. *International Journal of Sport Psychology, 14,* 105–115.

Eys, M. A., Loughead, T. M., Bray, S. R., & Carron, A. V. (2009). Development of a cohesion questionnaire for youth: The Youth Sport Environment Questionnaire. *Journal of Sport & Exercise Psychology, 31,* 390–408.

Eysenck, H. J. (1947). *Dimensions of personality.* London: Routledge & Kegan Paul.

Eysenck, M. W., Derakshan, N., Santos, R., & Calvo, M. G. (2007). Anxiety and cognitive performance: Attentional control theory. *Emotion, 7,* 336–353.

Feltz, D. L., Chase, M. A., Moritz, S. E., & Sullivan, P. J. (1999). A conceptual model of coaching efficacy: Preliminary investigation and instrument development. *Journal of Educational Psychology, 91,* 675–776.

Feltz, D. L., Short, S. E., & Sullivan, P. J. (2008). Self-efficacy in sport: Research and strategies for working with athletes, teams, and coaches. Champaign, IL: Human Kinetics.

Fenz, W. D., & Epstein, S. (1967). Gradients of physiological arousal in parachutists as a function of an approaching jump. *Psychosomatic Medicine, 29,* 33–51.

Festinger, L. (1954). A theory of social comparison processes. *Human Relations, 7,* 117–140.

Festinger, L. (1957). *A theory of cognitive dissonance.* Stanford, CA: Stanford University Press.

Fifer, A., Henschen, K., Gould, D., & Ravizza, K. (2008). What works when working with athletes. *The Sport Psychologist, 22,* 356–377.

Fletcher, D., & Hanton, S. (2003). Sources of organizational stress in elite sports performance. *The Sport Psychologist, 17,* 175–195.

Folkman, S. (1991). Coping across the life span: Theoretical issues. In E. M. Cummings, A. L. Greene, & K. H. Karraker (Eds.), *Life-span developmental psychology: Perspectives on stress and coping* (pp. 3–19). Hillsdale, NJ: Erlbaum.

Folkman, S., & Lazarus, R. S. (1988). *Manual for the Ways of Coping Questionnaire.* Palo Alto, CA: Consulting Psychologists Press.

Frank, M. G., & Gilovich, T. (1988). The dark side of self- and social perception: Black uniforms and aggression in professional sports. *Journal of Personality and Social Psychology, 54,* 74–85.

Freeman, P., & Rees, T. (2010). Perceived social support from teammates: Direct and stress-buffering effects on self-confidence. *European Journal of Sports Sciences, 10,* 59–67.

Furley, P., Memmert, D., & Heller, C. (2010). The dark side of visual awareness in sport: Inattentional blindness in a real-world basketball task. *Attention, Perception, & Psychophysics, 72,* 1327–1337.

Gardner, F. L., & Moore, Z. E. (2007). *The psychology of enhancing human performance: The Mindfulness-Acceptance-Commitment (MAC) approach.* New York: Springer.

Gaudreau, P., & Blondin, J.-P. (2002). Development of a questionnaire for the assessment of coping strategies employed by athletes in competitive sport settings. *Psychology of Sport and Exercise, 3,* 1–34.

Gaudreau, P., Nicholls, A., & Levy, A. R. (2010). The ups and downs of coping and sport achievement: An episodic process analysis of within-person associations. *Journal of Sport and Exercise Psychology, 32,* 298–312.

Gee, C. J., Marshall, J. C., & King, J. F. (2010). Should coaches use personality assessments in the talent identification process? A 15 year predictive study on professional hockey players. *International Journal of Coaching Science, 4,* 25–34.

Giacobbi, P., Foore, B., & Weinberg, R. S. (2004). Broken clubs and expletives: The sources of stress and coping responses of skilled and moderately skilled golfers. *Journal of Applied Sport Psychology, 16,* 166–182.

Gigerenzer, G. (2004). Fast and frugal heuristics: The tools of bounded rationality. In D. J. Koehler & N. Harvey (Eds.), *Handbook of judgment and decision making*. Oxford: Blackwell.

Gigerenzer, G., Todd, P. M., & ABC Research Group (1999). *Simple heuristics that make us smart*. Oxford: Oxford University Press.

Gilbourne, D., & Richardson, D. (2006). Tales from the field: Personal reflections on the provision of psychological support in professional soccer. *Psychology of Sport and Exercise, 7*, 325–327.

Gill, D. L., & Williams, L. (2008). *Psychological dynamics of sport and exercise* (3rd ed.). Champaign, IL: Human Kinetics.

Gilovich, T., Vallone, R., & Tversky, A. (1985). The hot hand in basketball: On the misperception of random sequences. *Cognitive Psychology, 17*, 295–314.

Golby, J., Sheard, M., & Lavallee, D. (2003). A cognitive-behavioural analysis of mental toughness in national rugby league football teams. *Perceptual and Motor Skills, 96*, 455–462.

Goldberg, L. R., Johnson, J. A., Eber, H. W., Hogan, R., Ashton, M. C., Cloninger, C. R., & Gough, H. G. (2006). The international personality item pool and the future of public-domain personality measures. *Journal of Research in Personality, 40*, 84–96.

Goldstein, E. B. (2008). Cognitive Psychology: Connecting mind, research, and everyday experience. New York: Thomson Learning.

Goncalo, J., Flynn, F., & Kim, S. (2010). Are two narcissists better than one? The link between narcissism, perceived creativity, and creative performance. *Personality and Social Psychology Bulletin, 36*, 1484–1495.

Gould, D., & Carson, S. (2008). Life skills development through sport: Current status and future directions. *International Review of Sport and Exercise Psychology, 1*, 58–78.

Gray, R. (2004). Attending to the execution of a complex sensorimotor skill: Expertise differences, choking and slumps. *Journal of Experimental Psychology: Applied, 10*, 42–54.

Graydon, J., & Murphy, T. (1995). The effects of personality on social facilitation whilst performing a sports related task. *Personality and Individual Differences, 19*, 265–267.

Greenlees, I. (2007). Person perception and sport performance. In S. Jowett & D. Lavallee (Eds.), *Social psychology in sport* (pp. 195–208). Champaign, IL: Human Kinetics.

Greenlees, I. A., Bradley, A., Holder, T., & Thelwell, R. C. (2005). The impact of opponents' non-verbal behaviour on the first impressions and outcome expectations of table tennis players. *Psychology of Sport and Exercise, 6*, 103–115.

Greenlees, I. A., Buscombe, R., Thelwell, R. C., Holder, T., & Rimmer, M. (2005). Perception of opponents in tennis: The impact of opponents' clothing and body language on impression formation and outcome expectations. *Journal of Sport & Exercise Psychology, 27*, 39–52.

Greenlees, I., Dicks, M., Holder, T., & Thelwell, R. (2007). Order effects in sport: Examining the impact of order of information presentation on attributions of ability. *Psychology of Sport and Exercise, 8*, 477–489.

Greenlees, I., Graydon, J., & Maynard, I. (1999). The impact of collective efficacy beliefs on effort and persistence in a group task. *Journal of Sports Sciences, 17*, 151–158.

Greenlees, I., Graydon, J., & Maynard, I. (2000). The impact of individual efficacy beliefs on group goal commitment. *Journal of Sports Sciences, 18*, 451–459.

Greenlees, I., Thelwell, R., & Holder, T. (2006). Examining the efficacy of the concentration grid exercise as a concentration enhancement exercise. *Psychology of Sport and Exercise, 7*, 29–39.

Greenspan, M. J., & Feltz, D. L. (1989). Psychological interventions with athletes in competitive situations: A review. *The Sport Psychologist, 3*, 219–236.

Griffiths, P. E. (1997). *What emotions really are*. Chicago, IL: University of Chicago Press.

Gucciardi, D. F. (2009). Do developmental differences in mental toughness exist between specialized and invested Australian footballers? *Personality and Individual Differences, 47*, 985–989.

Gucciardi, D. F., & Gordon, S. (2009). Development and preliminary validation of the Cricket Mental Toughness Inventory (CMTI). *Journal of Sports Sciences, 27*,1293–1310.

Gucciardi, D. F., Gordon, S., & Dimmock, J. A. (2008). Towards an understanding of mental toughness in Australian football. *Journal of Applied Sport Psychology, 20*, 261–281.

Gucciardi, D. F., Gordon, S., & Dimmock, J. A. (2009a). Evaluation of a mental toughness training programme for youth-aged Australian footballers: I. A quantitative analysis. *Journal of Applied Sport Psychology, 21*, 307–323.

Gucciardi, D. F., Gordon, S., & Dimmock, J. A. (2009b). Advancing mental toughness research and theory using personal construct psychology. *International Review of Sport and Exercise Psychology, 2*, 54–72.

Gucciardi, D. F., Gordon, S., & Dimmock, J. A. (2009c). Development and preliminary validation of a mental toughness inventory for Australian football. *Psychology of Sport and Exercise, 10*, 201–209.

Gucciardi, D. F., Gordon, S., Dimmock, J. A., & Mallett, C. J. (2009). Understanding the coach's role in the development of mental toughness: Perspectives of elite Australian football coaches. *Journal of Sports Sciences, 27*, 1483–1496.

Gucciardi, D. F., Hanton, S., & Mallett, C. J. (2012). Progressing measurement in mental toughness: A case example of the Mental Toughness Questionnaire 48. *Sport, Exercise, and Performance Psychology, 1*, 194–214.

Gucciardi, D. F., & Jones, M. I. (2012). Beyond optimal performance: Mental toughness profiles and developmental success in adolescent cricketers. *Journal of Sport and Exercise Psychology, 34*, 16–36.

Hagemann, N., Strauss, B., & Leißing, J. (2008). When the referee sees red. *Psychological Science, 19*, 769–771.

Hagger, M. S., & Chatzisarantis, N. L. D. (2007). *Intrinsic motivation and self-determination in exercise and sport.* Champaign, IL: Human Kinetics.

Hanin Y. L. (2000). *Emotions in sport.* Champaign, IL: Human Kinetics.

Hanton, S., Fletcher, D., & Coughlan, G. (2005). Stress in elite sport performers: A comparative study of competitive and organizational stressors. *Journal of Sports Sciences, 23*, 1129–1141.

Hanton, S., Thomas, O., & Maynard, I. (2004). Competitive anxiety responses in the week leading up to competition: The role of intensity, direction and frequency dimensions. *Psychology of Sport and Exercise, 5*(2), 169–181.

Hardman, D. (2009). *Judgments and decision making: Psychological perspectives.* Chichester, UK: BPS-Blackwell.

Hardy, J. (2006). Speaking clearly: A critical review of the self-talk literature. *Psychology of Sport and Exercise, 7*, 81–97.

Hardy, J., Gammage, K., & Hall, C. (2001). A descriptive study of athlete self-talk. *The Sport Psychologist, 15*, 306–318.

Hardy, J., Hall, C. R., & Hardy, L. (2004). A note on athletes' use of self-talk. *Journal of Applied Sport Psychology, 16*, 251–257.

Hardy, L. (1990). A catastrophe model of anxiety and performance. In J. G. Jones & L. Hardy (Eds.), *Stress and performance in sport.* Chichester, UK: Wiley.

Hardy, L. (1997). The Coleman Roberts Griffith Address: Three myths about applied consultancy work. *Journal of Applied Sport Psychology, 9*, 277–294.

Hardy, L. (2012). Comment on McCarthy, Wilson, Keegan, & Smith. *Sport and Exercise Psychology Review, 8*(2), 17–21.

Hardy, L., Jones, G., & Gould, D. (1996). *Understanding psychological preparation for sport: Theory and practice of elite performers.* Chichester, UK: Wiley.

Hardy, L., Roberts, R., Thomas, P. R., & Murphy, S. M. (2010). Test of performance strategies (TOPS): Instrument refinement using confirmatory factor analysis. *Psychology of Sport and Exercise, 11*, 27–35.

Harker, L., & Keltner, D. (2001). Expressions of positive emotion in women's college year book pictures and their relationship to personality and life outcomes across adulthood. *Journal of Personality and Social Psychology, 80*, 112–124.

Harris, D. V., & Harris, B. L. (1984). *The athlete's guide to sports psychology: Mental skills for physical people.* New York: Leisure Press.

References

Harwood, C., Spray, C. M., & Keegan, R. (2008). Achievement goal theories in sport. In T. S. Horn (Ed.), *Advances in sport psychology* (3rd ed., pp. 157–185). Champaign, IL: Human Kinetics.

Hatzigeorgiadis, A., & Biddle, S. J. H. (2000). Assessing cognitive interference in sport: Development of the Thought Occurrence Questionnaire for Sport. *Anxiety, Stress and Coping, 13*, 65–86.

Hatzigeorgiadis, A., Zourbanos, N., Galanis, E., & Theodorakis, Y. (2011). Self-talk and sports performance: A meta-analysis. *Perspectives on Psychological Science, 6*, 348–356.

Hatzigeorgiadis, A., Zourbanos, N., Goltsios, C., & Theodorakis, Y. (2008). Investigating the functions of self-talk: The effects of motivational self-talk on self-efficacy and performance in young tennis players. *The Sport Psychologist, 22*, 458–471.

Heider, F. (1958). The psychology of interpersonal relations. New York: Wiley.

Hemmings, B., & Holder, T. (2009). *Applied sport psychology: A case-based approach.* Chichester, UK: Wiley-Blackwell.

Hill, R. A., & Barton, R. A. (2005). Red enhances human performance in contests. *Nature, 435*(7040), 293.

Hill, D. M., Hanton, S., Matthews, N., & Fleming, S. (2010). Choking in sport: A review. *International Review of Sport and Exercise Psychology, 3*, 24–39.

Høigaard, R., Fuglestad, S., Peters, D. M., De Cuyper, B., De Backer, M., & Boen, F. (2010). Role satisfaction mediates the relationship between role ambiguity and social loafing among elite women handball players. *Journal of Applied Sport Psychology, 22*, 408–419.

Holt, N. L., & Dunn, J. G. H. (2004). Longitudinal idiographic analyses of appraisal and coping responses in sport. *Psychology of Sport and Exercise, 5*, 213–222.

Horsburgh, V. A., Schermer, J. A., Veselka, L., & Vernon, P. A. (2009). A behavioural genetic study of mental toughness and personality. *Personality and Individual Differences, 46*, 100–105.

Hughes, S. L., Case, H. S., Stuempfle, K. J., & Evans, D. S. (2003). Personality profiles of Iditasport ultra-marathon participants. *Journal of Applied Sport Psychology, 15*, 256–261.

Jackson, B., Dimmock, J. A., Gucciardi, D. F., & Grove, J. R. (2010). Relationship commitment in athletic dyads: Actor and partner effects for big five self- and other-ratings. *Journal of Research in Personality, 44*, 641–648.

Jackson, B., Dimmock, J. A., Gucciardi, D. F., & Grove, J. R. (2011). Personality traits and relationship perceptions in coach–athlete dyads: Do opposites really attract? *Psychology of Sport and Exercise, 12*, 222–230.

Jacob, C. S., & Carron, A. V. (1996). Sources of status in sport teams. *International Journal of Sport Psychology, 27*, 369–382.

Jamieson, J. P. (2010). The home field advantage in athletics: A meta-analysis. *Journal of Applied Social Psychology, 40*,1819–1848.

John, O. P., Naumann, L. P., & Soto, C. J. (2008). Paradigm shift to the integrative big five trait taxonomy: History, measurement, and conceptual issues. In O. P. John, R. W. Robins & L. A. Pervin (Eds.), *Handbook of personality: Theory and research* (3rd ed., pp. 114–158). New York: Guilford Press.

Jones, G., Hanton, S., & Connaughton, D. (2002). What is this thing called mental toughness? An investigation of elite performers. *Journal of Applied Sport Psychology, 14*, 205–218.

Jones, G., Hanton, S., & Connaughton, D. (2007). A framework of mental toughness in the world's best performers. *The Sport Psychologist, 21*, 243–264.

Jones, M. V. (2012). Emotion regulation and sport performance. In S. M. Murphy (Ed.), *The Oxford handbook of sport and performance psychology* (pp. 154–172). New York: Oxford University Press.

Jones, M. V., Bray, S. R., & Lavallee, D. (2007). All the World's a stage: Impact of an audience on sport performance. In S. Jowett & D. Lavallee (Eds.), *Social psychology in sport* (pp. 103–113). Champaign, IL: Human Kinetics.

Jones, M. V., Lane, A. M., Bray, S. R., Uphill, M., & Catlin, J. (2005). Development and validation of the Sport Emotion Questionnaire. *Journal of Sport & Exercise Psychology, 27*, 407–431.

Jones, M. V., Mace, R. D., Bray, S. R., MacRae, A. W., & Stockbridge, C. (2002). The impact of motivational imagery on the emotional state and self-efficacy levels of novice climbers. *Journal of Sport Behavior, 25*, 57–73.

Jones, M. V., Meijen, C., McCarthy, P. J., & Sheffield, D. (2009). A theory of challenge and threat states in athletes. *International Review of Sport and Exercise Psychology, 2*, 161–180.

Jones, M. V., Paull, G. C., & Erskine, J. (2002). The impact of a team's aggressive reputation on the decisions of association football referees. *Journal of Sports Sciences, 20*, 991–1000.

Kahneman, D. (1973). *Attention and effort.* Englewood Cliffs, NJ: Prentice Hall.

Kahneman, D., & Tversky, A. (1979). Prospect theory: An analysis of decision under risk. *Econometrica, 47(2)*, 263–291.

Kaiseler, M., Polman, R. C. J., & Nicholls, A. R. (2012). Effects of the big five personality dimensions on appraisal coping, and coping effectiveness in sport. *European Journal of Sport Science, 12*, 62–72.

Kamata, A., Tenebaum, G., & Hanin, Y. L. (2002). Individual zone of optimal functioning (IZOF): A probabilistic estimation. *Journal of Sport & Exercise Psychology, 24*, 189–208.

Karimian, M., Kashefolhagh, F., Dadashi, M. S., & Chharbaghi, Z. (2010). The effect of relaxation and mental imagery on self-efficacy, competitive anxiety and sportive performance. *British Journal of Sports Medicine, 44*, S57.

Kelly, G. A. (1991). *The psychology of personal constructs: A theory of personality* (Vol. 1). London: Routledge (original work published 1955).

Kingston, K. M., & Hardy, L. (1997). Effects of different types of goals on processes that support performance. *The Sport Psychologist, 11*, 277–293.

Koehler, D. J., & Harvey, N. (2004). *Blackwell handbook of judgment and decision making.* Malden, MA: Blackwell.

Kowalski, K. C., & Crocker, P. R. E. (2001). Development and validation of the Coping Function Questionnaire for adolescents in sport. *Journal of Sport and Exercise Psychology, 23*, 136–155.

Kraus, M. W., Huang, C., & Keltner, D. (2010). Tactile communication, cooperation, and performance: An ethological study of the NBA. *Emotion, 10*, 745–749.

Kyllo, L. B., & Landers, D. M. (1995). Goal setting in sport and exercise: A research synthesis to resolve the controversy. *Journal of Sport & Exercise Psychology, 17*, 117–137.

Lane, A. M., Harwood, C., & Nevill, A. M. (2005). Confirmatory factor analysis of the Thought Occurrence Questionnaire for Sport (TOQS) among adolescent athletes. *Anxiety, Stress & Coping, 18*, 245–254.

Lane, A. M., Sewell, D. F., Terry, P. C., Bartram, D., & Nesti, M. S. (1999). Confirmatory factor analysis of the competitive state anxiety inventory-2. *Journal of Sports Sciences, 17*, 505–512.

Latané, B., Williams, K., & Harkins, S. (1979). Many hands make light the work: The causes and consequences of social loafing. *Journal of Personality and Social Psychology, 37*, 822–832.

Lavallee, D., Kremer, J., Moran, A., & Williams, M. (2012). *Sport psychology: Contemporary themes* (2nd ed.). London, UK: Palgrave.

Lazarus, A. A. (1981). *The practice of multimodal therapy.* New York: McGraw-Hill.

Lazarus, R. S. (1991). *Emotion and adaptation.* New York: Oxford University.

Lazarus, R. S. (1999). *Stress and emotion: A new synthesis.* New York: Springer.

Lazarus, R. S. (2000). How emotions influence performance in competitive sports. *The Sport Psychologist, 14*, 229–252.

Lazarus, R. S., & Folkman, S. (1984). *Stress, appraisal and coping.* New York: Springer.

Le Foll, D., Rascle, O., & Higgins, N. C. (2008). Attributional feedback-induced changes in functional and dysfunctional attributions, expectations of success, hopefulness, and short-term persistence in a novel sport. *Psychology of Sport and Exercise, 9*, 77–101.

Lewin, K. (1948) *Resolving social conflicts.* New York: Harper & Row.

Locke, E. A., Shaw, K. N., Saari, L. M., & Latham, G. P. (1981). Goal setting and task performance. *Psychological Bulletin, 90*, 125–152.

References

Loftus, E. F., & Palmer, J. C. (1974). Reconstruction of automobile destruction: An example of the interaction between language and memory. *Journal of Verbal Learning and Verbal Behaviour, 13*, 585–589.

Luepker, E. T. (2010). Purposes, characteristics, and contents for protecting our clients and ourselves. In S. J. Hanrahan & M. B. Andersen (Eds.), *Routledge handbook of applied sport psychology: A comprehensive guide for students and practitioners* (pp. 49–59). New York: Routledge.

Madden, C. C., Kirkby, R. J., & McDonald, D. (1989). Coping styles of competitive middle distance runners. *International Journal of Sport Psychology, 20*, 287–296.

Mandler, G. (1984). Mind and body: Psychology of emotions and stress. New York: Norton.

Martens, R., Vealey, R. S., & Burton, D. (1990) *Competitive anxiety in sport*. Champaign, IL: Human Kinetics.

Martin, K. A., Moritz, S. E., & Hall, C. R. (1999). Imagery use in sport: A literature review and applied model. *The Sport Psychologist, 13*, 245–268.

Martin, L. J., & Carron, A. V. (2012). Team attributions in sport: A meta-analysis. *Journal of Applied Sport Psychology, 24*, 157–174.

Martin, L. J., Carron, A. V., & Burke, S. M. (2009). Team building interventions in sport: A meta-analysis. *Sport and Exercise Psychology Review, 5*(2), 3–18.

Martin, L. J., Carron, A. V., Eys, M. A., & Loughead, T. M. (2012). Development of a cohesion inventory for children's sport teams. *Group Dynamics: Theory, Research, and Practice, 16*, 68–79.

Mascarenhas, D., O'Hare, D., & Plessner, H. (2006). The psychological and performance demands of association football refereeing. *International Journal of Sport Psychology, 37*, 99–120.

Masters, K. S., & Ogles, B. M. (1998). Associative and dissociative cognitive strategies in exercise and running: 20 years later what do we know? *The Sport Psychologist, 12*, 252–270.

Masters, R., & Maxwell, J. (2008). The theory of reinvestment. *International Review of Sport and Exercise Psychology, 1*, 160–183.

McAuley, E., Duncan, T., & Russell, D. (1992). Measuring causal attributions: The Revised Causal Dimension Scale (CDS-II). *Personality and Social Psychology Bulletin, 18*, 566–573.

McCarthy, P. J. (2011). Positive emotion in sport performance: Current status and future directions. *International Review of Sport and Exercise Psychology, 4*, 50–69.

McCarthy, P. J., Jones, M. V., & Clark-Carter, D. (2008). Understanding enjoyment in youth sport: A developmental perspective. *Psychology of Sport and Exercise, 9*, 142–156.

McCrae, R. R., & Costa, P. T. (1989). Reinterpreting the Myers-Briggs Type Indicator from the perspective of the five-factor model of personality. *Journal of Personality, 57*, 17–40.

McCrae, R. R., & Costa, P. T. (2008). The five-factor theory of personality. In O. P. John, R. W. Robins & L. A. Pervin (Eds.), *Handbook of personality: Theory and research* (3rd ed., pp. 159–181). New York: Guilford Press.

McCullagh, P., Law, B., & Ste-Marie, D. (2012). Modeling and performance. In S. M. Murphy (Ed.), *The Oxford handbook of sport and performance psychology* (pp. 250–272). New York: Oxford University Press.

McEwan, D., Martin Ginis, K. A., & Bray, S. R. (2012). 'With the game on his stick': The home (dis)advantage in National Hockey League shootouts. *Psychology of Sport and Exercise, 13*, 578–581.

McGraw, A. P., Mellers, B. A., & Tetlock, P. E. (2005). Expectations and emotions of Olympic athletes. *Journal of Experimental Social Psychology, 41*, 438–446.

McKay, J., Niven., A. G., Lavallee, D., & White, A. (2008). Sources of strain among elite UK track athletes. *The Sport Psychologist, 22*, 143–163.

McNair, D. M., Lorr, M., & Droppelman, L. F. (1971). *Manual for the Profile of Mood States*. San Diego, CA: Educational and Industrial Testing Services.

Medvec, V. H., Madey, S. F., & Gilovich, T. (1995). When less is more: Counterfactual thinking and satisfaction among Olympic medalists. *Journal of Personality and Social Psychology, 69*, 603–610.

Meijen, C., Jones, M., McCarthy, P. J., Sheffield, D., & Allen, M. S. (2013). Cognitive and affective components of challenge and threat states. *Journal of Sports Sciences*.

Mesagno, C., Harvey, J. T., & Janelle, C. M. (2011). Self-presentation origins of choking: Evidence from separate pressure manipulations. *Journal of Sport & Exercise Psychology*, *33*, 441–459.

Mesagno, C., Marchant, D., & Morris, T. (2009). Alleviating choking: The sounds of distraction. *Journal of Applied Sport Psychology*, *20*, 131–147.

Miller, D. T., & Ross, M. (1975). Self-serving biases in the attribution of causality: Fact or fiction? *Psychological Bulletin*, *82*, 213–225.

Milton, J., Solodkin, A., Hlustik, P., & Small, S. L. (2007). The mind of expert performance is cool and focused. *Neuroimage*, *35*, 804–813.

Mobbs, D., Hassabis, D., Seymour, B., Marchant, J. L., Weiskopf, N., Dolan, R. J., & Frith, C. D. (2009). Choking on the money: Reward-based performance decrements are associated with midbrain activity. *Psychological Science*, *20*, 955–962.

Moran, A. (2012a). Sport and exercise psychology: A critical introduction (2nd ed.). New York: Routledge.

Moran, A. (2012b). Concentration: Attention and performance. In S. M. Murphy (Ed.), *The Oxford handbook of sport and performance psychology* (pp. 117–130). New York: Oxford University Press.

Moran, A., Byrne, A., & McGlade, N. (2002). The effects of anxiety and strategic planning on visual search behaviour. *Journal of Sports Sciences*, *20*, 225–236.

Morgan, W. P., & Pollock, M. L. (1977). Psychologic characterization of the elite distance runner. *Annals of the New York Academy of Sciences*, *301*, 382–403.

Moritz, S. E., Feltz, D. L., Fahrbach, K. R., & Mack, D. E. (2000). The relation of self-efficacy measures to sport performance: A meta-analytic review. *Research Quarterly for Exercise and Sport*, *71*, 280–294.

Munroe, K., Estabrooks, P., Dennis, P., & Carron, A. V. (1999). A phenomenological analysis of group norms in sport teams. *The Sport Psychologist*, *13*, 171–182.

Muraven, M. (2010). Building self-control strength: Practising self-control leads to improved self-control performance. *Journal of Experimental Social Psychology*, *46*, 465–468.

Murphy, S., Nordin, S., & Cumming, J. (2008). Imagery in sport, exercise, and dance. In T. S. Horn (Ed.), *Advances in sport psychology* (3rd ed., pp. 297–324). Champaign, IL: Human Kinetics.

Myers, N. D., Feltz, D. L., & Short, S. E. (2004). Collective efficacy and team performance: A longitudinal study of collegiate football teams. *Group Dynamics: Theory, Research, and Practice*, *8*, 126–138.

Nicholls, A. R. (2010). *Coping in sport: Theory, methods, and related constructs*. New York: Nova.

Nicholls, A. R., & Ntoumanis, N. (2010). Traditional and new methods of assessing coping in sport. In A. R. Nicholls (Ed.), *Coping in sport: Theory, methods, and related constructs* (pp. 35–51). New York: Nova.

Nicholls, A. R., & Polman, R. C. J. (2007). Coping in sport: A systematic review. *Journal of Sports Sciences*, *25*, 11–31.

Nicholls, A., & Polman, R. C. J. (2008). Think aloud: Acute stress and coping strategies during golf performances. *Anxiety, Stress and Coping*, *21*, 283–294.

Nicholls, A. R., Polman, R. C. J., Levy, A. R., & Backhouse, S. H. (2008). Mental toughness, optimism, pessimism, and coping among athletes. *Personality and Individual Differences*, *44*, 1182–1192.

Nicholls, A. R., Polman, R. C. J., Levy, A. R., & Backhouse, S. H. (2009). Mental toughness in sport: Achievement level, gender, age, experience, and sport type differences. *Personality and Individual Differences*, *47*, 73–75.

Nicholls, A., Polman, R., Morley, D., & Taylor, N. J. (2009). Coping and coping effectiveness in relation to a competitive sport event: Pubertal status, chronological age, and gender among adolescent athletes. *Journal of Sport & Exercise Psychology*, *31*, 299–317.

References

Nicholls, A. R., & Thelwell, R. C. (2010). Coping conceptualised and unravelled. In A. R. Nicholls (Ed.), *Coping in sport: Theory, methods, and related constructs* (pp. 3–14). Hauppauge, NY: Nova.

Nicholls, J. G. (1984). Achievement motivation: Conceptions of ability, subjective experience, task choice, and performance. *Psychological Review, 91*, 328–346.

Nicholls, J. G. (1989). *The competitive ethos and democratic education.* Cambridge, MA: Harvard University Press.

Nideffer, R. M. (1976). Test of attentional and interpersonal style. *Journal of Personality and Social Psychology, 34*, 394–404.

Ntoumanis, N. (2012). A self-determination theory perspective on motivation in sport and physical education: Current trends and possible future directions. In G. C. Roberts & D. C. Treasure (Eds.), *Advances in motivation in sport and exercise* (3rd ed., pp. 91–128). Champaign, IL: Human Kinetics.

Ntoumanis, N., & Biddle, S. J. (1998). The relationship of coping and its perceived effectiveness to positive and negative affect in sport. *Personality and Individual Differences, 24*(6), 773–788.

Ntoumanis, N., & Biddle, S. J. H. (1999). A review of motivational climate in physical activity. *Journal of Sports Sciences, 17*, 643–665.

Oatley, K., Keltner, D., & Jenkins, J. M. (2006). *Understanding emotions* (2nd ed.). Oxford: Blackwell.

Orlick, T., & Partington, J. (1988). Mental links to excellence. *The Sport Psychologist, 2*, 105–130.

Otten, M. (2009). Choking vs clutch performance: A study of sport performance under pressure. *Journal of Sport and Exercise Psychology, 31*, 583–601.

Oudejans, R. R. D., Kuijpers, W., Kooijman, C. C., & Bakker, F. C. (2011). Thoughts and attention of athletes under pressure: Skill focus or performance worries? *Anxiety, Stress, & Coping, 24*, 59–73.

Park, S., Lavallee, D., & Tod, D. (2013). Athletes' career transition out of sport: A systematic review. *International Review of Sport and Exercise Psychology, 6*, 22–53.

Parkes, J. F., & Mallett, C. J. (2011). Developing mental toughness: Attributional style retraining in rugby. *The Sport Psychologist, 25*, 269–287.

Pensgaard, A. M., & Duda, J. L. (2003). Sydney 2000: The interplay between emotions, coping, and the performance of Olympic-level athletes. *The Sport Psychologist, 17*, 253–267.

Pervin, L. A., & Cervone, D. (2010). *Personality: Theory and research* (11th ed.). New York: Wiley.

Petrie, T. A., & Buntrock, C. (1995). Sexual attraction and the profession of sport psychology. *Journal of Applied Sport Psychology, 7*, S98.

Piedmont, R. L., Hill, D. C., & Blanco, S. (1999). Predicting athletic performance using the five-factor model of personality. *Personality and Individual Differences, 27*, 769–777.

Pizzera, A., & Raab, M. (2012). Perceptual judgments of sports officials are influenced by their motor and visual experience. *Journal of Applied Sport Psychology, 24*, 59–72.

Plessner, H. (1999). Expectation biases in gymnastics judging. *Journal of Sport & Exercise Psychology, 21*, 131–144.

Plessner, H., & Betsch, T. (2001). Sequential effects in important referee decisions: The case of penalties in soccer. *Journal of Sport and Exercise Psychology, 23*, 254–259.

Plessner, H., Schweizer, G., Brand, R., & O'Hare, D. (2009). A multiple-cue learning approach as the basis for understanding and improving soccer referees' decision making. *Progress in Brain Research, 174*, 151–158.

Plous, S. (1993). *The psychology of judgment and decision making.* New York: McGraw-Hill.

Poczwardowski, A., & Sherman, C. P. (2011). Revisions to the sport psychology service delivery (SPSD) heuristic: Explorations with experienced consultants. *The Sport Psychologist, 25*, 511–531.

Poczwardowski, A., Sherman, C. P., & Henschen, K. P. (1998). A sport psychology service delivery heuristic: Building on theory and practice. *The Sport Psychologist, 12*, 191–207.

Poliseo, J. M., & McDonough, M. H. (2012). Coping effectiveness in competitive sport: Linking goodness of fit and coping outcomes. *Sport, Exercise, and Performance Psychology, 1*, 106–119.

Pollard, R. (2002). Evidence of a reduced home advantage when a team moves to a new stadium. *Journal of Sports Sciences, 20*, 969–973.

Posner, M. I. (1980). Orienting of attention: The VIIth Sir Frederic Barlett lecture. *Quarterly Journal of Experimental Psychology, 32A*, 3–25.

Prapavessis, H., Carron, A. V., & Spink, K. S. (1996). Team building in sport. *International Journal of Sport Psychology, 27*, 269–285.

Raab, M., Gula, B., & Gigerenzer, G. (2012). The hot hand exists in volleyball and is used for allocation decisions. *Journal of Experimental Psychology: Applied, 18*, 81–94.

Ram, N., & McCullagh, P. (2003). Self-modeling: Does watching yourself perform influence physical and psychological performance? *The Sport Psychologist, 17*, 220–232.

Recht, L. D., Lew, R. A., & Schwartz, W. J. (1995). Baseball teams beaten by jet lag. *Nature, 377*, 583.

Rees, T., & Freeman, P. (2007). The effect of perceived and received support on self-confidence. *Journal of Sports Sciences, 25*, 1057–1065.

Rees, T., & Freeman, P. (2010). Social support and performance in a golf-putting experiment. *The Sport Psychologist, 18*, 333–348.

Rees, T., & Freeman, P. (2012). Coping in sport through social support. In J. Thatcher, M. Jones, & D. Lavallee (Eds.), *Coping and emotion in sport* (2nd ed., pp. 102–117). Abingdon, UK: Routledge.

Rees, T., Ingledew, D. K., & Hardy, L. (2005). Attribution in sport psychology: Seeking congruence between theory, research and practice. *Psychology of Sport and Exercise, 6*, 189–204.

Reeves, C. W., Nicholls, A. R., & McKenna, J. (2011). The effects of a coping intervention on coping self-efficacy, coping effectiveness, and subjective performance among adolescent soccer players. *International Journal of Sport and Exercise Psychology, 9*, 126–142.

Rhodes, R. E., & Smith, N. E. (2006). Personality correlates of physical activity: A review and meta-analysis. *British Journal of Sports Medicine, 40*, 958–965.

Ringelmann, M. (1913). Recherches sur les moteurs animés: Travail de l'homme [Research on animate sources of power: The work of man], *Annales de l'Institut National Agronomique, 12*, 1–40.

Roberts, G. C. (2012). Motivation in sport and exercise from an achievement goal theory perspective: After 30 years, where are we? In G. C. Roberts & D. C. Treasure (Eds.), *Advances in motivation in sport and exercise* (3rd ed., pp. 5–58). Champaign, IL: Human Kinetics.

Roberts, G. C., & Treasure, D. C. (2012). *Advances in motivation in sport and exercise* (3rd ed.). Champaign, IL: Human Kinetics.

Roberts, G. C., Treasure, D. C., & Balague, G. (1998). Achievement goals in sport: The development and validation of the perceptions of success questionnaire. *Journal of Sports Sciences, 16*, 337–347.

Rovio, E., Eskola, J., Kozub, S. A., Duda, J. L., & Lintunen, T. (2009). Can high group cohesion be harmful? A case study of a junior ice-hockey team. *Small Group Research, 40*, 421–435.

Ryan, E. D. (1980). Attribution, intrinsic motivation, and athletics: A replication and extension. In C. H. Nadeau, W. R. Halliwell, K. M. Newell, & G. C. Roberts (Eds.), *Psychology of motor behavior and sport* (pp. 19–26). Champaign, IL: Human Kinetics.

Ryan, R. M., & Deci, E. L. (2007). Active human nature: Self-determination theory and the promotion and maintenance of sport, exercise and health. In M. S. Hagger, & N. L. D. Chatzisarantis (Eds.), *Intrinsic motivation and self-determination in exercise and sport* (pp. 1–19). Champaign, IL: Human Kinetics.

Scanlan, T. K., Carpenter, P. J., Lobel, M., & Simons, J. P. (1993). Sources of enjoyment of youth sport athletes. *Pediatric Exercise Science, 5*, 275–285.

References

Scanlan, T. K., & Simons, J. P. (1992). The construct of sport enjoyment. In G. C. Roberts (Ed.), *Motivation in sport and exercise* (pp. 199–215). Champaign, IL: Human Kinetics.

Scanlan, T. K., Stein, G. L., & Ravizza, K. (1991). An in-depth study of former elite figure skaters: III. Sources of stress. *Journal of Sport & Exercise Psychology, 13*, 103–120.

Schurr, K. T., Ashley, M. A., & Joy, K. J. (1977). A multivariate analysis of male athlete personality characteristics: Sport type and success. *Multivariate Experimental Clinical Research, 3*, 53–68.

Schurr, K. T., Ruble, V. E., Nisbet, J., & Wallace, D. (1984). Myers-Briggs Type Inventory characteristics of more and less successful players on an American football team. *Journal of Sport Behavior, 7*, 47–57.

Sexton, T. L., & Whiston, S. C. (1994). The status of the counselling relationship: An empirical review, theoretical implications, and research directions. *The Counselling Psychologist, 22*, 6–78.

Shaw, M. (1976). *Group dynamics* (2nd ed.). New York: McGraw-Hill.

Sheard, M. (2009). A cross-national analysis of mental toughness and hardiness in elite rugby league teams. *Perceptual and Motor Skills, 109*, 213–223.

Sheard, M., Golby, J., & van Wersch, A. (2009). Progress toward construct validation of the sports mental toughness questionnaire (SMTQ). *European Journal of Psychological Assessment, 25*, 186–193.

Shin, D. S., & Lee, K. H. (1994). A comparative study of mental toughness between elite and non-elite female athletes. *Korean Journal of Sport Science, 6*, 85–102.

Short, J. A. C., & Sorrentino, R. M. (1986). Achievement, affiliation, and group incentives: A test of the overmotivation hypothesis. *Motivation and Emotion, 10*, 115–131.

Smith, R. E., Leffingwell, T. R., & Ptacek, J. T. (1999). Can people remember how they coped? Factors associated with discordance between same-day and retrospective reports. *Journal of Personality and Social Psychology, 76*, 1050–1061.

Spence, J. T., & Spence, K. W. (1966). The motivational components of manifest anxiety: Drive and drive stimuli. In C. D. Spielberger (Ed.), *Anxiety and behavior* (pp. 291–326). New York: Academic Press.

Standage, M., Duda, J. L., & Ntoumanis, N. (2003). Predicting motivational regulations in physical education: The interplay between dispositional goal orientations, motivational climate and perceived competence. *Journal of Sports Sciences, 21*, 631–647.

Standage, M., Duda, J. L., & Ntoumanis, N. (2005). A test of self-determination theory in school physical education. *British Journal of Educational Psychology, 75*, 411–433.

Stanovich, K. E., & West, R. F. (2000). Individual differences in reasoning: Implications for the rationality debate. *Behavioral and Brain Sciences, 23*, 645–726.

Starek, J., & McCullagh, P. (1999). The effect of self-modeling on the performance of beginning swimmers. *The Sport Psychologist, 13*, 269–287.

Steiner, I. (1972). *Group process and productivity*. San Diego, CA: Academic Press.

Stevens, L. M., & Andersen, M. B. (2007). Transference and countertransference in sport psychology service delivery: Part II. Two case studies on the erotic. *Journal of Applied Sport Psychology, 19*, 270–287.

Summitt, P. H., & Jenkins, S. (1998). *Reach for the summit: The definite dozen system for succeeding at whatever you do*. New York: Broadway.

Tajfel, H., & Turner, J. C. (1986). The social identity theory of intergroup behavior. In S. Worchel & L. W. Austin (Eds.), *Psychology of intergroup relations*. Chicago, IL: Nelson-Hall.

Tauer, J. M., Guenther, C. L., & Rozek, C. (2009). Is there a home choke in decisive playoff basketball games? *Journal of Applied Sport Psychology, 21*, 148–162.

Taylor, J., & Schneider, B. A. (1992). The Sport-Clinical Intake Protocol: A comprehensive interview instrument for applied sport psychology. *Professional Psychology: Research and Practice, 23*, 318–325.

Thatcher, J., & Day, M. C. (2008). Re-appraising stress appraisals: The underlying properties of stress in sport. *Psychology of Sport and Exercise, 9*, 318–335.

Thatcher, J., Jones, M., & Lavallee, D. (2011). *Coping and emotion in sport* (2nd ed.). Abingdon, UK: Routledge.

Thelan, H. A. (1949). Group dynamics in instruction: The principle of least group size. *School Review, 57,* 139–148.

Thelwell, R., Such, B. A., Weston, N. J., Such, J. D., & Greenlees, I. A. (2010). Developing mental toughness: Perceptions of elite female gymnasts. *International Journal of Sport and Exercise Psychology, 8,* 170–188.

Thelwell, R., Weston, N., & Greenlees, I. (2005). Defining and understanding mental toughness within soccer. *Journal of Applied Sport Psychology, 17,* 326–332.

Tok, S. (2011). The big five personality traits and risky sport participation. *Social Behavior and Personality, 39,* 1105–1112.

Treasure, D. C., Monson, J., & Lox, C. L. (1996). Relationship between self-efficacy, wrestling performance, and affect prior to competition. *The Sport Psychologist, 10,* 73–83.

Triplett, N. (1898). The dynamogenic factors in pacemaking and competition. *American Journal of Psychology, 9,* 507–533.

Turner, M. J., Jones, M. V., Sheffield, D., & Cross, S. L. (2012). Cardiovascular indices of challenge and threat states predict competitive performance. *International Journal of Psychophysiology, 86,* 48–57.

Unkelbach, C., & Memmert, D. (2010). Crowd noise as a cue in referee decisions contributes to the home advantage. *Journal of Sport & Exercise Psychology, 32,* 483–498.

Uphill, M. A., & Jones, M. V. (2007). Antecedents of emotions in elite athletes: A cognitive motivational relational perspective. *Research Quarterly for Exercise and Sport, 78,* 79–89.

van de Pol, P. K. C., Kavussanu, M., & Ring, C. (2012). Goal orientations, perceived motivational climate, and motivational outcomes in football: A comparison between training and competition contexts. *Psychology of Sport and Exercise, 13,* 491–499.

Van Lange, P. A. M., Kruglanski, A. W., & Higgins E. T. (2012). *Handbook of theories of social psychology* (Vol. 1). London: Sage.

Vanden Auweele, Y., Opdenacker, J., Vertommen, T., Boen, F., Van Niekerk, L., De Martelaer, K., & De Cuyper, B. (2008). Unwanted sexual experiences in sport: Perceptions and reported prevalence among Flemish female student-athletes. *International Journal of Sport and Exercise Psychology, 6*(4), 354–365.

Vealey, R. S. (1986). Conceptualization of sport-confidence and competitive orientation: Preliminary investigation and instrument development. *Journal of Sport Psychology, 8,* 221–246.

Vealey, R. S. (2002). *Personality and sport behavior.* In T. Horn (Ed.), Advances in sport psychology (2nd ed., pp. 43–82). Champaign, IL: Human Kinetics.

Volkwein, K. A. E., Schnell, F. I., Sherwood, D., & Livezy, A. (1997). Sexual harassment in sport. *International Review for the Sociology of Sport, 32,* 283–295.

Wallace, H. M., & Baumeister, R. F. (2002). The effects of success versus failure feedback on further self-control. *Self and Identity, 1,* 35–41.

Wallace, H. M., Baumeister, R. F., & Vohs, K. D. (2005). Audience support and choking under pressure: A home disadvantage? *Journal of Sports Sciences, 23,* 429–438.

Ward, G. D., Sandstedt, S. D., Cox, R. H., & Beck, N. C. (2005). Athlete-counselling competencies for US psychologists working with athletes. *The Sport Psychologist, 19,* 318–334.

Watson, D., Clark, L., & Tellegen, A. (1988). Development and validation of brief measures of positive and negative affect: The PANAS scales. *Journal of Personality and Social Psychology, 54,* 1063–1070.

Wegner, D. M. (1994). Ironic processes of mental control. *Psychological Review, 101,* 34–52.

Wegner, D. M., Ansfield, M., & Pilloff, D. (1998). The putt and the pendulum: Ironic effects of the mental control of action. *Psychological Science, 9,* 196–199.

Weinberg, R., Miller, A., & Horn, T. (2012). The influence of a self-talk intervention on collegiate cross-country runners. *International Journal of Sport and Exercise Psychology, 10,* 123–134.

References

Weiner, B. (1985). An attributional theory of achievement motivation and emotion. *Psychological Review, 92*, 548–573.

Weiner, B. (2012). An attribution theory of motivation. In P. A. M. Van Lange, A. W. Kruglanski, & E. T. Higgins (Eds.), *Handbook of theories of social psychology* (Vol. 1, pp. 135–155). London: Sage.

Weston, N., Greenlees, I., & Thelwell, R. (2013). A review of Butler and Hardy's (1992) performance profiling procedure within sport. *International Review of Sport and Exercise Psychology, 6*, 1–21.

Williams, J. M. (2010). *Applied sport psychology: Personal growth to peak performance.* New York: McGraw-Hill.

Wilson, M. (2008). From processing efficiency to attentional control: A mechanistic account of the anxiety–performance relationship. International *Review of Sport and Exercise Psychology, 1*, 184–201.

Wilson, M., Chattington, M., Marple-Horvat, D. E., & Smith, N. C. (2007). A comparison of self-focus versus attentional explanations of choking. *Journal of Sport & Exercise Psychology, 29*, 439–456.

Wilson, M., Smith, N. C., & Holmes, P. S. (2007). The role of effort in influencing the effect of anxiety on performance: Testing the conflicting predictions of processing efficacy theory and the conscious processing hypothesis. *British Journal of Psychology, 98*, 411–428.

Wilson, M. R., Wood, G., & Vine, S. J. (2009). Anxiety, attentional control, and performance impairment in penalty kicks. *Journal of Sport & Exercise Psychology, 31*(6), 761–775.

Woodman, T., Akehurst, S., Hardy, L., & Beattie, S. (2010). Self-confidence and performance: A little self-doubt helps. *Psychology of Sport and Exercise, 11*, 467–470.

Woodman, T., & Davis, P. A. (2008). The role of repression in the incidence of ironic errors. *The Sport Psychologist, 22*, 183–196.

Woodman, T., Davis, P. A., Hardy, L., Callow, N., Glasscock, I., & Yuill-Proctor, J. (2009). Emotions and sport performance: An exploration of happiness, hope, and anger. *Journal of Sport & Exercise Psychology, 31*, 169–188.

Woodman, T., & Hardy, L. (2001a). Stress and anxiety. In R. N. Singer, H. A. Hausenblas & C. M. Janelle (Eds.), Handbook of sport psychology (pp. 290–318). New York: Wiley.

Woodman, T., & Hardy, L. (2001b). A case study of organisational stress in elite sport. *Journal of Applied Sport Psychology, 13*, 207–238.

Woodman, T., & Hardy, L. (2003). The relative impact of cognitive anxiety and self-confidence upon sports performance: A meta-analysis. *Journal of Sports Sciences, 21*, 443–457.

Woodman, T., Roberts, R., Hardy, L., Callow, N., & Rogers, C. H. (2011). There is an I in TEAM: Narcissism and social loafing. *Research Quarterly for Exercise and Sport, 82*, 285–290.

Wulf, G., Höß, M., & Prinz, W. (1998). Instructions for motor learning: Differential effects of internal versus external focus of attention. *Journal of Motor Behavior, 30*, 169–179.

Wulf, G., & Lewthwaite, R. (2010). Effortless motor learning? An external focus of attention enhances movement effectiveness and efficiency. In B. Bruya (Ed.), Effortless attention: *A new perspective in attention and action* (pp. 75–101). Cambridge, MA: MIT Press.

Yerkes, R. M., & Dodson, J. D. (1908).The relation of strength of stimulus to rapidity of habit-formation. Journal of Comparative *Neurology and Psychology, 18*, 459–482.

Zajonc, R. B. (1965). Social facilitation. *Science, 149*(3681), 269–274.

Index

Note: Note page entries in **bold** refer to glossary definitions

ability 26, 27
abuse of clients by practitioners 142
achievement goal theory 18–20, 23
aggression and colour 113
agreeableness 4, 5, 8, 10, 11, 12
Allport, Gordon 4
Andersen, Mark 132
anxiety **159**
  attentional control theory 37, 65–6, 69
  cognitive 35, 36
  conscious processing hypothesis 36–7, 41
  definition 34
  and effort 37
  mental imagery, effects of 148
  multidimensional anxiety theory 35–6
  and performance 41, 67
  pre-competitive 39
  somatic 35–6
  theories of 34–7
  and threat 40
appraisals 39
  cognitive 81
apprehension 92
arousal 35, 40, **159**
  definition 34
  effect on attention 67
  physiological 35, 148
  sports requiring high arousal 41
Asch, Solomon 116
assessment of athletes 143–5
assessments
  'at risk' sports people 12
  to predict sport performance 7–8
  trait based 6
  type-based 6
associations, learned 111–12
associative attention strategy 72
attention
  definition 63
  strategies 69–72
  self-talk (to improve attention) 147
  System 2 108

attentional control theory 37, 41, 65
attentional focus manipulation 70
attitude/mindset 127
attribution
  causal 117–18
  globality 26
  measurement 26–7
  universality 26
attribution biases 25
attribution retraining 27, **159**
attribution theory 24–28
attribution theory of achievement
     motivation (ATAM) 25–6
audience, effect on behaviour 7, 12, 92–3
autonomy 21, 22, 23
avoidance coping 78

Bandura, Albert 52
BASIC ID 145
behaviour prediction
  approaches to 5
behaviours 25, 26
  and emotion 32
  and environmental factors 125
  heritability 125
behavioural approach 141
bias, self-serving 25, 117–18
'big five' model of personality 4–5, 6,
  for predicting athletic performance 7–8
body language 56, 116
bounded rationality concept 110, **159**
burnout 129

CANOE 5
catastrophe theory 35
Cattell, Raymond 4
causal attribution 115, 117–18
challenge 126–7
  and threat 40, 81–2, 127
'choking' 66–7, 94

client, relationship with 149
closure 150
clutch performances 67
coaches 55–6
cognitive appraisal 39, 81
cognitive consonance 114, **159**
cognitive dissonance 114–15, **159**
cognitive irrelevance 114, **159**
cognitive-motivational-relational theory
    (CMRT) 81
cognitive neuroscience 69
cognitive restructuring 148
cognitive skills 85
cohesion
  building 99–100
  measurement 99
  social 98
  task 98
  team 98–100
collective efficacy 55, 99, **159**
commitment 126, 127
competence 18, 21, 23
competition 40,
  and coping 81
  pressure 109
  and social support 85
competitive stress 79–80, 81
competitiveness 38
concentration 61–72
  attentional control theory 37, 41, 65
  definition 63
  distraction 64–5, 66–7
  divided attention 63
  enhancement 69–72
  explicit monitory theory 67
  filter model 64
  focus of attention 65–6, 70, 72
  ironic processes 65
  measurement 68–9
  cognitive neuroscience 69
  mental practice 71
  models 63–5
  performance goals 71
  pre-performance routines 71
  resource model 64
  selective attention 63
  spotlight model 64
  theories 63–9
concentration grid 69

confidence 27, 126–7, 129, 132
  coach 55–6
  overconfidence 57
  see also self-confidence
conscientiousness 4, 5, 7–8, 10, 11
conscious processing hypothesis 36–7, 41
constancy 129
control 126–7, 129
controllability 25, 26, 27
coordination, loss of in group 95
coping 39, 76–86
  and age 83
  and control of situation 84–5
  definition 77
  and emotion 81–2
  and gender 83
  measurement 82
  and mental toughness 129–130
  performance 83
  population-based differences 82–3
  process 77–8
  questionnaires 82
  research 81–3
  retirement 83
  self-control 85
  smiling 85–6
  social support 85
  strategies 78, 84–6
  styles 77–8
  task oriented strategies 83
  team sports 83
coping effectiveness 84–6, **160**
CSAI-2 42, 50, 54
CSAI-2R 50
coping strategies 7
contextual dependence 111–15
  biases in memory 112–14
  cognitive consonance 114
  cognitive dissonance 114–15
  cognitive irrelevance 114
  learned associations 111–12
counterfactual thinking 117, **160**
creativity and narcissism 11

decision field theory (DFT) 110
decision making 106–18
  colour, influence of 113
  contextual dependence 111–15

definition 107
influence of prior decisions 112–13
primacy effect 116
team reputation 113
theories 109–10
understanding the process 107–8
developmental studies 124–5
deviance, ingroup 96
dissociative attention strategy 72
distraction 64–5, 66–7
dominant response tendency 92
drive theory 35
Duchenne smiles 86

efficacy
collective 55, 99
coaching 55–6
proxy 56
role 97–8
see also self-efficacy
effort 26, 27
and anxiety 37
expenditure 78
social loafing 95–6
electroencephalography (EEG) 69, **160**
emotion 7, 25, 26, 31–43
challenge and threat 40
cognitive appraisal 39
controlling 42–3, 129
coping 39, 78, 81–2
counterfactual thinking 117
definition 33
effect on behaviour 32
individual zones of optimalfunctioning
(IZOF) 39–40
measurement 41–2
mental imagery 147
mental toughness 129–30
negative 38, 40, 41, 81, 82, 85
negatively valanced 35, 40
observer ratings 42
and performance 41–3
physiological markers 42
positive 38, 40, 41, 81, 82, 85–6
positively valanced 35, 40
psychological variable,as a 124–5
restricting factor 110
sports requiring fine motor skills 41

sports requiring high arousal 41
theories of 38–40
understanding emotion 33-4
emotion-focused coping 78, 82, 84–5
emotional regulation pitfalls 43
emotional states 53
endurance events 72
enjoyment 38
ethics and personality research 11–12
ethics and sport psychologists 140–2, 145
evaluation of consultancy 150
existential approach 141
expectations 25, 26, 27, 50
experience 109, 129
explanation, psychology of 24
explicit monitoring 66
external regulation 22
extraversion 4, 5, 6, 7, 8, 9, 10, 11, 12
Eysenck, Hans 4,

failure 26
fatigue 65
feedback 23
Festinger, Leon 114
focus of attention 65–6, 70, 108
external 72
internal 72
4Cs 126–7, 128
functional magnetic resonance
imaging (fMRI) 69, **160**
fundamental attribution error 24–5, **160**

Galen 4, 5
game location factors 93
Gestalt approach 141
goal orientation 23
ego 18–19, 20
task 18–19, 20, 23
goal setting 42–3, 100, 144, 146
goals
approach focused 18
avoidance focused 18
mastery 18, 19, 20
measuring 19
motivational climate 19–20
outcome 71, 146, **161**
performance 18–19, 71, 146

process 71, 146
team 100
goodness-of-fit model 84
group norms 96–7, 99, **160**
groups
    definition 91
    ingroup deviance 96
    least group size 95
    optimal size 94–95, 96
    performance 11, 12, 90
    processes 90–100
    productivity 91–2, 95
    Ringelmann effect 96
    roles within group 96, 97–8
    self-serving bias 118
    social facilitation 92–3
    social loafing 96, 97, 99
    status 97, 99
    structure 96
    see also teams
groupthink 99, **160**

hardiness 126
Heider, Fritz 24
Hippocrates 4, 5
home advantage 93–4
hot hand effect 112

identified regulation 22
imagery 42–3, 52, 57, 78, 146, 147–8, **160**
    types of 148
    see also mental practice
individual zones of optimal functioning
    (IZOF) 39–40
individual performance within team 95
ingroup deviance 96, **160**
inhibition function 37
inverted U hypothesis 34–5
integrated regulation 22
interpersonal skills 85
interviews 5, 123–4, 143, 144–5
introjected regulation 22
introversion 5, 12
ironic processes 65

judgement 104–18
    causal attribution 115, 117–18
    colour, influence of 113
    and decision making 107
    definition 107
    memory, role of 112
    person perception 115, 116
    personal performances 115–18
    primacy effect 116
    social comparison 115, 117

Lazarus, Arnold 145
Lazarus's cognitive-motivational-relational
    theory 38–9
leadership issues
    social cohesion 98
    and stress 80
life skills, development of 9
locus of causality 25, 26
logical analysis 78
longevity 86
luck 26

mastery climate development 20
memory
    alterations 114
    biases in 112–14
mental practice 71
mental toughness 122–32
    age differences 124, 129–30
    and athletic success 129–30
    attributes 123, 127
    confidence, constancy and control 129
    definition 123–4, 125–6
    development of 131–2
    gender differences 129–30
    heritability 125
    developmental studies 124–5
    measurement 128–9
    pain tolerance 128
    predictor of success 130
    problems with 132
    population-based differences 129
    psychological variables 124–5
    and sport performance 126–30
mental weakness 124
modelling 52, 57
mood states 3,
motivation 16–28, 39
    achievement goal theory 18–20

amotivation 22, 23
  attribution theory 25–6
  definition 17
  extrinsic 22
  intrinsic 22–3
  mental imagery 147
  Ringelmann effect 95
  role conflict 98
motivational climate 19–20, **161**
motor control and self-talk 147
motor planning 69
motor skills, sports requiring fine 41

narcissism 11, 67
needs 21, 23
negative emotions 38, 40, 41, 81, 82, 85,
    160
NEO inventory 6
neuroticism 4, 5, 6, 7–8, 10

observations 5
  observer ratings of emotion 42
OCEAN 4
openness 4, 5, 6, 8, 10, 11
optimal zone 39–40
optimism 129
organisational stress 79, 80
outcome expectations 50
overconfidence 57, **161**

parental involvement 38
PEN model of personality 4
performance 34–7
  and coaching 56
  and cohesion 98, 99
  and coping 83
  dominant response tendency 92
  and effect of distance travelled 93
  and emotion 41–3
  evaluation 144
  expectations 50
  goals 71, **161**
  group size 94–5
  home advantage 93–4
  individual within team 95
  mental imagery 148
  and order of appearance 112

physical touch 43
  Ringelmann effect 95
  role 97–8
  and self-doubt 55, 124, 132
  and self-efficacy 54
  and self-talk 147
  social facilitation 92
  sports psychologists 139–40
  team 55, 56, 99
  see also audience, effect on behaviour
person-centred approach 141
person perception 115, 116
personal goals 42
personal stress 79
personality 1–12
  adjectives 4
  as a predictor of participation in sport
      9–10
  assessments 6
  definition 3, 4
  development due to participation insport
      9, 10
  differences, population-based 8–9
  dimensions 4
  effect on relationships 10–11
  gender differences 8
  heritability 125
  hierarchical structure 4
  measurement of 5–6
  models of personality structure 3–5
  psychological variables 124–5
  and sport performance 7, 11–12
  tests 5–8, 12
  traits 4, 5, 10, 124–5
physical touch, importance of in improving
      performance 43
physiological markers of emotion 42
physiological toughness 128
Piedmont, Ralph 7–8
positive emotions 38, 40, 41, 81, 82,
      85–6, **161**
positive mental rehearsal 57
  see also imagery
positive self-persuasion 52, 55, 57
  see also self-talk
Positive and Negative Affect Schedule 41
positon emission tomography (PET) 69, **161**
pre-performance routines 71, **161**
pressure 66–7, 70

competition 109
explicit monitoring theory 67
home crowd 94
primacy effect 116
problem-focused coping 78, 82, 84–5
process gains 92
productivity, group 91–2
Profile of Mood States 41
progress, monitoring 144
prospect theory 109
proxy efficacy 56, **161**
psychoanalytic approach 141
psychological approaches 141
psychological skills training(PST) 146–9, **161**
psychological needs 21, 23
psychologists
    effectiveness 149–50
    role 138, 139–48
psychometric testing 144, 145
psychotism 4

questionnaires 5–6
    achievement goals 19
    Australian Football Mental Toughness
        Inventory (AFMTI) 129
    Child Sport Environment Questionnaire 99
    cohesion 99
    coping 82
    Cricket Mental Toughness Inventory
        (CMTI) 129
    CSAI-2 42, 50, 54
    CSAI-2R 50
    Group Environment Questionnaire 99
    measurement of emotion 41–2
    measurement of mental toughness 128–9
    Mental Toughness Questionnaire 48
        (MTQ-48) 128–9
    Perceptions of Success 19
    performance profile 144
    self-confidence 50
    Sports Mental Toughness Questionnaire
        (SMTQ) 129
    State Sports Confidence Inventory 50
    Task and Ego Orientation in Sport 19
    Test of Attentional and Interpersonal
        Style (TAIS) 68–9
    Test of Performance Strategies-2
        (TOPS-2) 144

Thought Occurrence Questionnaire for
    Sport (TOQS) 68–9
2x2 Achievement Goal Questionnaire for
    Sport 19
Youth Sport Environment Questionnaire
    99

rational-emotive approach 141
reappraisal 42–3
record-keeping 145
relatedness 21
relationships 10–11
relaxation techniques 42–3, 78, 130, 146,
    148
restricted cognitive information-processing
    ability 110
rewards 22, 23, 67
Ringelmann effect 95, **162**
Ringelmann, Maximilien 95
risk-taking behaviour 129
roles (within group) 96, 97–8
    acceptance of 98
    clarity of 97–8
    conflict in 98
    efficacy 98
    formal 97
    informal 97
    satisfaction 98

satisficing 110
self-belief 124
self-confidence 47–57
    building 57, 147
    defining 49–50
    measurement 50, 54
    mental toughness 124
    and opponents 56
    optimal 57
    and self-doubt 55
    social support, effect on 85
    and sport performance 54–7
    and teams 55
self-control 85, **162**
self-determined behaviour, development
    of 23
self-determination theory (SDT) 21–4
self-doubt 55, 124, 132

self-efficacy 49–50, **162**
  building 57
  consequences 53
  determinants 52–3
  mastery experiences 52, 55
  physiological states 53, 55
  verbal persuasion 52, 55, 57
  vicarious experience (modelling) 52,
    55, 57
self-efficacy theory 51–3
self-esteem 50, 117–18, **162**
self-evaluation 128
self-reports 5–6, 7
  measurement of concentration 68–9
  measurement of emotion 41–2
  measurement of mental toughness 128–9
  self-confidence 50
self-serving bias 25, 117–18, **162**
self-talk (positive self-persuasion) 42–3, 52,
    55, 57, 130, 146, 147, **162**
  success of 147
  instructional 71
sexual interaction between practitioners
    and clients 142
shifting function 37
Simon, Herbert 110
simple heuristics 110
simulation training 70, **162**
16PF model of personality 4
smiling, benefits of 85–6
social comparison 115, 117
social cognitive theory 51
social facilitation 92–3, **162**
social loafing 95–6, 97, 99, **162**
Sport-Clinical Intake Protocol (SCIP) 144
sport performance and personality 7
sport psychology delivery 140–2
stability 25–7
status 97, 99
Steiner, Ivan 95
stress 65, **162**
  competitive 79–80
  definition 34
  environmental 80
  leadership issues 80

  organisational 79, 80
  personal 79, 80
  smiling, benefits of 85–6
  social support, effect on 85
  sources of 79–81
  team issues 80
stressors 76, 78, 84
  controllable 85
  types of 79–81
  uncontrollable 85
subjective expected utility theory (SEU) 109
System 1 108
System 2 108

TARGET 20
task difficulty 26
task mastery 18–19, 20, 23
team building 100
team confidence 55
teams
  audience effects 92–3
  building cohesion 100
  cohesion 98–100
  measurement of cohesion 99
  definition 91
  effectiveness 90
  goals 100
  home advantage 93–4
  individual performance 95
  optimal size 94
  performance 90, 93, 99
  self-serving bias 118
  and stress 80
  structure 91, 100
  see also groups
theory of challenge and threat states in
    athletes (TCTSA) 81–2
thought control 78
traits 4, 5, **162**
Triplett, Norman 92
twins 125

uncertainty 109
utility 109